First Person Past

American Autobiographies
Volume II

First Person Past

American Autobiographies
Volume II

EDITED BY

MARIAN J. MORTON

and

RUSSELL DUNCAN

BRANDYWINE PRESS · St. James, New York

ISBN 1-881089-29-0

1st Printing 1994

Telephone Orders: 1-800-345-1776

Printed in the United States of America

In gratitude for generous financial and technical support, we would like to dedicate First Person Past *to John Carroll University.*

CONTENTS

INTRODUCTION

First Person Past lets some fascinating people speak for themselves. These men and women participated in, shaped, and observed many of the most exciting and important events of United States history.

They wrote about that past and their own lives in a unique kind of historical literature, autobiography. Autobiography is a retrospective account of its author's life, which begins with his or her childhood and describes in narrative form a significant portion of that life. Novelist William Dean Howells described autobiography as "the most democratic" of American literary genres. This is an overstatement since most Americans have not had the inclination, the time, or the literary skills to write their life stories. Nevertheless, because most autobiography does not claim to be *belles lettres,* it has offered a voice to groups like women, African-Americans, Native Americans, and immigrants, whose writings have often been excluded from the literary canon.

From the hundreds of American autobiographies, we have chosen twelve for Volume II of *First Person Past* because they are interesting history and good literature. We have tried to preserve their literary and historical virtues as we edited them for inclusion in this single volume.

AUTOBIOGRAPHY AS HISTORY

The autobiographers in this volume reveal much about the private sides of American life. Woody Guthrie experienced the devastating impact of hard times on families; Mary Antin and Monica Sone, the generation gap between immigrant parents and children. Mary Jones, Anna Howard Shaw, and Frederic C. Howe struggled to redefine women's traditional roles, and Ron Kovic and Anne Moody, to express their sexuality.

These autobiographers also provided their personal perspectives on public events. Their first-hand accounts dramatize and authenticate much of the American story from Reconstruction in the South through the political and social unrest of the 1960s and 1970s.

The Civil War ended in 1865, but the conflict between the North and the South continued another dozen years while Congress tried to rebuild the nation and reconstruct the South. Tunis Campbell's imprisonment for trying to aid the freedmen illustrates the difficulties of that reconstruction.

Fueled by post-Civil War nationalism, the historic American belief in white Anglo-Saxon superiority became a driving force in domestic policy. The federal government abandoned its half-hearted efforts to guarantee equality of opportunity for black freedmen. Booker T. Washington's philosophy of racial accomodation responded to that abandonment. Government officials continued to confine Native Americans to reservations or to exterminate them when they resisted. Black Elk described that resistance and the painful death of the Plains Indians' way of life.

Native-born Americans of western European background were also made uneasy by the huge waves of "new" immigrants who arrived from eastern and southern Europe, distinguished by their dress, language, culture, and their Roman Catholic or Jewish religion. Concentrated in port cities and industrial centers, these newcomers exacerbated the problems of poverty, crime, and disease created by rapid, unplanned urban growth.

Searching for freedom and especially economic opportunity, immigrants like Mary Antin soon discovered that America's streets were not paved with gold. Yet many did find jobs in America's growing industries. Andrew Carnegie, an immigrant himself, described his own spectacular rise from rags to riches in the context of the country's emergence as an industrial giant.

Industrialization brought fierce competition, and employers and stockholders formed trusts, holding companies, and monopolies to offset the perils of the unstable marketplace. As workplaces and corporations became big business, working men and women offset their own loss of individual autonomy and power by joining unions—big labor. The American Federation of Labor, founded in 1881 and led by Samuel Gompers, emerged as the foremost advocate for organized labor. In general, only skilled workers belonged to AFL affiliates. An exception was the United Mine Workers of America, for which Mary "Mother" Jones was an organizer. Workers and employers clashed violently and constantly over wages, working conditions, and union recognition. Labor seldom won; employers like Andrew Carnegie had money and public opinion on their side.

By the 1890s labor unrest and worsening urban problems concerned growing numbers of middle-class Americans. Many set out to solve those problems, initiating the decades of reform and experimentation known as the Progressive era. Reformers, like Frederic C. Howe, hoped that city, state, and federal governments would improve the American economy, politics, and personal behavior.

The enfranchisement of all American women in 1920 by the passage of the Nineteenth Amendment expressed this belief that politics was a viable route to reform. As Anna Howard Shaw recounted, the struggle for the vote had been long and difficult, engaging several generations of American women since the 1848 Seneca Falls convention when a handful of bold women had first demanded that right.

Few Americans were untouched by the economic catastrophe of the Great Depression of the 1930s. Americans experienced joblessness, desperate poverty, and sometimes starvation. Woody Guthrie joined the thousands of transients who wandered the countryside hoping that the next stop would bring them closer to economic salvation.

The United States' entrance into World War II in December 1941 ended the Great Depression as it created millions of jobs in factories, offices, and the armed services. The war also brought the relocation of 112,000 Japanese-Americans like Monica Sone from their homes on the West Coast to internment camps in the interior of the country. Long suspect because of their race, Japanese immigrants to the United States—the *Isei* Japanese—had been prevented by immigration law from becoming citizens, heightening fears that they would betray the United States in war time. Their children—the *Nisei*—also suffered.

Patriotic slogans, advertising the war as a fight to preserve freedom and democracy, opportunities to earn decent wages and join the armed services, and the massive migration into northern cities, inspired African-Americans to renew their fight for equality at home. The National Association for the Advancement of Colored People continued to pursue racial justice through the legal system, achieving a landmark victory in the 1954 Supreme court case, *Brown v. The Board of Education of Topeka, Kansas*.

A new strategy, nonviolent direct resistance, was employed successfully in Montgomery, Alabama in 1955–56. Dr. Martin Luther King Jr. emerged as the country's leading apostle of nonviolent change. By the mid-1960s, however, as Southerners resisted peaceful integration with violence and the federal government remained only partially committed to racial equality, nonviolence began to lose its hold on young civil rights workers like Anne Moody.

The crusade for civil rights became the catalyst for the women's liberation movement and a student movement which challenged the political and cultural status quo. By the close of the 1960s, protest became focused on the United States' involvement in the war in Vietnam. Activists like Ron Kovic questioned both the political establishment and the moral and legal underpinnings of American foreign policy.

In the last decades of the nineteenth century, most native-born and immigrant Americans had confidently believed that the United States was the "promised land," where the dream of equality and justice could be achieved. A century later, however, that confidence had been gravely shaken.

AUTOBIOGRAPHY AS LITERATURE

Autobiography lives halfway between fact and fiction. Claiming that his or her story is a factual account of the past, the autobiographer puts that story together using some of the imaginative strategies of fiction.

The personal nature of autobiography means that many of its author's statements, unlike those of the historian, cannot be corroborated. The autobiographer's "facts" often exist only in his or her memory, a memory always selective and not always reliable. By necessity, the autobiographer has greater freedom and license to create and "make up" the past—in short, to write fiction.

The autobiographer also has greater freedom than the historian to make the story come out right. (Writing the story of your life may be the only way to live it over again without the mistakes or the boring parts.) The narrative usually takes the form of a journey: a journey through time, through space, or through spiritual travail. Anna Howard Shaw and Woody Guthrie journeyed across the continental United States; Mary Antin and Andrew Carnegie, across the Atlantic Ocean; and Black Elk, Frederic C. Howe, and Anne Moody, through emotional and intellectual torment. In both religious and secular autobiography, there is often a conversion experience which moves the plot forward.

Few of us like to appear naked in public. Neither does an autobiographer, who disguises his or her nakedness by creating someone to play his or her part throughout the story. This invented self—or persona—tells us how the autobiographer wishes to be perceived. Most authors construct a persona which is acceptable to his or her time and place. Reflecting the different expectations of their culture, men and women often portray themselves differently: men as solitary individuals, women as family members or maternal figures. Mary "Mother" Jones, an extremely unconventional woman, nevertheless assumed a conventional persona. Ron Kovic, a conventional boy, became an unconventional man.

Part of the autobiographer's disguise is the voice in which the author speaks, the language he or she uses. Black Elk spoke through stories of the past. Booker T. Washington's solemn prose contrasted with the dialect he put in the mouth of uneducated southern blacks. Moody wrote equally powerful "black" and "white" English. Woody Guthrie used language that was both poetic and politically appropriate as he dressed himself up as "just folks."

Even the most skillful writer of fiction, however, can get tripped up by reality. The "real," or historically determined, self may appear naked on the pages of the book. Even the "wizard of Tuskegee," Booker T. Washington, occasionally let his disguise drop. Sometimes an author's life contradicts the recounted life story.

Andrew Carnegie portrayed himself as a friend of labor despite his actions during the Homestead steel strike. Monica Sone insisted on a happy ending to her autobiography although the realities of her life suggested otherwise. Howe frequently confessed to despairing of reform but in reality never gave up.

Autobiography's plot is often predictable. Knowing how the journey has ended in the present, the author will predetermine its direction in the past. There are no surprises, no accidents, no chance happenings in the story of the rebel Mary "Mother" Jones. The stage was fully set in Mary Antin's Old World for her life in the New.

In no other historical genre are history and literature so intimately interwoven as in autobiography. Informative as fact and intriguing as fiction, autobiography challenges its readers to distinguish between them and to understand and enjoy both.

Marian Morton
Russell Duncan
John Carroll University

First Person Past

American Autobiographies
Volume II

TUNIS GULIC CAMPBELL
1812–1891

Tunis Campbell often shared the stage with Frederick Douglass at abolition meetings in the North before the Civil War. After the war, Campbell talked with President Ulysses Grant about enforcing equal treatment for the people freed by the war but still living in the South. Grant helped a little, but at the end of Reconstruction, a sixty-four-year-old Campbell found himself wearing chains and a prison uniform working as a convict-laborer hired out on a Georgia plantation.

He was born free in New Jersey. In an age when few African-Americans had any formal education, Campbell spent twelve years in an otherwise all-white Episcopal school in New York. He trained to be a missionary for the American Colonization Society which hoped to return all blacks to the newly-established country of Liberia in Africa. When he opted to fight against slavery in America instead of taking African-Americans to a foreign land, he joined the Methodist Church, founded an anti-colonization society and preached abolition.

After working in hotels in New York City and Boston, Campbell wrote the first American-published book on hotel management, Hotel Keepers, Head Waiters, and Housekeepers' Guide *(1848). When the Civil War began, Campbell was married, had three children (one an adopted son), and owned a partnership in a bread company in NYC. He offered to join the army, but the U.S. was not accepting black soldiers at that time. In 1862, he got a commission to go to Port Royal, South Carolina, where refugeed slaves were getting land. He was to help in resettling them.*

With the establishment in 1865 of the Bureau of Refugees, Freedmen and Abandoned Lands, Campbell was appointed a Bureau Agent to five Georgia islands. He set up schools, parceled out land, formed militia companies, and taught the ex-slaves about democracy. Beginning in 1867, after Congress took charge of Reconstruction, Georgia voters elected Campbell to the Constitutional Convention, state senate, and state legislature, as well as vice-president of the state's Republican party and local justice of the peace.

Campbell used his state offices to further black equality through legislation and by his associations with national Republican politicians. He used his local office as a judge to protect citizens along the Georgia coast in Darien, where he lived. He became the political boss of McIntosh County's Republican party and counseled blacks on labor contracts and civil rights.

1

By so doing he angered resurgent white reactionaries who refused to accept changes in the Southern way of life.

After white Democrats and their militant arm, the Ku Klux Klan, forced Georgia's only-elected Republican governor to flee the state, Northerners tired of fighting the South, and Grant insisted "Let us have peace," Campbell became a target for removal. His house was burned, his wife and son threatened, and his legislative office stripped from him. Campbell was sentenced to the penitentiary from which he was hired out for one year as a convict laborer for eight dollars to a rich landowner. Released in 1877, Campbell moved to Washington, D.C., and wrote his memoirs. From there his life is obscure. He died in 1891 and was buried in Boston.

Sufferings of the Rev. T. G. Campbell and His Family, in Georgia. *Washington, D.C.: Enterprise Publishing Co., 1877.*

I was born in Middlebrook, Somerset county, New Jersey, on the 1st day of April, in the year 1812. My father, (John Campbell, sr.,) was a blacksmith by trade. I had five sisters and four brothers. I was the youngest of all, except two sisters, and they were living near Middlebrook. When at the age of 5 years, a gentleman rode up on horseback and spoke to me, as I was playing with two of my sisters by the roadside. He inquired for my mother. We all knew him very well, for he lived in Middlebrook. He told my father and mother that he could get me in a school on Long Island, in the State of New York. I was subsequently sent to a school at Babylon, on Long Island. I was the only colored child in the school. The principal and assistants were very kind to me. At the age of 18 I returned home. I would not agree to go to Africa as a missionary, and from this period I commenced as an anti-slavery lecturer.

My father had removed to the city of New Brunswick, New Jersey. Here, in the year 1832, I formed an anti-colonization society, and then pledged myself never to leave this country until every slave was free on American soil—unless I went to learn something, or to get help to secure their liberation. I was brought up in (and intended to be sent out from) the Episcopal Church, but after leaving school I joined the Methodist Church; and except being mobbed many times while lecturing or preaching, and nearly killed once, there was nothing of note occurred, except that I was the first moral reformer and temperance lecturer that entered the Five Points, in the city of New York. After the work was begun, then noble-hearted white men stepped in; and where the old dens of thieves and pannel-houses stood, they have raised a mission house.

The mayor of Jersey City was kind enough to send a policeman down to the ferry, every Monday night, to protect me from the ferry, and back to the ferry, from the temperance meetings held in that city every Monday night; and through Divine Providence kind friends came forward and helped us to raise our school houses and churches in Jersey City during the years 1841, 1842, 1845, and 1846. I also, during the same time, labored in Brooklyn and Williamsburg in the same way.

I now pass to the year 1861. I was at this time a partner and general agent of the firm of Davies & Co., unfermented bread manufacturers, on the corner of Third avenue and Fourteenth street, in the city of New York....

TUNIS GULIC CAMPBELL

This was the first year of the war. Myself and other colored men offered to aid the Government in putting down the rebellion, but our services were refused—Secretary Seward replying that we were premature. In 1863 I sent a personal petition to the President, but got no answer. An old friend of mine in the city of New York asked me if I had got any answer to my Washington letter. I told him no. He then said, "Write again, and I will try what I can do for you." I did write again to President Lincoln; and in about a month after this I called to see my friend, and he had that very day received a package from the Secretary of War, upon opening which, I found a commission ordering me to report forthwith to General Saxton, at Hilton Head, in South Carolina; and there I remained with General Saxton, and did whatever was entrusted to me, I think, to his satisfaction. After the fall of Charleston I requested to be sent to the Sea Islands, in Georgia, and had assigned to me Burnside, Ausaba, Saint Catharines, Sapelo and Colonel's Islands, with orders to organize and establish governments on the Islands; protect freedmen and refugees for thirty miles back from the seashore; and I remained for two years governor on these Islands. I had three teachers brought from the North at my own expense, and paid them. Under my policy-plan (that of President Johnson) I was removed by General Tilson, who was then placed as head of the Freedman's Bureau, and military commander-in-chief of Georgia.

The schools which I had established on the Islands were broken up, and the people driven off—unless they work under contracts which were purposely made to cheat the freedmen out of their labor. Rebels, who before had appeared humble and repentant, now insisted that all colored men and women should sign these contracts; and when they refused, they would waylay them and beat them, telling them that they would have them back when the Yankees left the State.

I went to General Tilson at the time his headquarters were in Augusta, and told him that I could not go on the Islands with safety. I showed him my certificate as an Elder of the Zion Methodist Episcopal Church in America, with my commission from Right Rev. J. J. Clinton as missionary for the States of Georgia and Florida. He said, "That is all right; but I cannot give you any protection!" I now returned back to Savannah. I sent down to a little village called Thunder Bolt and got a sail boat to take me to the islands. In it I went to see the people, to tell them that if they would come over on the main land I would try to get a plantation called Belleville, which was owned by a gentleman of the name of Hopkins, in McIntosh county. There was 1,250 acres of land in this plantation, and he would not sell it for less than $14.50 per acre. Looking at the pitiful condition of the people, I agreed to give it; on which I advanced $1,000. As the people had to move with what they could only take in small boats, I got one flat-boat; but what with rain and storm, when we got to Belleville, it was almost worthless—for everything was burned up during the war on the place.

As the people dare not stay there without me, I therefore moved my own family into a camp made of old boards on the side and ends, and a Palmetto roof—for I had to have one to cook in, and the other to sleep in....

Under the Reconstruction Act of Congress I was appointed one of the registrars for the Second Senatorial District of Georgia—Liberty, McIntosh and Tatnall counties,—and subsequently was elected a member of the constitutional convention; and upon the submission of the constitutions to the people for ratification, I was elected Senator for the Second District of the State of Georgia....

[After being expelled from office because of his color, he went to Washington, D.C., met with Senator Charles Sumner and others, protested the expulsion and lobbied for a new Amendment, the Fifteenth, to guarantee voting rights. The national government returned Campbell to his senatorial seat and he worked to keep Georgia under military Reconstruction until Georgia Democrats were willing to acquiesce in the results of the Civil War Amendments.]

We all saw the danger of the State being admitted without some additional restriction, and this was brought by myself before the convention of colored men held in the city of Atlanta on February 3, 1871. I was by that convention elected a delegate at large to go to Washington and urge Congress to pass a law to protect loyal citizens in the Southern States. I arrived there in March, and found Congress just ready to adjourn; but, through the providence of God, the President issued his message to Congress, recommending to that body the consideration of the condition of loyal citizens in the Southern States, and the passage of some law looking to their protection. I had the honor of calling on the President at that time, and had assurance of his sanction to any bill passed by Congress for that purpose. The Ku-Klux Bill was passed, and of course my mission was accomplished.

Now the rebels became more enraged at me than ever. My friends informed me in Washington of plots layed to murder me on my way home, and advised me to stay in the North for a while; but without answering them, I came home before they thought I had left Washington, and went to work to find out, if possible, how they intended to kill me. The plan was this: Certain men were to come up from the country and watch for me going to or coming from the church at night, and kill me: then take my body a short distance in the woods, and leave something by it to make it appear that colored men from the country had done it. I pursued my inquiries until the statements made were fully corroborated by incidents that occurred at my own house and near the church. The parties were well known; and when they found that I was aware of their intentions, they had me arrested and taken to Savannah under the Ku-Klux Bill, before the United States Commissioner. It was another part of the programme to keep me in lawsuits, so as to compel me to leave the county to keep out of jail; or if I was put in jail, then break the jail at night and kill me in it. In any event, my life was to be taken.

I was compelled, on going up to the legislature last November, to leave my house at dusk, and go by land, to meet my son, who was waiting in Savannah for me. On my return, the captain of the steamer "Hardy" (a boat that stops at Darien coming and going to Savannah) refused to take me and another gentleman who was with me, and had my trunk put on the dock. After first taking our fare, he then came and gave it back to us, and ordered us on shore. All this was to get up a difficulty in Savannah; but being aware of their object, I at once ordered my things to be taken directly off the wharf, and crossed the country in a wagon, which took one day longer to get home. The only security that I now had for my life or property was this: The rebels knew that they would be held responsible by the loyal people of this country, both colored and white, for any injury that might be done to me....

[Georgia Democrats surged back into office in 1872 and began a systematic campaign to remove all black officeholders. As a state senator and a local justice of the peace (J.P.) in Darien, Campbell was a prime target. He found himself facing charges of judicial malfeasance in a case that had come before his J.P. court.]

My case charged false imprisonment of a man named Rafe. This man was charged with breaking into a house in which two families lived, and threatening to kill the two men—both heads of these families. Upon the affidavits of said parties I issued a warrant for his arrest, and upon a hearing, he was ordered to give a bond of $50 in each case to keep the peace for six months as towards these families, and to pay the costs of court, which he agreed to do. He went to get bondsmen; but came back and said he would not give bonds; upon which, I ordered him to be locked up; but he went and made an affidavit that he had given bonds, and then ran away.

I was indicted without having a notice to appear before the grand jury, and that charges had been preferred against me. When the regular term of court came it was adjourned, and no time was set. I had business in Washington, and went there. Upon my return home I found my dwelling-house had been burned, and the grocery and dry-goods store of my wife and son was also burned. That day the court met, and I was arrested the next day....

[After an all-white jury found him guilty but recommended "mercy," the judge sentenced him to jail. While his attorneys worked to appeal the conviction, he spent time in a prison camp.]

We then got papers ready while one of my counsel was speaking to move before Judge Hopkins, of the Atlanta Superior Court; and to do this, we had to dismiss it from before the Court of Ordinary. As soon as we dismissed it, irons were put upon me. I was then dragged to a covered wagon, and taken out of town, through by-roads, to a woods, when they made me get out and walk. Of course I took my time. When we got within a mile of a prison camp, two men came up on horseback and served papers upon the guard, ordering him to bring me back; but they not being officers, he refused. I was put in irons there, and that afternoon put to work, and the next day, until 2 o'clock, I worked, when I fell—being unable to work any longer.

The next morning it was raining. After they had breakfast I was taken by two men up to the guard tent, or headquarters, when they took off my chains. The captain of the guard showed me the order of court forbidding chains being put upon me, and ordering my return to Atlanta. After I had read it, he asked me when I expected my friends would send for me. "Why," I replied, "you are ordered by this to send me back, therefore they will not come." He then ordered a buggy to be brought, and ordered me put in, to be sent back to the Atlanta jail, in charge of a guard. I was carried to the jail by two men. When they laid me down upon the cell-floor, the men said, "He will soon die, for he is scarcely alive now." I asked one of the men to get me a little rice and milk. In about two hours he brought it. With difficulty I ate it, for I had not eaten anything for two days. The food given to prisoners was corn meal, mixed with water, without salt, made into an oval shape, and baked hard on the outside—but, as a general thing quite raw inside—and a piece of fat bacon, that eight persons to one would find raw. In going about they would pick up pieces of old-iron pots and kettles, and these were used for frying meat upon. Then they would break open the corn bread, and lay the pieces upon the coals and cook it—or rather burn it—so as to make it more palatable; but I could not eat it.

In the jail at Atlanta the food was better; but I had my meals brought from the hotel. As a general thing they kept them out in the office, until quite cold. I could never see the man who brought them. There were white prisoners who had their meals sent to them from some hotel, and the man would carry them in their cells.

Two or three days after my being brought back—I do not remember the day, for I was very sick—my lawyers brought me out again for a hearing before Judge Hopkins. I was carried up in a carriage....

[Judge Hopkins put him in an Atlanta jail while he ordered the McIntosh County court to accept bond in the case. It took a month for the lower court to comply.]

I was then brought out again, before Judge Hopkins, and gave bond. I now went down to Savannah, on my way home. I got to Savannah about 5 o'clock in the afternoon. The next day, at 2 o'clock p. m., I was arrested upon an old suit, which was not only out of date, but had been decided in my favor by the Supreme Court. In this case the judge refused to take bonds. I was then put in the jail in Savannah, which had been condemned by the grand jury on account of its unhealthiness. I was kept there for eight months and ten days. The first month I was kept in a cell down stairs, nine feet long and four and one-half feet wide. The prisoners were let out to walk in a hall six feet wide once in two weeks. Mr. Russell, after I had been there about four weeks, ordered me to go up stairs, and every day after that my cell was unlocked, and I was allowed to walk about the hall all day. My wife also made arrangement with a friend of ours to send me something to eat every day. She also sent me medicines, for her knowledge of the medicinal qualities of roots and herbs was very extensive.

I was attacked with a severe cough, and a swelling in my body, but was relieved of them by rubbing with a liniment and taking three doses a day of a syrup which was made by her.

I wrote a letter to President Grant, after I had been three or four months in jail, and, in answer, Attorney General Pierrepont informed me that he did not see how he could do anything for me. About three days after I got a communication from the Attorney General. I also received a letter from my wife, informing me of her having written to President Grant; and the same afternoon I received a communication from the Department of Justice, informing me that my wife (Mrs. Harriet Campbell) had written a letter to the President; and from statements made therein—said letter having been referred to him—that an immediate investigation should be made in my case. Just when I got through reading this letter I was ordered down to the office, and there I found the assistant attorney general for the State of Georgia—Colonel G. Thomas. He said that a dispatch had been received at Atlanta, ordering them to take my case into the United States Court. He had an affidavit drawn up, already for me to sign. He read it to me. I told him that was all right; but there was the other case before the Supreme Court of the State of Georgia, which ought also to be brought into the United States Court....

[When the Georgia Supreme Court refused to hear the case because of a legal technicality in the way the appeal had been filed and when the federal courts refused to intervene, Campbell resigned himself to defeat.]

On or about the 12th of January, 1876, the guard from the State prison came, about 7 o'clock a. m., and handcuffed me, and, with a chain about twelve feet long, dragged me along the streets of Savannah to the Central railroad, and then took me one hundred and forty miles from Savannah, to a prison camp on the plantation of Colonel Jack Smith's, in Washington county, State of Georgia. The weather was very cold, and they took me up in a wagon. I was helpless when we got there, at 1 o'clock in the night—my hands being chained together. I had a very bad fall in getting out of the wagon. I tried to get pen and ink, and finally did get pen, ink and paper, and wrote a letter to my wife. I suffered very much from my fall. They were clearing land, and ordered me to pile brush. It is impossible to describe the way in which prisoners were worked. They were taken out as soon as they could see—both winter and summer—and kept to work as long as it was light, with one hour for dinner. They had breakfast before daylight. If wood was to be cut, the strongest and most expert men with the ax were made leaders, and every other man had to keep stroke with him all day long; and if they failed to do so, they were beaten most unmercifully with a leather strop, or a buggy trace, and given from fifty to one hundred strokes, until they would keep up or die. I am well satisfied that four men in the camp where I was were whipped to death—and this was considered one of the best camps in the State. These beatings made men reckless, and they would rush here and there, like wild men, to get the favor of the guard. I must say that the guards were a low and brutal set of men, as a general thing. You could hear them all the time calling out to the men, "I don't hear those axs! Go in with those axs! Go in with those axs!" If a man could not stand the work, then he was reported, and of course beaten. Women were treated in the same manner. I was in this camp eleven months and twenty-one days.

Two women—one a prisoner and the other a hired woman (both colored)—had white babies—which shows the state of morals there. I preached in this camp. I was for three Sundays in chains; but the Monday morning after the third Sunday my chains were taken off, and I was put as overseer of the wheelwright and blacksmith shops. The keys of the store houses and cribs were given to me, as also the books for all accounts of work done on the place, or for our neighbors. Mr. and Mrs. Smith always, from that time, treated me very kindly. My meals came from their table. My wife sent me every month a box of nourishments and medicines—clothing, soda-crackers, sugar-cakes, pound-cake, strawberry and other preserves, pickled eggs, &c. Since I have been out of prison I found that my wife went to the principle keeper and stated my case to him, and through her statements he was induced to have my chains taken off. Yet I feel under many obligations to Colonel J. T. Smith and lady for their kindness to me.

My wife and daughter were, during my confinement, in the city of Atlanta; and every dollar that she had been able to collect from her customers was used up in trying to help me. She also made up medicine in the winter to sell; and in the summer, went into the woods around Atlanta and picked blackberries, and brought them to the city to sell; and from the fields brought strawberries in, and sold them. About three weeks before I got home—January 6, 1877—my little girl went out to work, so as to keep a room, that I might have a place to come once more, and be with them. She wrote all the letters sent to President Grant by her mother. In this connection, I must say that Mrs. Campbell (my wife) is a woman of remarkable good judgment, guided by firm Christian principles, and I have no language to express my thankfulness to God for both wife and child.

During the whole of this time I was in dread of the ku-klux, or parties of men who broke open jails and prison camps to get persons that they wanted out of the way.

BLACK ELK
1863–1950

Black Elk was a holy man of the Oglala band of Lakota (Sioux) who found himself a witness to the two most famous battles in history between Indians and the United States military. When he was thirteen, he took his first scalp as Sitting Bull, Crazy Horse, and Rain-in-the-Face defended their villages from the attack of George Armstrong Custer along the banks of the Little Bighorn River in Montana Territory. Fourteen years later, the sound of firing caused him to rush through the snow in South Dakota in time to watch the soldiers retreating from the massacre of two hundred Lakota men, women, and children at Wounded Knee.

Black Elk had been raised close to the earth in the old way of Lakota culture. At the age of five he learned to use a bow and ride a horse. He participated in bison hunts and followed the rhythms of the seasons from hunting ground to tribal gatherings. When courting, he snuck into tepees to steal away the woman of his desire. He led religious ceremonies that honored the bond of man with nature.

In the late 1860s, the Union Pacific Railroad split the bison herd in half and provided an artery for westward settlement. White pioneers believing in the manifest destiny of expansion and white superiority killed the buffalo and claimed the land. After years of resistance, the old way died for the Plains Indians.

Black Elk was a religious leader connected to the yesterdays of the ancestors through voices, visions, and premonitions. He first heard voices at age four; five years later he had a Great Vision in which he left his body and sat with the Powers of the World. They imparted understanding to him. Thereafter, and with the old way crumbling around him, Black Elk fixed upon the promises of the Other World for deliverance from the present one.

In 1931 as the United States suffered through the second year of the Great Depression—and as Woody Guthrie collected stories of the homeless—Black Elk told his story of the Lakota's five-decade-long depression to poet and historian John G. Neihardt. While critics argue over how much of the autobiography belongs to Black Elk and how much is derived from the skill of Neihardt, they agree that the story is true to Lakota traditions and the holy man's tone. Black Elk's son Ben, who had attended Carlisle Indian School in Pennsylvania, interpreted his father's words for Neihardt's transcription.

Black Elk Speaks *is the most influential autobiography in American Indian literature as told to a recorder. It is in a way a collective autobiography of the Indian experience on the upper Great Plains. Illustrating that alternative dreams and other nations died in the wake of the American Dream and nation, this collaborative autobiography is in the tradition that gave voice to classes, castes, and peoples who were outside the dominant power structure.*

Black Elk Speaks: Being the Life Story of a Holy Man of the Oglala Sioux, *1932. Reprint, Lincoln, NE: University of Nebraska Press, 1961. (Reprinted with permission.)*

So I know that it is a good thing I am going to do; and because no good thing can be done by any man alone, I will first make an offering and send a voice to the Spirit of the World, that it may help me to be true. See, I fill this sacred pipe with the bark of the red willow; but before we smoke it, you must see how it is made and what it means. These four ribbons hanging here on the stem are the four quarters of the universe. The black one is for the west where the thunder beings live to send us rain; the white one for the north, whence comes the great white cleansing wind; the red one for the east, whence springs the light and where the morning star lives to give men wisdom; the yellow for the south, whence come the summer and the power to grow.

But these four spirits are only one Spirit after all, and this eagle feather here is for that One, which is like a father, and also it is for the thoughts of men that should rise high as eagles do. Is not the sky a father and the earth a mother, and are not all living things with feet or wings or roots their children? And this hide upon the mouthpiece here, which should be bison hide, is for the earth, from whence we came and at whose breast we suck as babies all our lives, along with all the animals and birds and trees and grasses. And because it means all this, and more than any man can understand, the pipe is holy.

There is a story about the way the pipe first came to us. A very long time ago, they say, two scouts were out looking for bison; and when they came to the top of a high hill and looked north, they saw something coming a long way off, and when it came closer they cried out, "It is a woman!," and it was. Then one of the scouts, being foolish, had bad thoughts and spoke them; but the other said: "That is a sacred woman; throw all bad thoughts away." When she came still closer, they saw that she wore a fine white buckskin dress, that her hair was very long and that she was young and very beautiful. And she knew their thoughts and said in a voice that was like singing: "You do not know me, but if you want to do as you think, you may come." And the foolish one went; but just as he stood before her, there was a white cloud that came and covered them. And the beautiful young woman came out of the cloud, and when it blew away the foolish man was a skeleton covered with worms.

Then the woman spoke to the one who was not foolish: "You shall go home and tell your people that I am coming and that a big tepee shall be built for me in the center of the nation." And the man, who was very much afraid, went quickly and told the people, who did at once as they were told; and there around the big tepee they waited for the sacred woman. And after a while she came, very beautiful and singing, and as she went into the tepee this is what she sang:

"With visible breath I am walking.
A voice I am sending as I walk.

> In a sacred manner I am walking.
> With visible tracks I am walking.
> In a sacred manner I walk."

And as she sang, there came from her mouth a white cloud that was good to smell. Then she gave something to the chief, and it was a pipe with a bison calf carved on one side to mean the earth that bears and feeds us, and with twelve eagle feathers hanging from the stem to mean the sky and the twelve moons, and these were tied with a grass that never breaks. "Behold!" she said. "With this you shall multiply and be a good nation. Nothing but good shall come from it. Only the hands of the good shall take care of it and the bad shall not even see it." Then she sang again and went out of the tepee; and as the people watched her going, suddenly it was a white bison galloping away and snorting, and soon it was gone.

This they tell, and whether it happened so or not I do not know; but if you think about it, you can see that it is true.

Now I light the pipe, and after I have offered it to the powers that are one Power, and sent forth a voice to them, we shall smoke together. Offering the mouthpiece first of all to the One above—so—I send a voice:

Hey hey! hey hey! hey hey! hey hey! . . .

I am a Lakota of the Ogalala band. My father's name was Black Elk, and his father before him bore the name, and the father of his father, so that I am the fourth to bear it. He was a medicine man and so were several of his brothers. Also, he and the great Crazy Horse's father were cousins, having the same grandfather. My mother's name was White Cow Sees; her father was called Refuse-to-Go, and her mother, Plenty Eagle Feathers. I can remember my mother's mother and her father. My father's father was killed by the Pawnees when I was too little to know, and his mother, Red Eagle Woman, died soon after.

I was born in the Moon of the Popping Trees (December) on the Little Powder River in the Winter When the Four Crows Were Killed (1863), and I was three years old when my father's right leg was broken in the Battle of the Hundred Slain. From that wound he limped until the day he died, which was about the time when Big Foot's band was butchered on Wounded Knee (1890). He is buried here in these hills.

I can remember that Winter of the Hundred Slain as a man may remember some bad dream he dreamed when he was little, but I can not tell just how much I heard when I was bigger and how much I understood when I was little. It is like some fearful thing in a fog, for it was a time when everything seemed troubled and afraid.

I had never seen a Wasichu [white man] then, and did not know what one looked like; but every one was saying that the Wasichus were coming and that they were going to take our country and rub us all out and that we should all have to die fighting. It was the Wasichus who got rubbed out in that battle, and all the people were talking about it for a long while; but a hundred Wasichus was not much if there were others and others without number where those came from.

I remember once that I asked my grandfather about this. I said: "When the scouts come back from seeing the prairie full of bison somewhere, the people say the Wasichus are coming; and when strange men are coming to kill us all, they say the Wasichus are coming. What does it mean?" And he said, "That they are many."

BLACK ELK

When I was older, I learned what the fighting was about that winter and the next summer. Up on the Madison Fork the Wasichus had found much of the yellow metal that they worship and that makes them crazy, and they wanted to have a road up through our country to the place where the yellow metal was; but my people did not want the road. It would scare the bison and make them go away, and also it would let the other Wasichus come in like a river. They told us that they wanted only to use a little land, as much as a wagon would take between the wheels; but our people knew better. And when you look about you now, you can see what it was they wanted.

Once we were happy in our own country and we were seldom hungry, for then the two-leggeds and the four-leggeds lived together like relatives, and there was plenty for them and for us. But the Wasichus came, and they have made little islands for us and other little islands for the four-leggeds, and always these islands are becoming smaller, for around them surges the gnawing flood of the Wasichu; and it is dirty with lies and greed. . . .

When it was summer again we were camping on the Rosebud, and I did not feel so much afraid, because the Wasichus seemed farther away and there was peace there in the valley and there was plenty of meat. But all the boys from five or six years up were playing war. The little boys would gather together from the different bands of the tribe and fight each other with mud balls that they threw with willow sticks. And the big boys played the game called Throwing-Them-Off-Their-Horses, which is a battle all but the killing; and sometimes they got hurt. The horsebacks from the different bands would line up and charge upon each other, yelling; and when the ponies came together on the run, they would rear and flounder and scream in a big dust, and the riders would seize each other, wrestling until one side had lost all its men, for those who fell upon the ground were counted dead.

When I was older, I, too, often played this game. We were always naked when we played it, just as warriors are when they go into battle if it is not too cold, because they are swifter without clothes. Once I fell off on my back right in the middle of a bed of prickly pears, and it took my mother a long while to pick all the stickers out of me. I was still too little to play war that summer, but I can remember watching the other boys, and I thought that when we all grew up and were big together, maybe we could kill all the Wasichus or drive them far away from our country. . . .

I was four years old then, and I think it must have been the next summer that I first heard the voices. It was a happy summer and nothing was afraid, because in the Moon When the Ponies Shed (May) word came from the Wasichus that there would be peace and that they would not use the road any more and that all the soldiers would go away. The soldiers did go away and their towns were torn down; and in the Moon of Falling Leaves (November), they made a treaty with Red Cloud that said our country would be ours as long as grass should grow and water flow. You can see that it is not the grass and the water that have forgotten.

Maybe it was not this summer when I first heard the voices, but I think it was, because I know it was before I played with bows and arrows or rode a horse, and I was out playing alone when I heard them. It was like somebody calling me, and I thought it was my mother, but there was nobody there. This happened more than once, and always made me afraid, so that I ran home.

It was when I was five years old that my Grandfather made me a bow and some arrows. The grass was young and I was horseback. A thunder storm was coming from where the sun goes down, and just as I was riding into the woods along a creek, there was a kingbird sitting on a limb. This was not a dream, it happened. And I was going to shoot at the kingbird with the bow my Grandfather made, when the bird spoke and said: "The clouds all over are one-sided." Perhaps it meant that all the clouds were looking at me. And then it said: "Listen! A voice is calling you!" Then I looked up at the clouds, and two men were coming there, headfirst like arrows slanting down; and as they came, they sang a sacred song and the thunder was like drumming. I will sing it for you. The song and the drumming were like this:

> "Behold, a sacred voice is calling you;
> All over the sky a sacred voice is calling."

I sat there gazing at them, and they were coming from the place where the giant lives (north). But when they were very close to me, they wheeled about toward where the sun goes down, and suddenly they were geese. Then they were gone, and the rain came with a big wind and a roaring.

I did not tell this vision to any one. I liked to think about it, but I was afraid to tell it.

What happened after that until the summer I was nine years old is not a story. There were winters and summers, and they were good; for the Wasichus had made their iron road along the Platte and traveled there. This had cut the bison herd in two, but those that stayed in our country with us were more than could be counted, and we wandered without trouble in our land.

Now and then the voices would come back when I was out alone, like someone calling me, but what they wanted me to do I did not know. This did not happen very often, and when it did not happen, I forgot about it; for I was growing taller and was riding horses now and could shoot prairie chickens and rabbits with my bow. The boys of my people began very young to learn the ways of men, and no one taught us; we just learned by doing what we saw, and we were warriors at a time when boys now are like girls. . . .

[A nine-year-old Black Elk, wracked with illness, had a "Great Vision" of a flaming rainbow tepee occupied by his Lakota "Grandfathers." These "Great Powers" revealed to him the understanding that the earth and his people were concentric circles with a sacred tree in the center. After returning from his vision, and with his parents unaware that he "had been so far away," Black Elk's band followed the buffalo migration. His telling of the vision and subsequent visions made him a tribal holy man.]

I was ten years old that winter, and that was the first time I ever saw a Wasichu. At first I thought they all looked sick, and I was afraid they might just begin to fight us any time, but I got used to them.

That winter one of our boys climbed the flagpole and chopped it off near the top. This almost made bad trouble, for the soldiers surrounded us with their guns; but Red Cloud, who was living there, stood right in the middle without a weapon and made speeches to the Wasichus and to us. He said the boy who did it must be punished, and he told the Wasichus it was foolish for men to want to shoot grown people because their little boys did foolish things in play; and he asked them if they ever did foolish things for fun when they were boys. So nothing happened after all.

Red Cloud was a great chief, and he was an Ogalala. But at this time he was through with fighting. After the treaty he made with the Wasichus five years before (1868) he never fought again, and he was living with his band, the Bad Faces, at the Soldiers' Town. Crazy Horse was an Ogalala too, and I think he was the greatest chief of all.

In the Moon of the Red Grass Appearing (April) about thirty tepees of us broke camp and started for the Black Hills to cut tepee poles. We followed down Horse-Head-Cutting Creek to its mouth, and while we were camped there one day I was away from the village alone, when I heard a spotted eagle whistle. I looked up and there he was, hovering over me. The queer feeling came back very strong, and for a little while it seemed that I was in the world of my vision again.

From there we moved on to Buffalo Gap at the foot of the Hills, and my father and I went out alone to look for deer. We climbed up through the timber to the top of a big hill, and it was hard for my father, who was lame from the wound he got in the Battle of the Hundred Slain. When we were on top, my father looked down and said: "There are some yonder. You stay here, and I will go around them." Then the queer feeling came back, and I said without knowing why I said it: "No, father, stay here; for they are bringing them to us." He looked at me hard, and said: "Who is bringing them?" I could not answer; and after he had looked hard at me again, he said: "All right, son." So we lay down there in the grass and waited. They did come to us, and my father got two of them.

While we were butchering and I was eating some liver, I felt sorry that we had killed these animals and thought that we ought to do something in return. So I said: "Father, should we not offer one of these to the wild things?" He looked hard at me again for a while. Then he placed one of the deer with its head to the east, and, facing the west, he raised his hand and cried, "Hey-hey" four times and prayed like this: "Grandfather, the Great Spirit, behold me! To all the wild things that eat flesh, this I have offered that my people may live and the children grow up with plenty."

That was another happy summer, for the big trouble had not come yet. We cut plenty of tepee poles up along the creeks that came down the east side of the Black Hills, and there was all we wanted to eat, for the Hills were like a big food pack for our people. Iron Bull, a little boy my age, and I had great fun fishing. We always made an offering of bait to the fish, saying: "You who are down in the water with wings of red, I offer this to you; so come hither." Then when we caught the first fish, we would put it on a forked stick and kiss it. If we did not do this, we were sure the others would know and stay away. If we caught a little fish, we would kiss it and throw it back, so that it would not go and frighten the bigger fish. I don't know whether all this helped or not, but we always got plenty of fish, and our parents were proud of us. We tried to catch as many as we could so that people would think much of us. . . .

[Black Elk told how his people had been forced to leave the Black Hills and settle near Soldiers' Town (Fort Laramie) when soldiers under Pahushka (George Custer) entered the area.]

Afterward I learned that it was Pahuska [General Custer] who had led his soldiers into the Black Hills that summer to see what he could find. He had no right to go in there, because all that country was ours. Also the Wasichus had made a treaty with Red Cloud (1868) that said it would be ours as long as grass should grow and water flow. Later I learned too that Pahuska had found there much of the yellow metal that makes the Wasichus crazy; and that is what made the bad trouble, just as it did before, when the hundred were rubbed out.

Our people knew there was yellow metal in little chunks up there; but they did not bother with it, because it was not good for anything.

We stayed all winter at the Soldiers' Town, and all the while the bad trouble was coming fast; for in the fall we heard that some Wasichus had come from the Missouri River to dig in the Black Hills for the yellow metal, because Pahuska had told about it with a voice that went everywhere. Later he got rubbed out for doing that.

The people talked about this all winter. Crazy Horse was in the Powder River country and Sitting Bull was somewhere north of the Hills. Our people at the Soldiers' Town thought we ought to get together and do something. Red Cloud's people said that the soldiers had gone in there to keep the diggers out, but we, who were only visiting, did not believe it. We called Red Cloud's people "Hangs-Around-the-Fort," and our people said they were standing up for the Wasichus, and if we did not do something we should lose the Black Hills.

In the spring when I was twelve years old (1875), more soldiers with many wagons came up from the Soldiers' Town at the mouth of the Laramie River and went into the Hills. . . .

[In 1875 and 1876 when prospectors swarmed over the Black Hills looking for gold, a group of Lakota led by Crazy Horse—which included Black Elk and his family—split from the "Hangs-Around-the-Fort" people of Red Cloud. As the United States Army attempted to force compliance from the nonreservation-minded Indians, fighting broke out and increased.]

About the middle of the Moon of Making Fat (June) the whole village moved a little way up the River to a good place for a sun dance. The valley was wide and flat there, and we camped in a great oval with the river flowing through it, and in the center they built the bower of branches in a circle for the dancers, with the opening of it to the east whence comes the light. Scouts were sent out in all directions to guard the sacred place. Sitting Bull, who was the greatest medicine man of the nation at that time, had charge of this dance to purify the people and to give them power and endurance. It was held in the Moon of Fatness because that is the time when the sun is highest and the growing power of the world is strongest. I will tell you how it was done.

First a holy man was sent out all alone to find the waga chun, the holy tree that should stand in the middle of the dancing circle. Nobody dared follow to see what he did or hear the sacred words he would say there. And when he had found the right tree, he would tell the people, and they would come there singing, with flowers all over them. Then when they had gathered about the holy tree, some women who were bearing children would dance around it, because the Spirit of the Sun loves all fruitfulness. After that a warrior, who had done some very brave deed that summer, struck the tree, counting coup upon it; and when he had done this, he had to give gifts to those who had least of everything, and the braver he was, the more he gave away.

After this, a band of young maidens came singing, with sharp axes in their hands; and they had to be so good that nobody there could say anything against them, or that any man had ever known them; and it was the duty of any one who knew anything bad about any of them to tell it right before all the people there and prove it. But if anybody lied, it was very bad for him.

The maidens chopped the tree down and trimmed its branches off. Then chiefs, who were the sons of chiefs, carried the sacred tree home, stopping four times on the way, once for each season, giving thanks for each.

Now when the holy tree had been brought home but was not yet set up in the center of the dancing place, mounted warriors gathered around the circle of the village, and at a signal they all charged inward upon the center where the tree would stand, each trying to be the first to touch the sacred place; and whoever was the first could not be killed in war that year. When they all came together in the middle, it was like a battle, with the ponies rearing and screaming in a big dust and the men shouting and wrestling and trying to throw each other off the horses.

After that there was a big feast and plenty for everybody to eat, and a big dance just as though we had won a victory.

The next day the tree was planted in the center by holy men who sang sacred songs and made sacred vows to the Spirit. And the next morning nursing mothers brought their holy little ones to lay them at the bottom of the tree, so that the sons would be brave men and the daughters the mothers of brave men. The holy men pierced the ears of the little ones, and for each piercing the parents gave away a pony to some one who was in need.

The next day the dancing began, and those who were going to take part were ready, for they had been fasting and purifying themselves in the sweat lodges, and praying. First, their bodies were painted by the holy men. Then each would lie down beneath the tree as though he were dead, and the holy men would cut a place in his back or chest, so that a strip of rawhide, fastened to the top of the tree, could be pushed through the flesh and tied. Then the man would get up and dance to the drums, leaning on the rawhide strip as long as he could stand the pain or until the flesh tore loose.

We smaller boys had a good time during the two days of dancing, for we were allowed to do almost anything to tease the people, and they had to stand it. We would gather sharp spear grass, and when a man came along without a shirt, we would stick him to see if we could make him cry out, for everybody was supposed to endure everything. Also we made pop-guns out of young ash boughs and shot at the men and women to see if we could make them jump; and if they did, everybody laughed at them. The mothers carried water to their holy little ones in bladder bags, and we made little bows and arrows that we could hide under our robes so that we could steal up to the women and shoot holes in the bags. They were supposed to stand anything and not scold us when the water spurted out. We had a good time there.

Right after the sun dance was over, some of our scouts came in from the south, and the crier went around the circle and said: "The scouts have returned and they have reported that soldiers are camping up the river. So, young warriors, take courage and get ready to meet them."

While they were all getting ready, I was getting ready too, because Crazy Horse was going to lead the warriors and I wanted to go with him; but my uncle, who thought a great deal of me, said: "Young nephew, you must not go. Look at the helpless ones. Stay home, and maybe there will be plenty of fighting right here." So the war parties went on without me. Maybe my uncle thought I was too little to do much and might get killed.

Then the crier told us to break camp, and we moved over west towards the Greasy Grass [Little Bighorn] and camped at the head of Spring Creek while the war parties were gone. We learned later that it was Three Stars [General Crook] who fought with our people on the Rosebud that time. . . .

Crazy Horse whipped Three Stars on the Rosebud that day, and I think he could have rubbed the soldiers out there. He could have called many more warriors from the villages and he could have rubbed the soldiers out at daybreak, for they camped there in the dark after the fight.

He whipped the cavalry of Three Stars when they attacked his village on the Powder that cold morning in the Moon of the Snowblind (March). Then he moved farther west to the Rosebud; and when the soldiers came to kill us there, he whipped them and made them go back. Then he moved farther west to the valley of the Greasy Grass. We were in our own country all the time and we only wanted to be let alone. The soldiers came there to kill us, and many got rubbed out. It was our country and we did not want to have trouble.

We camped there in the valley along the south side of the Greasy Grass before the sun was straight above; and this was, I think, two days before the battle. It was a very big village and you could hardly count the tepees. Farthest up the stream toward the south were the Hunkpapas, and the Ogalalas were next. Then came the Minneconjous, the Sans Arcs, the Blackfeet, the Shyelas; and last, the farthest toward the north, were the Santees and Yanktonais. Along the side towards the east was the Greasy Grass, with some timber along it, and it was running full from the melting of the snow in the Big Horn Mountains. If you stood on a hill you could see the mountains off to the south and west. On the other side of the river, there were bluffs and hills beyond. Some gullies came down through the bluffs. On the westward side of us were lower hills, and there we grazed our ponies and guarded them. There were so many they could not be counted. . . .

[On June 25, 1876, Custer launched a two-pronged attack on the village along the Little Bighorn River in Montana. Black Elk described the initial confusion of the Indians before they rallied for "the rubbing out of Long Hair."]

"Crazy Horse is coming! Crazy Horse is coming!" Off toward the west and north they were yelling "Hoka hey!" like a big wind roaring, and making the tremolo; and you could hear eagle bone whistles screaming.

The valley went darker with dust and smoke, and there were only shadows and a big noise of many cries and hoofs and guns. On the left of where I was I could hear the shod hoofs of the soldiers' horses going back into the brush and there was shooting everywhere. Then the hoofs came out of the brush, and I came out and was in among men and horses weaving in and out and going upstream, and everybody was yelling, "Hurry! Hurry!" The soldiers were running upstream and we were all mixed there in the twilight and the great noise. I did not see much; but once I saw a Lakota charge at a soldier who stayed behind and fought and was a very brave man. The Lakota took the soldier's horse by the bridle, but the soldier killed him with a six-shooter. I was small and could not crowd in to where the soldiers were, so I did not kill anybody. There were so many ahead of me, and it was all dark and mixed up.

Soon the soldiers were all crowded into the river, and many Lakotas too; and I was in the water awhile. Men and horses were all mixed up and fighting in the water, and it was like hail falling in the river. Then we were out of the river, and people were stripping dead soldiers and putting the clothes on themselves. There was a soldier on the ground and he was still kicking. A Lakota rode up and said to me: "Boy, get off and scalp him." I got off and started to do it. He had short hair and my knife was not very sharp. He ground his teeth. Then I shot him in the forehead and got his scalp.

Many of our warriors were following the soldiers up a hill on the other side of the river. Everybody else was turning back down stream, and on a hill away down yonder above the Santee camp there was a big dust, and our warriors whirling around in and out of it just like swallows, and many guns were going off.

I thought I would show my mother my scalp, so I rode over toward the hill where there was a crowd of women and children. On the way down there I saw a very pretty young woman among a band of warriors about to go up to the battle on the hill, and she was singing like this:

"Brothers, now your friends have come!
Be brave! Be brave!
Would you see me taken captive?"

When I rode through the Ogalala camp I saw Rattling Hawk sitting up in his tepee with a gun in his hands, and he was all alone there singing a song of regret that went like this:

"Brothers, what are you doing that I can not do?"

When I got to the women on the hill they were all singing and making the tremolo to cheer the men fighting across the river in the dust on the hill. My mother gave a big tremolo just for me when she saw my first scalp.

I stayed there awhile with my mother and watched the big dust whirling on the hill across the river, and horses were coming out of it with empty saddles. . . .

After I showed my mother my first scalp, I stayed with the women awhile and they were all singing and making the tremolo. We could not see much of the battle for the big dust, but we knew there would be no soldiers left. There were many other boys about my age and younger up there with their mothers and sisters, and they asked me to go over to the battle with them. So we got on our ponies and started. While we were riding down hill toward the river we saw gray horses with empty saddles stampeding toward the water. We rode over across the Greasy Grass to the mouth of a gulch that led up through the bluff to where the fighting was.

Before we got there, the Wasichus were all down, and most of them were dead, but some of them were still alive and kicking. Many other little boys had come up by this time, and we rode around shooting arrows into the Wasichus. There was one who was squirming around with arrows sticking in him, and I started to take his coat, but a man pushed me away and took the coat for himself. Then I saw something bright hanging on this soldier's belt, and I pulled it out. It was round and bright and yellow and very beautiful and I put it on me for a necklace. At first it ticked inside, and then it did not any more. I wore it around my neck a long time before I found out what it was and how to make it tick again.

Then the women all came over and we went to the top of the hill. Gray horses were lying dead there, and some of them were on top of dead Wasichus and dead Wasichus were on top of them. There were not many of our own dead there, because they had been picked up already; but many of our men were killed and wounded. They shot each other in the dust. I did not see Pahuska, and I think nobody knew which one he was. There was a soldier who was raising his arms and groaning. I shot an arrow into his forehead, and his arms and legs quivered. I saw some Lakotas holding another Lakota up. I went over there, and it was Chase-in-the-Morning's brother, who was called Black Wasichu. He had been shot through the right shoulder downward, and the bullet stopped in his left hip, because he was hanging on the side of his horse when he was hit. They were trying to give him some medicine. He was my cousin, and his father and my father were so angry over this, that they went and butchered a Wasichu and cut him open. The Wasichu was fat, and his meat looked good to eat, but we did not eat any.

There was a little boy, younger than I was, who asked me to scalp a soldier for him. I did, and he ran to show the scalp to his mother. While we were there, most of the warriors chased the other soldiers back to the hill where they had their pack mules. After awhile I got tired looking around. I could smell nothing but blood, and I got sick of it. So I went back home with some others. I was not sorry at all. I was a happy boy. Those Wasichus had come to kill our mothers and fathers and us, and it was our country. When I was in the brush up there by the Hunkpapas, and the first soldiers were shooting, I knew this would happen. I thought that my people were relatives to the thunder beings of my vision, and that the soldiers were very foolish to do this. . . .

[A month after the battle with Custer, the village broke into several groups. Sitting Bull led a large group into "Grandmother's Land" (Canada) to escape U.S. army reprisals; Black Elk stayed with Crazy Horse to fight for their land.]

Wherever we went, the soldiers came to kill us, and it was all our own country. It was ours already when the Wasichus made the treaty with Red Cloud, that said it would be ours as long as grass should grow and water flow. That was only eight winters before, and they were chasing us now because we remembered and they forgot.

After that we started west again, and we were not happy anymore, because so many of our people had untied their horses' tails and gone over to the Wasichus. We went back deep into our country, and most of the land was black from the fire, and the bison had gone away. We camped on the Tongue River where there was some cottonwood for the ponies; and a hard winter came on early. It snowed much; game was hard to find, and it was a hungry time for us. Ponies died, and we ate them. They died because the snow froze hard and they could not find the grass that was left in the valleys and there was not enough cottonwood to feed them all. There had been thousands of us together that summer, but there were not two thousand now.

News came to us there in the Moon of the Falling Leaves (November) that the Black Hills had been sold to the Wasichus and also all the country west of the

Hills—the country we were in then. I learned when I was older that our people did not want to do this. The Wasichus went to some of the chiefs alone and got them to put their marks on the treaty. Maybe some of them did this when they were crazy from drinking the minne wakan (holy water, whiskey) the Wasichus gave them. I have heard this; I do not know. But only crazy or very foolish men would sell their Mother Earth. Sometimes I think it might have been better if we had stayed together and made them kill us all. . . .

[Finally, cold, starving, and outgunned, Black Elk's group surrendered at Fort Laramie. After the soldiers killed Crazy Horse and moved the tribe to a reservation, a few Indians, including a fifteen-year-old Black Elk, fled to Canada. The soldiers soon forced them to return. Black Elk spent much time in visions and ceremonies as the Lakota searched for deliverance.]

You have noticed that everything an Indian does is in a circle, and that is because the Power of the World always works in circles, and everything tries to be round. In the old days when we were a strong and happy people, all our power came to us from the sacred hoop of the nation, and so long as the hoop was unbroken, the people flourished. The flowering tree was the living center of the hoop, and the circle of the four quarters nourished it. The east gave peace and light, the south gave warmth, the west gave rain, and the north with its cold and mighty wind gave strength and endurance. This knowledge came to us from the outer world with our religion. Everything the Power of the World does is done in a circle. The sky is round, and I have heard that the earth is round like a ball, and so are all the stars. The wind, in its greatest power, whirls. Birds make their nests in circles, for theirs is the same religion as ours. The sun comes forth and goes down again in a circle. The moon does the same, and both are round. Even the seasons form a great circle in their changing, and always come back again to where they were. The life of a man is a circle from childhood to childhood, and so it is in everything where power moves. Our tepees were round like the nests of birds, and these were always set in a circle, the nation's hoop, a nest of many nests, where the Great Spirit meant for us to hatch our children.

But the Wasichus have put us in these square boxes. Our power is gone and we are dying, for the power is not in us any more. You can look at our boys and see how it is with us. When we were living by the power of the circle in the way we should, boys were men at twelve or thirteen years of age. But now it takes them very much longer to mature.

Well, it is as it is. We are prisoners of war while we are waiting here. But there is another world. . . .

It was in the summer of my twentieth year (1883) that I performed the ceremony of the elk. That fall, they say, the last of the bison herds was slaughtered by the Wasichus. I can remember when the bison were so many that they could not be counted, but more and more Wasichus came to kill them until there were only heaps of bones scattered where they used to be. The Wasichus did not kill them to eat; they killed them for the metal that makes them crazy, and they took only the hides to sell. Sometimes they did not even take the hides, only the tongues; and I have heard that fire-boats came down the Missouri River loaded with dried bison tongues. You can see that the men who did this were crazy. Sometimes they did not even take the tongues; they just killed and killed because they liked to do that. When we hunted bison, we killed only what we needed. And when there was nothing left but heaps of bones, the Wasichus came and gathered up even the bones and sold them.

All our people now were settling down in square gray houses, scattered here and there across this hungry land, and around them the Wasichus had drawn a line to keep them in. The nation's hoop was broken, and there was no center any longer for the flowering tree. The people were in despair. They seemed heavy to me, heavy and dark; so heavy that it seemed they could not be lifted; so dark that they could not be made to see any more. Hunger was among us often now, for much of what the Great Father in Washington sent us must have been stolen by Wasichus who were crazy to get money. There were many lies, but we could not eat them. The forked tongue made promises.

I kept on curing the sick for three years more, and many came to me and were made over; but when I thought of my great vision, which was to save the nation's hoop and make the holy tree to bloom in the center of it, I felt like crying, for the sacred hoop was broken and scattered. The life of the people was in the hoop, and what are many little lives if the life of those lives be gone?

But late in my twenty-third summer (1886), it seemed that there was a little hope. There came to us some Wasichus who wanted a band of Ogalalas for a big show that the other Pahuska had. They told us this show would go across the big water to strange lands, and I thought I ought to go, because I might learn some secret of the Wasichu. . . .

[For two years, Black Elk toured the Eastern United States and Europe as part of Buffalo Bill Cody's Wild West Show. He returned to his tribe in 1889 just as news that a Paiute mystic, Wovoka, had spoken to the Great Spirit: "the Great Spirit told him how to save the Indian peoples and make the Wasichus disappear and bring back all the bison and the people who were dead and how there would be a new earth." The secret to this messianic resurrection was in the ceremony of the Ghost Dance—a phenomenon that spread quickly among the Plains Indians, but was strongest among the militant Lakota.]

Afterwhile I heard that north of Pine Ridge at the head of Cheyenne Creek, Kicking Bear had held the first ghost dance, and that people who danced had seen their dead relatives and talked to them. The next thing I heard was that they were dancing on Wounded Knee Creek just below Manderson.

I did not believe yet, but I wanted to find out things, because all this was sitting more and more strongly in my heart since my father died. Something seemed to tell me to go and see. For awhile I kept from going, but at last I could not any more. So I got on my horse and went to this ghost dance on Wounded Knee Creek below Manderson.

I was surprised, and could hardly believe what I saw; because so much of my vision seemed to be in it. The dancers, both women and men, were holding hands in a big circle, and in the center of the circle they had a tree painted red with most of its branches cut off and some dead leaves on it. This was exactly like the part of my vision where the holy tree was dying, and the circle of the men and women holding hands was like the sacred hoop that should have power to make the tree to bloom again. I saw too that the sacred articles the people had offered were scarlet, as in my vision, and all their faces were painted red. Also, they used the pipe and the eagle feathers. I sat there looking on and feeling sad. It all seemed to be from my great vision somehow and I had done nothing yet to make the tree to bloom.

Then all at once great happiness overcame me, and it all took hold of me right there. This was to remind me to get to work at once and help to bring my people back into the sacred hoop, that they might again walk the red road in a sacred manner pleasing to the Powers of the Universe that are One Power. I remembered how the spirits had taken me to the center of the earth and shown me the good things, and how my people should prosper. I remembered how the Six Grandfathers had told me that through their power I should make my people live and the holy tree should bloom. I believed my vision was coming true at last, and happiness overcame me.

When I went to the dance, I went only to see and to learn what the people believed; but now I was going to stay and use the power that had been given me. The dance was over for that day, but they would dance again next day, and I would dance with them. . . .

[Black Elk came to believe in the power of the Ghost Dance and had visions as he participated.]

I was floating head first through the air. My arms were stretched out, and all I saw at first was a single eagle feather right in front of me. Then the feather was a spotted eagle dancing on ahead of me with his wings fluttering, and he was making the shrill whistle that is his. My body did not move at all, but I looked ahead and floated fast toward where I looked.

There was a ridge right in front of me, and I thought I was going to run into it, but I went right over it. On the other side of the ridge I could see a beautiful land where many, many people were camping in a great circle. I could see that they were happy and had plenty. Everywhere there were drying racks full of meat. The air was clear and beautiful with a living light that was everywhere. All around the circle, feeding on the green, green grass, were fat and happy horses; and animals of all kinds were scattered all over the green hills, and singing hunters were returning with their meat.

I floated over the tepees and began to come down feet first at the center of the hoop where I could see a beautiful tree all green and full of flowers. When I touched the ground, two men were coming toward me, and they wore holy shirts made and painted in a certain way. They came to me and said: "It is not yet time to see your father, who is happy. You have work to do. We will give you something that you shall carry back to your people, and with it they shall come to see their loved ones."

I knew it was the way their holy shirts were made that they wanted me to take back. They told me to return at once, and then I was out in the air again, floating fast as before. When I came right over the dancing place, the people were still dancing, but it seemed they were not making any sound. I had hoped to see the withered tree in bloom, but it was dead.

Then I fell back into my body, and as I did this I heard voices all around and above me, and I was sitting on the ground. Many were crowding around, asking me what vision I had seen. I told them just what I had seen, and what I brought back was the memory of the holy shirts the two men wore. . . .

[Throughout 1890, he danced and hoped for fulfillment of the prophecy. His people were under the control of the soldiers at the Pine Ridge Agency.]

We camped on White River, then on White Clay, then on Cheyenne Creek north of Pine Ridge. Most of the Ogalalas were camping near there too.

It was about this time that bad news came to us from the north. We heard that some policemen from Standing Rock had gone to arrest Sitting Bull on Grand River, and that he would not let them take him; so there was a fight, and they killed him.

It was now near the end of the Moon of Popping Trees, and I was twenty-seven years old (December, 1890). We heard that Big Foot was coming down from the Badlands with nearly four hundred people. Some of these were from Sitting Bull's band. They had run away when Sitting Bull was killed, and joined Big Foot on Good River. There were only about a hundred warriors in this band, and all the others were women and children and some old men. They were all starving and freezing, and Big Foot was so sick that they had to bring him along in a pony drag. They had all run away to hide in the Badlands, and they were coming in now because they were starving and freezing. When they crossed Smoky Earth River, they followed up Medicine Root Creek to its head. Soldiers were over there looking for them. The soldiers had everything and were not freezing and starving. Near Porcupine Butte the soldiers came up to the Big Foots, and they surrendered and went along with the soldiers to Wounded Knee Creek where the Brenan store is now.

It was in the evening when we heard that the Big Foots were camped over there with the soldiers, about fifteen miles by the old road from where we were. It was the next morning (December 29, 1890) that something terrile happened.

That evening before it happened, I went in to Pine Ridge and heard these things, and while I was there, soldiers started for where the Big Foots were. These made about five hundred soldiers that were there next morning. When I saw them starting I felt that something terrible was going to happen. That night I could hardly sleep at all. I walked around most of the night.

In the morning I went out after my horses, and while I was out I heard shooting off toward the east, and I knew from the sound that it must be wagon-guns (cannon) going off. The sounds went right through my body, and I felt that something terrible would happen.

When I reached camp with the horses, a man rode up to me and said: "Hey-hey-hey! The people that are coming are fired on! I know it!"

I saddled up my buckskin and put on my sacred shirt. . . .

[On December 29, 1890, at Wounded Knee, quick tempers, exacerbated by white fears over the Ghost Dance, led to the massacre of Big Foot's (formerly Sitting Bull's) followers before Black Elk's group could mobilize to help them.]

By now many other Lakotas, who had heard the shooting, were coming up from Pine Ridge, and we all charged on the soldiers. They ran eastward toward where the trouble began. We followed down along the dry gulch, and what we saw was terrible. Dead and wounded women and children and little babies were scattered all along there where they had been trying to run away. The soldiers had followed along the gulch, as they ran, and murdered them in there. Sometimes they were in heaps because they had huddled together, and some were scattered all along. Sometimes bunches of them had been killed and torn to pieces where the wagon guns hit them. I saw a little baby trying to suck its mother, but she was bloody and dead.

There were two little boys at one place in this gulch. They had guns and they had been killing soldiers all by themselves. We could see the soldiers they had killed. The boys were all alone there, and they were not hurt. These were very brave little boys.

When we drove the soldiers back, they dug themselves in, and we were not enough people to drive them out from there. In the evening they marched off up Wounded Knee Creek, and then we saw all that they had done there.

Men and women and children were heaped and scattered all over the flat at the bottom of the little hill where the soldiers had their wagon-guns, and westward up the dry gulch all the way to the high ridge, the dead women and children and babies were scattered.

When I saw this I wished that I had died too, but I was not sorry for the women and children. It was better for them to be happy in the other world, and I wanted to be there too. But before I went there I wanted to have revenge. I thought there might be a day, and we should have revenge.

After the soldiers marched away, I heard from my friend, Dog Chief, how the trouble started, and he was right there by Yellow Bird when it happened. This is the way it was:

In the morning the soldiers began to take all the guns away from the Big Foots, who were camped in the flat below the little hill where the monument and burying ground are now. The people had stacked most of their guns, and even their knives, by the tepee where Big Foot was lying sick. Soldiers were on the little hill and all around, and there were soldiers across the dry gulch to the south and over east along Wounded Knee Creek too. The people were nearly surrounded, and the wagon-guns were pointing at them.

Some had not yet given up their guns, and so the soldiers were searching all the tepees, throwing things around and poking into everything. There was a man called Yellow Bird, and he and another man were standing in front of the tepee where Big Foot was lying sick. They had white sheets around and over them, with eyeholes to look through, and they had guns under these. An officer came to search them. He took the other man's gun, and then started to take Yellow Bird's. But Yellow Bird would not let go. He wrestled with the officer, and while they were wrestling, the gun went off and killed the officer. Wasichus and some others have said he meant to do this, but Dog Chief was standing right there, and he told me it was not so. As soon as the gun went off, Dog Chief told me, an officer shot and killed Big Foot who was lying sick inside the tepee.

Then suddenly nobody knew what was happening, except that the soldiers were all shooting and the wagon-guns began going off right in among the people.

Many were shot down right there. The women and children ran into the gulch and up west, dropping all the time, for the soldiers shot them as they ran. There were only about a hundred warriors and there were nearly five hundred soldiers. The warriors rushed to where they had piled their guns and knives. They fought soldiers with only their hands until they got their guns.

Dog Chief saw Yellow Bird run into a tepee with his gun, and from there he killed soldiers until the tepee caught fire. Then he died full of bullets.

It was a good winter day when all this happened. The sun was shining. But after the soldiers marched away from their dirty work, a heavy snow began to fall. The wind came up in the night. There was a big blizzard, and it grew very cold. The snow drifted deep in the crooked gulch, and it was one long grave of butchered women and children and babies, who had never done any harm and were only trying to run away. . . .

[Many Lakota left the Pine Ridge Agency to fight, but after a few weeks the January temperature, lack of food and shelter, and United States army soon brought them to realize that the long struggle for independence had ended in defeat.]

We wanted a much bigger war-party so that we could meet the soldiers and get revenge. But this was hard, because the people were not all of the same mind, and they were hungry and cold. We had a meeting there, and were all ready to go out with more warriors, when Afraid-of-His-Horses came over from Pine Ridge to make peace with Red Cloud, who was with us there.

Our party wanted go to out and fight anyway, but Red Cloud made a speech to us something like this: "Brothers, this is a very hard winter. The women and children are starving and freezing. If this were summer, I would say to keep on fighting to the end. But we cannot do this. We must think of the women and children and that it is very bad for them. So we must make peace, and I will see that nobody is hurt by the soldiers."

The people agreed to this, for it was true. So we broke camp next day and went down from the O-ona-gazhee to Pine Ridge, and many, many Lakotas were already there. Also, there were many, many soldiers. They stood in two lines with their guns held in front of them as we went through to where we camped.

And so it was all over.

I did not know then how much was ended. When I look back now from this high hill of my old age, I can still see the butchered women and children lying heaped and scattered all along the crooked gulch as plain as when I saw them with eyes still young. And I can see that something else died there in the bloody mud, and was buried in the blizzard. A people's dream died there. It was a beautiful dream.

And I, to whom so great a vision was given in my youth,—you see me now a pitiful old man who has done nothing, for the nation's hoop is broken and scattered. There is no center any longer, and the sacred tree is dead.

ANDREW CARNEGIE
1835–1919

Countless Americans know something of the story of the poor Scottish boy who, as an example of American free enterprise, emigrated to the United States in 1848, lived an honest life, worked hard to support his family and himself, seized opportunity, and expanded his personal wealth beyond what Aladdin could do with a magic lamp. At one time, he was the richest person in the world. Once he reached the top, he turned around and proved his virtue by giving away his $350,000,000 fortune to charity, education, and world peace.

Andrew Carnegie lived that life and wrote about it. He was well aware that his story embodied the American Dream, and he never tired of telling others about it. That the dream required at the time certain preconditions that he fulfilled makes him all the more representative of an American folk type. He arrived in the United States with the right skin color, gender, religion, and country of origin at a place and time where rapid industrialization was providing new opportunities for white males with luck and ambition; and he had both.

In depicting his rise as something anyone could achieve in the United States, Carnegie wrote a sermon—in the tradition of Benjamin Franklin and Booker T. Washington—on the Protestant work ethic and American distinctiveness. But Carnegie was someone Franklin and Washington were not, an immigrant in a nation of immigrants. Carnegie's autobiography surpasses theirs as promise and proof of individual success and national meaning.

He worked in a textile mill and later, as a delivery boy, taught himself telegraphy. One of his bosses, Thomas A. Scott, liked the boy's work habits and the boy himself and began to promote him to ever higher positions in the Pennsylvania Railroad Company. After Manifest Destiny and the Civil War built a nation and provided an insatiable appetite for railroad construction, Carnegie invested his savings in a steel-making plant near Pittsburgh. He prospered by scientific management and by paying low wages. The Gilded Age of American business consolidation built his and other fortunes. In an era of unrestrained competition celebrated by popularizers and social commentators, federal and state governments and the Supreme Court intervened to protect both entrepreneurs and securely established capitalists.

Carnegie was an enigmatic acquisitor of money who felt guilty about piling up wealth. Upon his retirement from business, Carnegie separated himself from the other robber barons of his time by donating most of his money to philanthropic causes. His propagandist autobiography must be read with a view to the ideology of the American Dream and the Gospel of Wealth that permeates the text.

Autobiography of Andrew Carnegie, *1920. Reprint, Boston: Houghton Mifflin Company, 1986.*

To begin, then, I was born in Dunfermline, in the attic of the small one-story house, corner of Moodie Street and Priory Lane, on the 25th of November, 1835, and, as the saying is, "of poor but honest parents, of good kith and kin." Dunfermline had long been noted as the center of the damask trade in Scotland. My father, William Carnegie, was a damask weaver, the son of Andrew Carnegie after whom I was named. . . .

As my father succeeded in the weaving business we removed from Moodie Street to a much more commodious house in Reid's Park. My father's four or five looms occupied the lower story; we resided in the upper, which was reached, after a fashion common in the older Scottish houses, by outside stairs from the pavement. It is here that my earliest recollections begin, and, strangely enough, the first trace of memory takes me back to a day when I saw a small map of America. It was upon rollers and about two feet square. Upon this my father, mother, Uncle William, and Aunt Aitken were looking for Pittsburgh and pointing out Lake Erie and Niagara. Soon after my uncle and Aunt Aitken sailed for the land of promise. . . .

The change from hand-loom to steam-loom weaving was disastrous to our family. My father did not recognize the impending revolution, and was struggling under the old system. His looms sank greatly in value, and it became necessary for that power which never failed in any emergency—my mother—to step forward and endeavor to repair the family fortune. She opened a small shop in Moodie Street and contributed to the revenues which, though slender, nevertheless at that time sufficed to keep us in comfort and "respectable." . . .

One of the chief enjoyments of my childhood was the keeping of pigeons and rabbits. I am grateful every time I think of the trouble my father took to build a suitable house for these pets. Our home became headquarters for my young companions. My mother was always looking to home influences as the best means of keeping her two boys in the right path. She used to say that the first step in this direction was to make home pleasant; and there was nothing she and my father would not do to please us and the neighbors' children who centered about us.

My first business venture was securing my companions' services for a season as an employer, the compensation being that the young rabbits, when such came, should be named after them. The Saturday holiday was generally spent by my flock in gathering food for the rabbits. My conscience reproves me to-day, looking back, when I think of the hard bargain I drove with my young playmates, many of whom were content to gather dandelions and clover for a whole season with me, conditioned upon this unique reward—the poorest return ever made to labor. Alas! what else had I to offer them! Not a penny.

I treasure the remembrance of this plan as the earliest evidence of organizing power upon the development of which my material success in life has hung—a success not to be attributed to what I have known or done myself, but to the faculty of knowing and choosing others who did know better than myself.

Precious knowledge this for any man to possess. I did not understand steam machinery, but I tried to understand that much more complicated piece of mechanism—man. . . .

With the introduction and improvement of steam machinery, trade grew worse and worse in Dunfermline for the small manufacturers, and at last a letter was written to my mother's two sisters in Pittsburgh stating that the idea of our going to them was seriously entertained—not, as I remember hearing my parents say, to benefit their own condition, but for the sake of their two young sons. Satisfactory letters were received in reply. The decision was taken to sell the looms and furniture by auction. And my father's sweet voice sang often to mother, brother, and me:

> "To the West, to the West, to the land of the free,
> Where the mighty Missouri rolls down to the sea;
> Where a man is a man even though he must toil
> And the poorest may gather the fruits of the soil."

The proceeds of the sale were most disappointing. The looms brought hardly anything, and the result was that twenty pounds more were needed to enable the family to pay passage to America. Here let me record an act of friendship performed by a lifelong companion of my mother—who always attracted stanch friends because she was so stanch herself—Mrs. Henderson, by birth Ella Ferguson, the name by which she was known in our family. She boldly ventured to advance the needful twenty pounds, my Uncles Lauder and Morrison guaranteeing repayment. Uncle Lauder also lent his aid and advice, managing all the details for us, and on the 17th day of May, 1848, we left Dunfermline. My father's age was then forty-three, my mother's thirty-three. I was in my thirteenth year, my brother Tom in his fifth year—a beautiful white-haired child with lustrous black eyes, who everywhere attracted attention.

I had left school forever, with the exception of one winter's night-schooling in America, and later a French night-teacher for a time, and, strange to say, an elocutionist from whom I learned how to declaim. I could read, write, and cipher, and had begun the study of algebra and of Latin. A letter written to my Uncle Lauder during the voyage, and since returned, shows that I was then a better penman than now. I had wrestled with English grammar, and knew as little of what it was designed to teach as children usually do. I had read little except about Wallace, Bruce, and Burns; but knew many familiar pieces of poetry by heart. I should add to this the fairy tales of childhood, and especially the "Arabian Nights," by which I was carried into a new world. I was in dreamland as I devoured those stories.

On the morning of the day we started from beloved Dunfermline, in the omnibus that ran upon the coal railroad to Charleston, I remember that I stood with tearful eyes looking out of the window until Dunfermline vanished from view, the last structure to fade being the grand and sacred old Abbey. During my first fourteen years of absence my thought was almost daily, as it was that morning, "When shall I see you again?" . . .

We sailed from the Broomielaw of Glasgow in the 800-ton sailing ship Wiscasset. During the seven weeks of the voyage, I came to know the sailors quite well, learned the names of the ropes, and was able to direct the passengers to answer the call of the boatswain, for the ship being undermanned, the aid of the

ANDREW CARNEGIE

passengers was urgently required. In consequence I was invited by the sailors to participate on Sundays, in the one delicacy of the sailors' mess, plum duff. I left the ship with sincere regret.

The arrival at New York was bewildering. I had been taken to see the Queen at Edinburgh, but that was the extent of my travels before emigrating. Glasgow we had not time to see before we sailed. New York was the first great hive of human industry among the inhabitants of which I had mingled, and the bustle and excitement of it overwhelmed me. . . .

My father was induced by emigration agents in New York to take the Erie Canal by way of Buffalo and Lake Erie to Cleveland, and thence down the canal to Beaver—a journey which then lasted three weeks, and is made to-day by rail in ten hours. There was no railway communication then with Pittsburgh, nor indeed with any western town. The Erie Railway was under construction and we saw gangs of men at work upon it as we traveled. Nothing comes amiss to youth, and I look back upon my three weeks as a passenger upon the canal-boat with unalloyed pleasure. All that was disagreeable in my experience has long since faded from recollection, excepting the night we were compelled to remain upon the wharf-boat at Beaver waiting for the steamboat to take us up the Ohio to Pittsburgh. This was our first introduction to the mosquito in all its ferocity. My mother suffered so severely that in the morning she could hardly see. We were all frightful sights, but I do not remember that even the stinging misery of that night kept me from sleeping soundly. I could always sleep, never knowing "horrid night, the child of hell."

Our friends in Pittsburgh had been anxiously waiting to hear from us, and in their warm and affectionate greeting all our troubles were forgotten. We took up our residence with them in Allegheny City. A brother of my Uncle Hogan had built a small weaver's shop at the back end of a lot in Rebecca Street. This had a second story in which there were two rooms, and it was in these (free of rent, for my Aunt Aitken owned them) that my parents began housekeeping. My uncle soon gave up weaving and my father took his place and began making tablecloths, which he had not only to weave, but afterwards, acting as his own merchant, to travel and sell, as no dealers could be found to take them in quantity. He was compelled to market them himself, selling from door to door. The returns were meager in the extreme.

As usual, my mother came to the rescue. There was no keeping her down. In her youth she had learned to bind shoes in her father's business for pin-money, and the skill then acquired was now turned to account for the benefit of the family. Mr. Phipps, father of my friend and partner Mr. Henry Phipps, was, like my grandfather, a master shoemaker. He was our neighbor in Allegheny City. Work was obtained from him, and in addition to attending to her household duties—for, of course, we had no servant—this wonderful woman, my mother, earned four dollars a week by binding shoes. Midnight would often find her at work. In the intervals during the day and evening, when household cares would permit, and my young brother sat at her knee threading needles and waxing the thread for her, she recited to him, as she had to me, the gems of Scottish minstrelsy which she seemed to have by heart, or told him tales which failed not to contain a moral.

This is where the children of honest poverty have the most precious of all advantages over those of wealth. The mother, nurse, cook, governess, teacher, saint, all in one; the father, exemplar, guide, counselor, and friend! Thus were my brother and I brought up. What has the child of millionaire or nobleman that counts compared to such a heritage?

My mother was a busy woman, but all her work did not prevent her neighbors from soon recognizing her as a wise and kindly woman whom they could call upon for counsel or help in times of trouble. Many have told me what my mother did for them. So it was in after years wherever we resided; rich and poor came to her with their trials and found good counsel. She towered among her neighbors wherever she went.

The great question now was, what could be found for me to do. I had just completed my thirteenth year, and I fairly panted to get to work that I might help the family to a start in the new land. The prospect of want had become to me a frightful nightmare. My thoughts at this period centered in the determination that we should make and save enough of money to produce three hundred dollars a year—twenty-five dollars monthly, which I figured was the sum required to keep us without being dependent upon others. Every necessary thing was very cheap in those days.

The brother of my Uncle Hogan would often ask what my parents meant to do with me, and one day there occurred the most tragic of all scenes I have ever witnessed. Never can I forget it. He said, with the kindest intentions in the world, to my mother, that I was a likely boy and apt to learn; and he believed that if a basket were fitted out for me with knickknacks to sell, I could peddle them around the wharves and make quite a considerable sum. I never knew what an enraged woman meant till then. My mother was sitting sewing at the moment, but she sprang to her feet with outstretched hands and shook them in his face.

"What! my son a peddler and go among rough men upon the wharves! I would rather throw him into the Allegheny River. Leave me!" she cried, pointing to the door, and Mr. Hogan went.

She stood a tragic queen. The next moment she had broken down, but only for a few moments did tears fall and sobs come. Then she took her two boys in her arms and told us not to mind her foolishness. There were many things in the world for us to do and we could be useful men, honored and respected, if we always did what was right. . . .

Soon after . . . my father found it necessary to give up hand-loom weaving and to enter the cotton factory of Mr. Blackstock, an old Scotsman in Allegheny City, where we lived. In this factory he also obtained for me a position as bobbin boy, and my first work was done there at one dollar and twenty cents per week. It was a hard life. In the winter father and I had to rise and breakfast in the darkness, reach the factory before it was daylight, and, with a short interval for lunch, work till after dark. The hours hung heavily upon me and in the work itself I took no pleasure; but the cloud had a silver lining, as it gave me the feeling that I was doing something for my world—our family. I have made millions since, but none of those millions gave me such happiness as my first week's earnings. I was now a helper of the family, a breadwinner, and no longer a total charge upon my parents. . . .

One evening, early in 1850, when I returned home from work, I was told that Mr. David Brooks, manager of the telegraph office, had asked my Uncle Hogan if he knew where a good boy could be found to act as messenger. Mr. Brooks and my uncle were enthusiastic draught-players, and it was over a game of draughts that this important inquiry was made. Upon such trifles do the most momentous consequences hang. A word, a look, an accent, may affect the destiny not only of individuals, but of nations. He is a bold man who calls anything a trifle. Who was it who, being advised to disregard trifles, said he always would if any one could tell him what a trifle was? The young should remember that upon trifles the best gifts of the gods often hang. . . .

The interview was successful. I took care to explain that I did not know Pittsburgh, that perhaps I would not do, would not be strong enough; but all I wanted was a trial. He asked me how soon I could come, and I said that I could stay now if wanted. And, looking back over the circumstance, I think that answer might well be pondered by young men. It is a great mistake not to seize the opportunity. The position was offered to me; something might occur, some other boy might be sent for. Having got myself in I proposed to stay there if I could. Mr. Brooks very kindly called the other boy—for it was an additional messenger that was wanted—and asked him to show me about, and let me go with him and learn the business. I soon found opportunity to run down to the corner of the street and tell my father that it was all right, and to go home and tell mother that I had got the situation.

And that is how in 1850 I got my first real start in life. From the dark cellar running a steam-engine at two dollars a week, begrimed with coal dirt, without a trace of the elevating influences of life, I was lifted into paradise, yes, heaven, as it seemed to me, with newspapers, pens, pencils, and sunshine about me. There was scarcely a minute in which I could not learn something or find out how much there was to learn and how little I knew. I felt that my foot was upon the ladder and that I was bound to climb. . . .

With all their pleasures the messenger boys were hard worked. Every other evening they were required to be on duty until the office closed, and on these nights it was seldom that I reached home before eleven o'clock. On the alternating nights we were relieved at six. This did not leave much time for self-improvement, nor did the wants of the family leave any money to spend on books. There came, however, like a blessing from above, a means by which the treasures of literature were unfolded to me.

Colonel James Anderson—I bless his name as I write—announced that he would open his library of four hundred volumes to boys, so that any young man could take out, each Saturday afternoon, a book which could be exchanged for another on the succeeding Saturday. My friend, Mr. Thomas N. Miller, reminded me recently that Colonel Anderson's books were first opened to "working boys," and the question arose whether messenger boys, clerks, and others, who did not work with their hands, were entitled to books. My first communication to the press was a note, written to the "Pittsburgh Dispatch," urging that we should not be excluded; that although we did not now work with our hands, some of us had done so, and that we were really working boys. Dear Colonel Anderson promptly enlarged the classification. So my first appearance as a public writer was a success.

My dear friend, Tom Miller, one of the inner circle, lived near Colonel Anderson and introduced me to him, and in this way the windows were opened in the walls of my dungeon through which the light of knowledge streamed in. Every day's toil and even the long hours of night service were lightened by the book which I carried about with me and read in the intervals that could be snatched from duty. And the future was made bright by the thought that when Saturday came a new volume could be obtained. In this way I became familiar with Macaulay's essays and his history, and with Bancroft's "History of the United States," which I studied with more care than any other book I had then read. Lamb's essays were my special delight, but I had at this time no knowledge of the great master of all, Shakespeare, beyond the selected pieces in the school books. My taste for him I acquired a little later at the old Pittsburgh Theater.

John Phipps, James R. Wilson, Thomas N. Miller, William Cowley— members of our circle—shared with me the invaluable privilege of the use of Colonel Anderson's library. Books which it would have been impossible for me to obtain elsewhere were, by his wise generosity, placed within my reach; and to him I owe a taste for literature which I would not exchange for all the millions that were ever amassed by man. Life would be quite intolerable without it. Nothing contributed so much to keep my companions and myself clear of low fellowship and bad habits as the beneficence of the good Colonel. . . . It was from my own early experience that I decided there was no use to which money could be applied so productive of good to boys and girls who have good within them and ability and ambition to develop it, as the founding of a public library in a community which is willing to support it as a municipal institution. . . .

> **[At seventeen after teaching himself telegraphy, he became an operator and then a clerk for Pennsylvania Railroad superintendent Thomas A. Scott. Carnegie's father died in 1855 and he persuaded his mother to mortgage their house for $500 with which he made his first stock market investment. The next year he joined the anti-slavery wing of the new Republican Party.]**

Mr. Scott was promoted to be the general superintendent of the Pennsylvania Railroad in 1856, taking Mr. Lombaert's place; and he took me, then in my twenty-third year, with him to Altoona. This breaking-up of associations in Pittsburgh was a sore trial, but nothing could be allowed to interfere for a moment with my business career. My mother was satisfied upon this point, great as the strain was upon her. Besides, "follow my leader" was due to so true a friend as Mr. Scott had been. . . .

Mr. Scott remained at Altoona for about three years when deserved promotion came to him. . . . To part with Mr. Scott was hard enough; to serve a new official in his place I did not believe possible. The sun rose and set upon his head so far as I was concerned. The thought of my promotion, except through him, never entered my mind.

He returned from his interview with the president at Philadelphia and asked me to come into the private room in his house which communicated with the office. He told me it had been settled that he should remove to Philadelphia. Mr. Enoch Lewis, the division superintendent, was to be his successor. I listened with great interest as he approached the inevitable disclosure as to what he was going to do with me. He said finally:

"Now about yourself. Do you think you could manage the Pittsburgh Division?"

I was at an age when I thought I could manage anything. I knew nothing that I would not attempt, but it had never occurred to me that anybody else, much less Mr. Scott, would entertain the idea that I was as yet fit to do anything of the kind proposed. I was only twenty-four years old, but my model then was Lord John Russell, of whom it was said he would take the command of the Channel Fleet tomorrow. So would Wallace or Bruce. I told Mr. Scott I thought I could.

"Well," he said, "Mr. Potts" (who was then superintendent of the Pittsburgh Division) "is to be promoted to the transportation department in Philadelphia and

I recommended you to the president as his successor. He agreed to give you a trial. What salary do you think you should have?"

"Salary," I said, quite offended; "what do I care for salary? I do not want the salary; I want the position. It is glory enough to go back to the Pittsburgh Division in your former place. You can make my salary just what you please and you need not give me any more than what I am getting now."

That was sixty-five dollars a month.

"You know," he said, "I received fifteen hundred dollars a year when I was there; and Mr. Potts is receiving eighteen hundred. I think it would be right to start you at fifteen hundred dollars, and after a while if you succeed you will get the eighteen hundred. Would that be satisfactory?"

"Oh, please," I said, "don't speak to me of money!". . . .

Upon our return to Pittsburgh in 1860 we rented a house in Hancock Street, now Eighth Street, and resided there for a year or more. Any accurate description of Pittsburgh at that time would be set down as a piece of the grossest exaggeration. The smoke permeated and penetrated everything. If you placed your hand on the balustrade of the stair it came away black; if you washed face and hands they were as dirty as ever in an hour. The soot gathered in the hair and irritated the skin, and for a time after our return from the mountain atmosphere of Altoona, life was more or less miserable. We soon began to consider how we could get to the country, and fortunately at that time Mr. D. A. Stewart, then freight agent for the company, directed our attention to a house adjoining his residence at Homewood. We moved there at once and the telegraph was brought in, which enabled me to operate the division from the house when necessary.

Here a new life was opened to us. There were country lanes and gardens in abundance. Residences had from five to twenty acres of land about them. The Homewood Estate was made up of many hundreds of acres, with beautiful woods and glens and a running brook. We, too, had a garden and a considerable extent of ground around our house. The happiest years of my mother's life were spent here among her flowers and chickens and the surroundings of country life. Her love of flowers was a passion. She was scarcely ever able to gather a flower. Indeed I remember she once reproached me for pulling up a weed, saying "it was something green." I have inherited this peculiarity and have often walked from the house to the gate intending to pull a flower for my button-hole and then left for town unable to find one I could destroy.

With this change to the country came a whole host of new acquaintances. Many of the wealthy families of the district had their residences in this delightful suburb. It was, so to speak, the aristocratic quarter. To the entertainments at these great houses the young superintendent was invited. The young people were musical and we had musical evenings a plenty. I heard subjects discussed which I had never known before, and I made it a rule when I heard these to learn something about them at once. I was pleased every day to feel that I was learning something new. . . .

[The Civil War began and Assistant Secretary of War Thomas Scott called Carnegie to Washington to work for the war effort.]

Soon after this I returned to Washington and made my headquarters in the War Building with Colonel Scott. As I had charge of the telegraph department, as well as the railways, this gave me an opportunity of seeing President Lincoln, Mr. Seward, Secretary Cameron, and others; and I was occasionally brought in personal contact with these men, which was to me a source of great interest. Mr. Lincoln would occasionally come to the office and sit at the desk awaiting replies to telegrams, or perhaps merely anxious for information.

All the pictures of this extraordinary man are like him. He was so marked of feature that it was impossible for any one to paint him and not produce a likeness. He was certainly one of the most homely men I ever saw when his features were in repose; but when excited or telling a story, intellect shone through his eyes and illuminated his face to a degree which I have seldom or never seen in any other. His manners were perfect because natural; and he had a kind word for everybody, even the youngest boy in the office. His attentions were not graduated. They were the same to all, as deferential in talking to the messenger boy as to Secretary Seward. His charm lay in the total absence of manner. It was not so much, perhaps, what he said as the way in which he said it that never failed to win one. I have often regretted that I did not note down carefully at the time some of his curious sayings, for he said even common things in an original way. I never met a great man who so thoroughly made himself one with all men as Mr. Lincoln. As Secretary Hay so well says, "It is impossible to imagine any one a valet to Mr. Lincoln; he would have been his companion." He was the most perfect democrat, revealing in every word and act the equality of men. . . .

[Carnegie became seriously ill from sunstroke and took leave for recuperation in a colder climate.]

During the Civil War the price of iron went up to something like $130 per ton. Even at that figure it was not so much a question of money as of delivery. The railway lines of America were fast becoming dangerous for want of new rails, and this state of affairs led me to organize in 1864 a rail-making concern at Pittsburgh. There was no difficulty in obtaining partners and capital, and the Superior Rail Mill and Blast Furnaces were built.

In like manner the demand for locomotives was very great, and with Mr. Thomas N. Miller I organized in 1866 the Pittsburgh Locomotive Works, which has been a prosperous and creditable concern—locomotives made there having obtained an enviable reputation throughout the United States. It sounds like a fairy tale to-day to record that in 1906 the one-hundred-dollar shares of this company sold for three thousand dollars—that is, thirty dollars for one. Large annual dividends had been paid regularly and the company had been very successful—sufficient proof of the policy: "Make nothing but the very best." We never did.

When at Altoona I had seen in the Pennsylvania Railroad Company's works the first small bridge built of iron. It proved a success. I saw that it would never do to depend further upon wooden bridges for permanent railway structures. An important bridge on the Pennsylvania Railroad had recently burned and the traffic had been obstructed for eight days. Iron was the thing. I proposed to H. J. Linville, who had designed the iron bridge, and to John L. Piper and his partner, Mr. Schiffler, who had charge of bridges on the Pennsylvania line, that they should come to Pittsburgh and I would organize a company to build iron bridges. It was the first company of its kind. I asked my friend, Mr. Scott, of the Pennsylvania Railroad, to go with us in the venture, which he did. Each of us paid for a one fifth interest, or $1250. My share I borrowed from the bank. Looking back at it now the sum seemed very small, but "tall oaks from little acorns grow."

In this way was organized in 1862 the firm of Piper and Schiffler which was merged into the Keystone Bridge Company in 1863—a name which I remember I was proud of having thought of as being most appropriate for a bridge-building concern in the State of Pennsylvania, the Keystone State. From this beginning iron bridges came generally into use in America, indeed, in the world at large so far as I know. My letters to iron manufacturers in Pittsburgh were sufficient to insure the new company credit. Small wooden shops were erected and several bridge structures were undertaken. Cast-iron was the principal material used, but so well were the bridges built that some made at that day and since strengthened for heavier traffic, still remain in use upon various lines. . . .

As I became acquainted with the manufacture of iron I was greatly surprised to find that the cost of each of the various processes was unknown. Inquiries made of the leading manufacturers of Pittsburgh proved this. It was a lump business, and until stock was taken and the books balanced at the end of the year, the manufacturers were in total ignorance of results. I heard of men who thought their business at the end of the year would show a loss and had found a profit, and *vice-versa*. I felt as if we were moles burrowing in the dark, and this to me was intolerable. I insisted upon such a system of weighing and accounting being introduced throughout our works as would enable us to know what our cost was for each process and especially what each man was doing, who saved material, who wasted it, and who produced the best results.

To arrive at this was a much more difficult task than one would imagine. Every manager in the mills was naturally against the new system. Years were required before an accurate system was obtained, but eventually, by the aid of many clerks and the introduction of weighing scales at various points in the mill, we began to know not only what every department was doing, but what each one of the many men working at the furnaces was doing, and thus to compare one with another. One of the chief sources of success in manufacturing is the introduction and strict maintenance of a perfect system of accounting so that responsibility for money or materials can be brought home to every man. Owners who, in the office, would not trust a clerk with five dollars without having a check upon him, were supplying tons of material daily to men in the mills without exacting an account of their stewardship by weighing what each returned in the finished form. . . .

[He invested in the newly discovered Pennsylvania oil fields and visited European manufactures. In 1867 he moved with his mother to New York City, became friends with J. P. Morgan, and invested in the Pullman Sleeping Car Company and the Union Pacific Railroad.]

The small shops put up originally for the Keystone Bridge Company had been leased for other purposes and ten acres of ground had been secured in Lawrenceville on which new and extensive shops were erected. Repeated additions to the Union Iron Mills had made them the leading mills in the United States for all sorts of structural shapes. Business was promising and all the surplus earnings I was making in other fields were required to expand the iron business. I had become interested, with my friends of the Pennsylvania Railroad Company, in building some railways in the Western States, but gradually withdrew from all such enterprises and made up my mind to go entirely contrary to the adage not to put all one's eggs in one basket. I determined that the proper policy was "to put all good eggs in one basket and then watch that basket."

I believe the true road to preeminent success in any line is to make yourself master in that line. I have no faith in the policy of scattering one's resources, and in my experience I have rarely if ever met a man who achieved preeminence in money-making—certainly never one in manufacturing—who was interested in many concerns. The men who have succeeded are men who have chosen one line and stuck to it. It is surprising how few men appreciate the enormous dividends derivable from investment in their own business. There is scarcely a manufacturer in the world who has not in his works some machinery that should be thrown out and replaced by improved appliances; or who does not for the want of additional machinery or new methods lose more than sufficient to pay the largest dividend obtainable by investment beyond his own domain. And yet most business men whom I have known invest in bank shares and in far-away enterprises, while the true gold mine lies right in their own factories.

I have tried always to hold fast to this important fact. It has been with me a cardinal doctrine that I could manage my own capital better than any other person, much better than any board of directors. The losses men encounter during a business life which seriously embarrass them are rarely in their own business, but in enterprises of which the investor is not master. My advice to young men would be not only to concentrate their whole time and attention on the one business in life in which they engage, but to put every dollar of their capital into it. If there be any business that will not bear extension, the true policy is to invest the surplus in first-class securities which will yield a moderate but certain revenue if some other growing business cannot be found. As for myself my decision was taken early. I would concentrate upon the manufacture of iron and steel and be master in that. . . .

[He used chemistry and scientific management to make better steel at cheaper prices under the principle of "economies of scale." He took a vacation trip around the world in 1878.]

The rapid substitution of steel for iron in the immediate future had become obvious to us. Even in our Keystone Bridge Works, steel was being used more and more in place of iron. King Iron was about to be deposed by the new King Steel, and we were becoming more and more dependent upon it. We had about concluded in 1886 to build alongside of the Edgar Thomson Mills new works for the manufacture of miscellaneous shapes of steel when it was suggested to us that the five or six leading manufacturers of Pittsburgh, who had combined to build steel mills at Homestead, were willing to sell their mills to us.

These works had been built originally by a syndicate of manufacturers, with the view of obtaining the necessary supplies of steel which they required in their various concerns, but the steel-rail business, being then in one of its booms, they had been tempted to change plans and construct a steel-rail mill. They had been able to make rails as long as prices remained high, but, as the mills had not been specially designed for this purpose, they were without the indispensable blast furnaces for the supply of pig iron, and had no coke lands for the supply of fuel. They were in no condition to compete with us. . . .

A further extension of our business was the establishing of the Hartman Steel Works at Beaver Falls, designed to work into a hundred various forms the product of the Homestead Mills. So now we made almost everything in steel from a wire nail up to a twenty-inch steel girder, and it was then not thought probable that we should enter into any new field.

It may be interesting here to note the progress of our works during the decade 1888 to 1897. In 1888 we had twenty millions of dollars invested; in 1897 more than double or over forty-five millions. The 600,000 tons of pig iron we made per annum in 1888 was trebled; we made nearly 2,000,000. Our product of iron and steel was in 1888, say, 2000 tons per day; it grew to exceed 6000 tons. Our coke works then embraced about 5000 ovens; they were trebled in number, and our capacity, then 6000 tons, became 18,000 tons per day. Our Frick Coke Company in 1897 had 42,000 acres of coal land, more than two thirds of the true Connells-ville vein. Ten years hence increased production may be found to have been equally rapid. It may be accepted as an axiom that a manufacturing concern in a growing country like ours begins to decay when it stops extending.

To make a ton of steel one and a half tons of iron stone has to be mined, transported by rail a hundred miles to the Lakes, carried by boat hundreds of miles, transferred to cars, transported by rail one hundred and fifty miles to Pittsburgh; one and a half tons of coal must be mined and manufactured into coke and carried fifty-odd miles by rail; and one ton of limestone mined and carried one hundred and fifty miles to Pittsburgh. How then could steel be manufactured and sold without loss at three pounds for two cents? This, I confess, seemed to me incredible, and little less than miraculous, but it was so.

America is soon to change from being the dearest steel manufacturing country to the cheapest. Already the shipyards of Belfast are our customers. This is but the beginning. Under present conditions America can produce steel as cheaply as any other land, notwithstanding its higher-priced labor. There is no labor so cheap as the dearest in the mechanical field, provided it is free, contented, zealous, and reaping reward as it renders service. And here America leads.

One great advantage which America will have in competing in the markets of the world is that her manufacturers will have the best home market. Upon this they can depend for a return upon capital, and the surplus product can be exported with advantage, even when the prices received for it do not more than cover actual cost, provided the exports be charged with their proportion of all expenses. The nation that has the best home market, especially if products are standardized, as ours are, can soon outsell the foreign producer. The phrase I used in Britain in this connection was: "The Law of the Surplus." It afterward came into general use in commercial discussions.

While upon the subject of our manufacturing interests, I may record that on July 1, 1892, during my absence in the Highlands of Scotland, there occurred the one really serious quarrel with our workmen in our whole history. For twenty-six years I had been actively in charge of the relations between ourselves and our men, and it was the pride of my life to think how delightfully satisfactory these had been and were. I hope I fully deserved what my chief partner, Mr. Phipps, said in his letter to the "New York Herald," January 30, 1904, in reply to one who had declared I had remained abroad during the Homestead strike, instead of flying back to support my partners. It was to the effect that "I was always disposed to yield to the demands of the men, however unreasonable"; hence one or two of my partners did not wish me to return. Taking no account of the reward that comes from feeling that you and your employees are friends and judging only from economical results, I believe that higher wages to men who respect their employers and are happy and contented are a good investment, yielding, indeed, big dividends.

The manufacture of steel was revolutionized by the Bessemer open-hearth and basic inventions. The machinery hitherto employed had become obsolete, and our firm, recognizing this, spent several millions at Homestead reconstructing and enlarging the works. The new machinery made about sixty per cent more steel than the old. Two hundred and eighteen tonnage men (that is, men who were paid by the ton of steel produced) were working under a three years' contract, part of the last year being with the new machinery. Thus their earnings had increased almost sixty per cent before the end of the contract.

The firm offered to divide this sixty per cent with them in the new scale to be made thereafter. That is to say, the earnings of the men would have been thirty per cent greater than under the old scale and the other thirty per cent would have gone to the firm to recompense it for its outlay. The work of the men would not have been much harder than it had been hitherto, as the improved machinery did the work. This was not only fair and liberal, it was generous, and under ordinary circumstances would have been accepted by the men with thanks. But the firm was then engaged in making armor for the United States Government, which we had declined twice to manufacture and which was urgently needed. It had also the contract to furnish material for the Chicago Exhibition. Some of the leaders of the men, knowing these conditions, insisted upon demanding the whole sixty per cent, thinking the firm would be compelled to give it. The firm could not agree, nor should it have agreed to such an attempt as this to take it by the throat and say, "Stand and deliver." It very rightly declined. Had I been at home nothing would have induced me to yield to this unfair attempt to extort.

Up to this point all had been right enough. The policy I had pursued in cases of difference with our men was that of patiently waiting, reasoning with them, and showing them that their demands were unfair; but never attempting to employ new men in their places—never. The superintendent of Homestead, however, was assured by the three thousand men who were not concerned in the dispute that they could run the works, and were anxious to rid themselves of the two hundred and eighteen men who had banded themselves into a union and into which they had hitherto refused to admit those in other departments—only the "heaters" and "rollers" of steel being eligible.

My partners were misled by this superintendent, who was himself misled. He had not had great experience in such affairs, having recently been promoted from a subordinate position. The unjust demands of the few union men, and the opinion of the three thousand non-union men that they were unjust, very naturally led him into thinking there would be no trouble and that the workmen would do as they had promised. There were many men among the three thousand who could take, and wished to take, the places of the two hundred and eighteen—at least so it was reported to me.

It is easy to look back and say that the vital step of opening the works should never have been taken. All the firm had to do was to say to the men: "There is a labor dispute here and you must settle it between yourselves. The firm has made you a most liberal offer. The works will run when the dispute is adjusted, and not till then. Meanwhile your places remain open to you." Or, it might have been well if the superintendent had said to the three thousand men, "All right, if you will come and run the works without protection," thus throwing upon them the responsibility of protecting themselves—three thousand men as against two hundred and eighteen. Instead of this it was thought advisable (as an additional precaution by the state officials, I understand) to have the sheriff with guards to protect the thousands against the hundreds. The leaders of the latter were violent and aggressive men; they had guns and pistols, and, as was soon proved, were able to intimidate the thousands. . . .

I was traveling in the Highlands of Scotland when the trouble arose, and did not hear of it until two days after. Nothing I have ever had to meet in all my life, before or since, wounded me so deeply. No pangs remain of any wound received in my business career save that of Homestead. It was so unnecessary. The men were outrageously wrong. The strikers, with the new machinery, would have made from four to nine dollars a day under the new scale—thirty per cent more than they were making with the old machinery. While in Scotland I received the following cable from the officers of the union of our workmen:

"Kind master, tell us what you wish us to do and we shall do it for you."

This was most touching, but, alas, too late. The mischief was done, the works were in the hands of the Governor; it was too late. . . .

[Carnegie blamed labor problems on misunderstandings by labor leaders, not the men, and insisted that he had always done what was fair.]

It is for the interest of the employer that his men shall make good earnings and have steady work. The sliding scale enables the company to meet the market; and sometimes to take orders and keep the works running, which is the main thing for the working-men. High wages are well enough, but they are not to be compared with steady employment. The Edgar Thomson Mills are, in my opinion, the ideal works in respect to the relations of capital and labor. I am told the men in our day, and even to this day (1914) prefer two to three turns, but three turns are sure to come. Labor's hours are to be shortened as we progress. Eight hours will be the rule—eight for work, eight for sleep, and eight for rest and recreation.

There have been many incidents in my business life proving that labor troubles are not solely found upon wages. I believe the best preventive of quarrels to be recognition of, and sincere interest in, the men, satisfying them that you really care for them and that you rejoice in their success. This I can sincerely say—that I always enjoyed my conferences with our workmen, which were not always in regard to wages, and that the better I knew the men the more I liked them. They have usually two virtues to the employer's one, and they are certainly more generous to each other.

Labor is usually helpless against capital. The employer, perhaps, decides to shut up the shops; he ceases to make profits for a short time. There is no change in his habits, food, clothing, pleasures—no agonizing fear of want. Contrast this with his workman whose lessening means of subsistence torment him. He has few comforts, scarcely the necessities for his wife and children in health, and for the sick little ones no proper treatment. It is not capital we need to guard, but helpless labor. If I returned to business to-morrow, fear of labor troubles would not enter my mind, but tenderness for poor and sometimes misguided though well-meaning laborers would fill my heart and soften it; and thereby soften theirs.

BOOKER TALIAFERRO WASHINGTON
1856–1915

Booker T. Washington spoke only briefly with the greatest black agitator in American history—Frederick Douglass. His ideas came under attack from the next great African American combatant against the country's racist institutions, William Edward Burghardt DuBois. Washington stands between those two giants, a man who lifted himself up from slavery to be the most influential black power broker in the turn-of-the-century United States.

From 1872 to 1875 he enrolled as a work/study student at Hampton Institute before teaching school in Malden, West Virginia, attending a Baptist seminary in Washington, D.C., working in a law office, and returning to his alma mater as a teacher. He then coordinated Hampton's efforts to teach Indians and to institute a night school.

In 1881, Hampton's founder, General Samuel Chapman Armstrong, supported and encouraged his protégé to direct the establishment of Tuskegee Institute in Alabama. For thirty-four years Washington promoted Tuskegee and, in 1915, the college had over 100 buildings, 1500 students and 200 professors.

Washington was a conservative who carefully refused to criticize white leaders or Southern prejudice. The reason that Reconstruction failed, he argued, was that it had concentrated on the right to vote instead of providing jobs and economic support. Washington determined that politics only inflamed passion and that, if they expected to rise, blacks must demonstrate their worth through vocational skills.

In 1895, the death of Douglass and Washington's "Atlanta Compromise" speech made him the most powerful black leader in the country. Whites thrilled to hear him accept social segregation and restrictions on the ballot. DuBois called him an accommodationist who abandoned civil rights efforts; the black Boston editor William Monroe Trotter excoriated him as a "Black Benedict Arnold." But in the 1890s, with over one hundred blacks a year being lynched, Washington's program of telling whites at least something of what they wanted to hear and his advice for black solidarity and community self-help seemed expedient. For this the label Uncle Tom still sticks to this ambiguous man.

Washington promoted the Protestant ethic of hard work, cleanliness, perseverance, and morality in the tradition of Benjamin Franklin; but whereas Franklin was a white man in a progressive Northern city, Washington was an ex-slave in the reactionary South. Up From Slavery *became an immediate classic because whites hoped that Washington was the*

*"representative man" of his race, able to succeed according to the myth of
the American Dream. Andrew Carnegie supported Washington's efforts
through contributions to Tuskegee Institute. Washington used the autobiography to promote Tuskegee and himself.*

Up From Slavery: An Autobiography. *NY: Doubleday, 1901.*

I was born a slave on a plantation in Franklin County, Virginia. I am not quite
sure of the exact place or exact date of my birth, but at any rate I suspect I must
have been born somewhere and at some time. As nearly as I have been able to
learn, I was born near a cross-roads post-office called Hale's Ford, and the year
was 1858 or 1859. I do not know the month or the day. The earliest impressions I
can now recall are of the plantation and the slave quarters—the latter being the
part of the plantation where the slaves had their cabins.

My life had its beginning in the midst of the most miserable, desolate, and
discouraging surroundings. This was so, however, not because my owners were
especially cruel, for they were not, as compared with many others. I was born in
a typical log cabin, about fourteen by sixteen feet square. In this cabin I lived with
my mother and a brother and sister till after the Civil War, when we were all
declared free.

Of my ancestry I know almost nothing. In the slave quarters, and even later, I
heard whispered conversations among the coloured people of the tortures which
the slaves, including, no doubt, my ancestors on my mother's side, suffered in the
middle passage of the slave ship while being conveyed from Africa to America. I
have been unsuccessful in securing any information that would throw any accurate
light upon the history of my family beyond my mother. She, I remember, had a
half-brother and a half-sister. In the days of slavery not very much attention was
given to family history and family records—that is, black family records. My
mother, I suppose, attracted the attention of a purchaser who was afterward my
owner and hers. Her addition to the slave family attracted about as much attention as the purchase of a new horse or cow. Of my father I know even less than of
my mother. I do not even know his name. I have heard reports to the effect that
he was a white man who lived on one of the near-by plantations. Whoever he was,
I never heard of his taking the least interest in me or providing in any way for my
rearing. But I do not find especial fault with him. He was simply another unfortunate victim of the institution which the Nation unhappily had engrafted upon it at
that time.

The cabin was not only our living-place, but was also used as the kitchen for
the plantation. My mother was the plantation cook. The cabin was without glass
windows; it had only openings in the side which let in the light, and also the cold,
chilly air of winter. There was a door to the cabin—that is, something that was
called a door—but the uncertain hinges by which it was hung, and the large cracks
in it, to say nothing of the fact that it was too small, made the room a very uncomfortable one. In addition to these openings there was, in the lower right-hand
corner of the room, the "cat-hole,"—a contrivance which almost every mansion
or cabin in Virginia possessed during the ante-bellum period. The "cat-hole" was
a square opening, about seven by eight inches, provided for the purpose of letting
the cat pass in and out of the house at will during the night. In the case of our
particular cabin I could never understand the necessity of this convenience, since

BOOKER TALIAFERRO WASHINGTON

there were at least a half-dozen other places in the cabin that would have accommodated cats. There was no wooden floor in our cabin, the naked earth being used as a floor. In the centre of the earthen floor there was a large, deep opening covered with boards, which was used as a place in which to store sweet potatoes during the winter. An impression of this potato-hole is very distinctly engraved upon my memory, because I recall that during the process of putting the potatoes in or taking them out I would often come into possession of one or two, which I roasted and thoroughly enjoyed. There was no cooking-stove on our plantation, and all the cooking for the whites and slaves my mother had to do over an open fireplace, mostly in pots and "skillets." While the poorly built cabin caused us to suffer with cold in the winter, the heat from the open fireplace in summer was equally trying.

The early years of my life, which were spent in the little cabin, were not very different from those of thousands of other slaves. My mother, of course, had little time in which to give attention to the training of her children during the day. She snatched a few moments for our care in the early morning before her work began, and at night after the day's work was done. One of my earliest recollections is that of my mother cooking a chicken late at night, and awakening her children for the purpose of feeding them. How or where she got it I do not know. I presume, however, it was procured from our owner's farm. Some people may call this theft. If such a thing were to happen now, I should condemn it as theft myself. But taking place at the time it did, and for the reason that it did, no one could ever make me believe that my mother was guilty of thieving. She was simply a victim of the system of slavery. I cannot remember having slept in a bed until after our family was declared free by the Emancipation Proclamation. Three children—John, my older brother, Amanda, my sister, and myself—had a pallet on the dirt floor, or, to be more correct, we slept in and on a bundle of filthy rags laid upon the dirt floor.

I was asked not long ago to tell something about the sports and pastimes that I engaged in during my youth. Until that question was asked it had never occurred to me that there was no period of my life that was devoted to play. From the time that I can remember anything, almost every day of my life has been occupied in some kind of labour; though I think I would now be a more useful man if I had had time for sports. . . .

I had no schooling whatever while I was a slave, though I remember on several occasions I went as far as the schoolhouse door with one of my young mistresses to carry her books. The picture of several dozen boys and girls in a schoolroom engaged in study made a deep impression upon me, and I had the feeling that to get into a schoolhouse and study in this way would be about the same as getting into paradise.

So far as I can now recall, the first knowledge that I got of the fact that we were slaves, and that freedom of the slaves was being discussed, was early one morning before day, when I was awakened by my mother kneeling over her children and fervently praying that Lincoln and his armies might be successful, and that one day she and her children might be free. In this connection I have never been able to understand how the slaves throughout the South, completely ignorant as were the masses so far as books or newspapers were concerned, were able to keep themselves so accurately and completely informed about the great National questions that were agitating the country. From the time that Garrison,

Lovejoy, and others began to agitate for freedom, the slaves throughout the South kept in close touch with the progress of the movement. Though I was a mere child during the preparation for the Civil War and during the war itself, I now recall the many late-at-night whispered discussions that I heard my mother and the other slaves on the plantation indulge in. These discussions showed that they understood the situation, and that they kept themselves informed of events by what was termed the "grape-vine" telegraph. . . .

I cannot remember a single instance during my childhood or early boyhood when our entire family sat down to the table together, and God's blessing was asked, and the family ate a meal in a civilized manner. On the plantation in Virginia, and even later, meals were gotten by the children very much as dumb animals get theirs. It was a piece of bread here and a scrap of meat there. It was a cup of milk at one time and some potatoes at another. Sometimes a portion of our family would eat out of the skillet or pot, while some one would eat from a tin plate held on the knees, and often using nothing but the hands with which to hold the food. . . .

Finally the war closed, and the day of freedom came. It was a momentous and eventful day to all upon our plantation. We had been expecting it. Freedom was in the air, and had been for months. Deserting soldiers returning to their homes were to be seen every day. Others who had been discharged, or whose regiments had been paroled, were constantly passing near our place. The "grave-vine telegraph" was kept busy night and day. The news and mutterings of great events were swiftly carried from one plantation to another. In the fear of "Yankee" invasions, the silverware and other valuables were taken from the "big house," buried in the woods, and guarded by trusted slaves. Woe be to any one who would have attempted to disturb the buried treasure. The slaves would give the Yankee soldiers, food, drink, clothing—anything but that which had been specifically intrusted to their care and honour. As the great day drew nearer, there was more singing in the slave quarters than usual. It was bolder, had more ring, and lasted later into the night. Most of the verses of the plantation songs had some reference to freedom. True, they sung those same verses before, but they had been careful to explain that the "freedom" in these songs referred to the next world, and had no connection with life in this world. Now they gradually threw off the mask; and were not afraid to let it be known that the "freedom" in their songs meant freedom of the body in this world. The night before the eventful day, word was sent to the slave quarters to the effect that something unusual was going to take place at the "big house" the next morning. There was little, if any, sleep that night. All was excitement and expectancy. Early the next morning word was sent to all the slaves, old and young, to gather at the house. In company with my mother, brother, and sister, and a large number of other slaves, I went to the master's house. All of our master's family were either standing or seated on the veranda of the house, where they could see what was to take place and hear what was said. There was a feeling of deep interest, or perhaps sadness, on their faces, but not bitterness. As I now recall the impression they made upon me, they did not at the moment seem to be sad because of the loss of property, but rather because of parting with those whom they had reared and who were in many ways very close to them. The most distinct thing that I now recall in connection with the scene was that some man who seemed to be a stranger (a United States officer, I presume) made a little speech and then read a rather long paper—the Emancipation Proclamation, I think. After the reading we were told that we were all free, and could go when and where we pleased. My mother, who was standing by my side, leaned over and kissed her children, while tears of joy ran down her cheeks. She explained to us what it all meant, that this was the day for which she had been praying, but fearing that she would never live to see.

For some minutes there was great rejoicing, and thanksgiving, and wild scenes of ecstasy. But there was no feeling of bitterness. In fact, there was pity among the slaves for our former owners. The wild rejoicing on the part of the emancipated coloured people lasted but for a brief period, for I noticed that by the time they returned to their cabins there was a change in their feelings. The great responsibility of being free, of having charge of themselves, of having to think and plan for themselves and their children, seemed to take possession of them. It was very much like suddenly turning a youth of ten or twelve years out into the world to provide for himself. In a few hours the great questions with which the Anglo-Saxon race had been grappling for centuries had been thrown upon these people to be solved. These were the questions of a home, a living, the rearing of children, education, citizenship, and the establishment and support of churches. Was it any wonder that within a few hours the wild rejoicing ceased and a feeling of deep gloom seemed to pervade the slave quarters? To some it seemed that, now that they were in actual possession of it, freedom was a more serious thing than they had expected to find it. Some of the slaves were seventy or eighty years old; their best days were gone. They had no strength with which to earn a living in a strange place and among strange people, even if they had been sure where to find a new place of abode. To this class the problem seemed especially hard. Besides, deep down in their hearts there was a strange and peculiar attachment to "old Marster" and "old Missus," and to their children, which they found it hard to think of breaking off. With these they had spent in some cases nearly a half-century, and it was no light thing to think of parting. Gradually, one by one, stealthily at first, the older slaves began to wander from the slave quarters back to the "big house" to have a whispered conversation with their former owners as to the future.

After the coming of freedom there were two points upon which practically all the people on our place were agreed, and I find that this was generally true throughout the South: that they must change their names, and that they must leave the old plantation for at least a few days or weeks in order that they might really feel sure that they were free.

In some way a feeling got among the coloured people that it was far from proper for them to bear the surname of their former owners, and a great many of them took other surnames. This was one of the first signs of freedom. When they were slaves, a coloured person was simply called "John" or "Susan." There was seldom occasion for more than the use of one name. If "John" or "Susan" belonged to a white man by the name of "Hatcher," sometimes he was called "John Hatcher," or as often "Hatcher's John." But there was a feeling that "John Hatcher" or "Hatcher's John" was not the proper title by which to denote a freeman; and so in many cases "John Hatcher" was changed to "John S. Lincoln" or "John S. Sherman," the initial "S" standing for no name, it being simply a part of what the coloured man proudly called his "entitles."

As I have stated, most of the coloured people left the old plantation for a short while at least, so as to be sure, it seemed, that they could leave and try their freedom on to see how it felt. After they had remained away for a time, many of the older slaves, especially, returned to their old homes and made some kind of contract with their former owners by which they remained on the estate. . . .

[His stepfather, Washington Ferguson, moved the family to Malden, West Virginia, where Washington worked in a salt mine, a coal mine, and as a house servant.]

From the time that I can remember having any thoughts about anything, I recall that I had an intense longing to learn to read. I determined, when quite a small child, that, if I accomplished nothing else in life, I would in some way get enough education to enable me to read common books and newspapers. Soon after we got settled in some manner in our new cabin in West Virginia, I induced my mother to get hold of a book for me. How or where she got it I do not know, but in some way she procured an old copy of Webster's "blue-black" spelling-book, which contained the alphabet, followed by such meaningless words as "ab," "ba," "ca," "da." I began at once to devour this book, and I think that it was the first one I ever had in my hands. I had learned from somebody that the way to begin to read was to learn the alphabet, so I tried in all the ways I could think of to learn it,—all of course without a teacher, for I could find no one to teach me. At that time there was not a single member of my race anywhere near us who could read, and I was too timid to approach any of the white people. In some way, within a few weeks, I mastered the greater portion of the alphabet. In all my efforts to learn to read my mother shared fully my ambition, and sympathized with me and aided me in every way that she could. Though she was totally ignorant, so far as mere book knowledge was concerned, she had high ambitions for her children, and a large fund of good, hard, common sense which seemed to enable her to meet and master every situation. If I have done anything in life worth attention, I feel sure that I inherited the disposition from my mother.

In the midst of my struggles and longing for an education, a young coloured boy who had learned to read in the state of Ohio came to Malden. As soon as the coloured people found out that he could read, a newspaper was secured, and at the close of nearly every day's work this young man would be surrounded by a group of men and women who were anxious to hear him read the news contained in the papers. How I used to envy this man! He seemed to me to be the one young man in all the world who ought to be satisfied with his attainments.

About this time the question of having some kind of a school opened for the coloured children in the village began to be discussed by members of the race. . . .

From the time when I could remember anything, I had been called simply "Booker." Before going to school it had never occurred to me that it was needful or appropriate to have an additional name. When I heard the school-roll called, I noticed that all of the children had at least two names, and some of them indulged in what seemed to me the extravagance of having three. I was in deep perplexity, because I knew that the teacher would demand of me at least two names, and I had only one. By the time the occasion came for the enrolling of my name, an idea occurred to me which I thought would make me equal to the situation; and so, when the teacher asked me what my full name was, I calmly told him "Booker Washington," as if I had been called by that name all my life; and by that name I have since been known. Later in life I found that my mother had given me the name of "Booker Taliaferro" soon after I was born, but in some way that part of my name seemed to disappear, and for a long while was forgotten, but as soon as I found out about it I revived it, and made my full name "Booker Taliaferro Washington." I think there are not many men in our country who have had the privilege of naming themselves in the way that I have. . . .

[Washington longed for additional schooling and enrolled at Hampton Institute in Virginia, some 500 miles from his home.]

As soon as possible after reaching the grounds of the Hampton Institute, I presented myself before the head teacher for assignment to a class. Having been so long without proper food, a bath and change of clothing, I did not, of course, make a very favourable impression upon her, and I could see at once that there were doubts in her mind about the wisdom of admitting me as a student. I felt that I could hardly blame her if she got the idea that I was a worthless loafer or tramp. For some time she did not refuse to admit me, neither did she decide in my favour, and I continued to linger about her, and to impress her in all the ways I could with my worthiness. In the meantime I saw her admitting other students, and that added greatly to my discomfort, for I felt, deep down in my heart, that I could do as well as they, if I could only get a chance to show what was in me.

After some hours had passed, the head teacher said to me: "The adjoining recitation-room needs sweeping. Take the broom and sweep it."

It occurred to me at once that here was my chance. Never did I receive an order with more delight. I knew that I could sweep, for Mrs. Ruffner had thoroughly taught me how to do that when I lived with her.

I swept the recitation-room three times. Then I got a dusting-cloth and I dusted it four times. All the woodwork around the walls, every bench, table, and desk, I went over four times with my dusting-cloth. Besides, every piece of furniture had been moved and every closet and corner in the room had been thoroughly cleaned. I had the feeling that in a large measure my future depended upon the impression I made upon the teacher in the cleaning of that room. When I was through, I reported to the head teacher. She was a "Yankee" woman who knew just where to look for dirt. She went into the room and inspected the floor and closets; then she took her handkerchief and rubbed it on the woodwork about the walls, and over the table and benches. When she was unable to find one bit of dirt on the floor, or a particle of dust on any of the furniture, she quietly remarked, "I guess you will do to enter this institution."

I was one of the happiest souls on earth. The sweeping of that room was my college examination, and never did any youth pass an examination for entrance into Harvard or Yale that gave him more genuine satisfaction. I have passed several examinations since then, but I have always felt that this was the best one I ever passed.

I have spoken of my own experience in entering the Hampton Institute. Perhaps few, if any, had anything like the experience that I had, but about that same period there were hundreds who found their way to Hampton and other institutions after experiencing something of the same difficulties that I went through. The young men and women were determined to secure an education at any cost.

The sweeping of the recitation-room in the manner that I did it seems to have paved the way for me to get through Hampton. Miss Mary F. Mackie, the head teacher, offered me a position as janitor. This, of course, I gladly accepted, because it was a place where I could work out nearly all the cost of my board. The work was hard and taxing, but I stuck to it. I had a large number of rooms to care for, and had to work late into the night, while at the same time I had to rise by four o'clock in the morning, in order to build the fires and have a little time in which to prepare my lessons. . . .

Life at Hampton was a constant revelation to me; was constantly taking me into a new world. The matter of having meals at regular hours, of eating on a tablecloth, using a napkin, the use of the bathtub and of the toothbrush, as well as the use of sheets upon the bed, were all new to me.

I sometimes feel that almost the most valuable lesson I got at the Hampton Institute was in the use and value of the bath. I learned there for the first time some of its value, not only in keeping the body healthy, but in inspiring self-respect and promoting virtue. In all my travels in the South and elsewhere since leaving Hampton I have always in some way sought my daily bath. To get it sometimes when I have been the guest of my own people in a single-roomed cabin has not always been easy to do, except by slipping away to some stream in the woods. I have always tried to teach my people that some provision for bathing should be a part of every house.

For some time, while a student at Hampton, I possessed but a single pair of socks, but when I had worn these till they became soiled, I would wash them at night and hang them by the fire to dry, so that I might wear them again the next morning.

The charge for my board at Hampton was ten dollars per month. I was expected to pay a part of this in cash and to work out the remainder. . . .

[He worked and studied his way through Hampton, graduating in June 1875 as one of the "honour" students.]

I was completely out of money when I graduated. In company with other Hampton students, I secured a place as a table waiter in a summer hotel in Connecticut, and managed to borrow enough money with which to get there. I had not been in this hotel long before I found out that I knew practically nothing about waiting on a hotel table. The head waiter, however, supposed that I was an accomplished waiter. He soon gave me charge of a table at which there sat four or five wealthy and rather aristocratic people. My ignorance of how to wait upon them was so apparent that they scolded me in such a severe manner that I became frightened and left their table, leaving them sitting there without food. As a result of this I was reduced from the position of waiter to that of a dish-carrier.

But I determined to learn the business of waiting, and did so within a few weeks and was restored to my former position. I have had the satisfaction of being a guest in this hotel several times since I was a waiter there.

At the close of the hotel season I returned to my former home in Malden [West Virginia] and was elected to teach the coloured school at that place. This was the beginning of one of the happiest periods of my life. I now felt that I had the opportunity to help the people of my home town to a higher life. I felt from the first that mere book education was not all that the young people of that town needed. I began my work at eight o'clock in the morning, and, as a result, it did not end until ten o'clock at night. In addition to the usual routine of teaching,

I taught the pupils to comb their hair, and to keep their hands and faces clean, as well as their clothing. I gave special attention to teaching them the proper use of the tooth-brush and the bath. In all my teaching I have watched carefully the influence of the tooth-brush, and I am convinced that there are few single agencies of civilization that are more far-reaching.

There were so many of the older boys and girls in the town, as well as men and women, who had to work in the daytime but still were craving an opportunity for some education, that I soon opened a night-school. From the first, this was crowded every night, being about as large as the school that I taught in the day. The efforts of some of the men and women, who in many cases were over fifty years of age, to learn, were in some cases very pathetic.

My day and night school work was not all that I undertook. I established a small reading-room and a debating society. On Sundays I taught two Sunday-schools, one in the town of Malden in the afternoon, and the other in the morning at a place three miles distant from Malden. In addition to this, I gave private lessons to several young men whom I was fitting to send to the Hampton Institute. Without regard to pay and with little thought of it, I taught any one who wanted to learn anything that I could teach him. I was supremely happy in the opportunity of being able to assist somebody else. I did receive, however, a small salary from the public fund, for my work as a public-school teacher.

During the time that I was a student at Hampton my older brother, John, not only assisted me all that he could, but worked all of the time in the coal-mines in order to support the family. He willingly neglected his own education that he might help me. It was my earnest wish to help him to prepare to enter Hampton, and to save enough money to assist him in his expenses there. Both of these objects I was successful in accomplishing. In three years my brother finished the course at Hampton, and he is now holding the important position of Superintendent of Industries at Tuskegee [a technical and agricultural school for Negroes, founded by Washington in Alabama]. When he returned from Hampton, we both combined our efforts and savings to send our adopted brother, James, through the Hampton Institute. This we succeeded in doing, and he is now the postmaster at the Tuskegee Institute. The year 1877, which was my second year of teaching in Malden, I spent very much as I did the first.

It was while my home was at Malden that what was known as the "Ku Klux Klan" was in the height of its activity. The "Ku Klux" were bands of men who had joined themselves together for the purpose of regulating the conduct of the coloured people, especially with the object of preventing the members of the race from exercising any influence in politics. They corresponded somewhat to the "patrollers" of whom I used to hear a great deal during the days of slavery, when I was a small boy. The "patrollers" were bands of white men—usually young men—who were organized largely for the purpose of regulating the conduct of the slaves at night in such matters as preventing the slaves from going from one plantation to another without passes, and for preventing them from holding any kind of meetings without permission and without the presence at these meetings of at least one white man.

Like the "patrollers" the "Ku Klux" operated almost wholly at night. They were, however, more cruel than the "patrollers." Their objects, in the main, were to crush out the political aspirations of the Negroes, but they did not confine themselves to this, because schoolhouses as well as churches were burned by them, and many innocent persons were made to suffer. During this period not a few coloured people lost their lives. . . .

I found Tuskegee to be a town of about two thousand inhabitants, nearly one-half of whom were coloured. It was in what was known as the Black Belt of the South. In the county in which Tuskegee is situated the coloured people out-numbered the whites by about three to one. In some of the adjoining and near-by counties the proportion was not far from six coloured persons to one white.

I have often been asked to define the term "Black Belt." So far as I can learn, the term was first used to designate a part of the country which was distinguished by the colour of the soil. The part of the country possessing this thick, dark, and naturally rich soil was, of course, the part of the South where the slaves were most profitable, and consequently they were taken there in the largest numbers. Later and especially since the war, the term seems to be used wholly in a political sense—that is, to designate the counties where the black people outnumbered the white.

Before going to Tuskegee I had expected to find there a building and all the necessary apparatus ready for me to begin teaching. To my disappointment, I found nothing of the kind. I did find, though, that which no costly building and apparatus can supply,—hundreds of hungry, earnest souls who wanted to secure knowledge.

Tuskegee seemed an ideal place for the school. It was in the midst of the great bulk of the Negro population, and was rather secluded, being five miles from the main line of railroad, with which it was connected by a short line. During the days of slavery, and since, the town had been a centre for the education of the white people. This was an added advantage, for the reason that I found the white people possessing a degree of culture and education that is not surpassed by many locali-ties. While the coloured people were ignorant, they had not, as a rule degraded and weakened their bodies by vices such as are common to the lower class of people in the large cities. In general, I found the relations between the two races pleasant. For example, the largest, and I think at that time the only hardware store in the town was owned and operated jointly by a coloured man and a white man. This copartnership continued until the death of the white partner.

I found that about a year previous to my going to Tuskegee some of the coloured people who had heard something of the work of education being done at Hampton had applied to the state Legislature, through their representatives, for a small appropriation to be used in starting a normal school in Tuskegee. This re-quest the Legislature had complied with to the extent of granting an annual appro-priation of two thousand dollars. I soon learned, however, that this money could be used only for the payment of the salaries of the instructors, and that there was no provision for securing land, buildings, or apparatus. The task before me did not seem a very encouraging one. It seemed much like making bricks without straw. The coloured people were overjoyed, and were constantly offering their ser-vices in any way in which they could be of assistance in getting the school started.

My first task was to find a place in which to open the school. After looking the town over with some care, the most suitable place that could be secured seemed to be a rather dilapidated shanty near the coloured Methodist church, together with the church itself as a sort of assembly-room. Both the church and the shanty were in about as bad condition as was possible. I recall that during the first months of school that I taught in this building it was in such poor repair that, whenever it rained, one of the older students would very kindly leave his lessons to hold an umbrella over me while I heard the recitations of the others. I remember, also, that on more than one occasion my landlady held an umbrella over me while I ate breakfast.

At the time I went to Alabama the coloured people were taking considerable interest in politics, and they were very anxious that I should become one of them politically, in every respect. They seemed to have a little distrust of strangers in this regard. I recall that one man, who seemed to have been designated by the others to look after my political destiny, came to me on several occasions and said, with a good deal of earnestness: "We wants you to be sure to vote jes' like we votes. We can't read de newspapers very much, but we knows how to vote, an' we wants you to vote jes' like we votes." He added: "We watches de white man, and we keeps watching de white man till we finds out which way de white man's gwine to vote; an' when we finds out which way de white man's gwine to vote, den we votes 'xactly de other way. Den we know we's right."

I am glad to add, however, that at the present time the disposition to vote against the white man merely because he is white is largely disappearing, and the race is learning to vote from principle, for what the voter considers to be for the best interests of both races.

I reached Tuskegee, as I have said, early in June, 1881. The first month I spent in finding accommodations for the school, and in travelling through Alabama, examining into the actual life of the people, especially in the country districts, and in getting the school advertised among the class of people that I wanted to have attend it. The most of my travelling was done over the country roads, with a mule and a cart or a mule and a buggy wagon for conveyance. I ate and slept with the people, in their little cabins. I saw their farms, their schools, their churches. Since, in the case of the most of these visits, there had been no notice given in advance that a stranger was expected, I had the advantage of seeing the real, everyday life of the people.

In the plantation districts I found that, as a rule the whole family slept in one room, and that in addition to the immediate family there sometimes were relatives, or others not related to the family, who slept in the same room. On more than one occasion I went outside the house to get ready for bed, or to wait until the family had gone to bed. They usually contrived some kind of a place for me to sleep, either on the floor or in a special part of another's bed. Rarely was there any place provided in the cabin where one could bathe even the face and hands, but usually some provision was made for this outside the house, in the yard.

The common diet of the people was fat pork and corn bread. At times I have eaten in cabins where they had only corn bread and "black-eye peas" cooked in plain water. The people seemed to have no other idea than to live on this fat meat and corn bread,—the meat, and the meal of which the bread was made, having been bought at a high price at a store in town, notwithstanding the fact that the land all about the cabin homes could easily have been made to produce nearly every kind of garden vegetable that is raised anywhere in the country. Their one object seemed to be to plant nothing but cotton; and in many cases cotton was planted up to the very door of the cabin. . . .

After consultation with the citizens of Tuskegee, I set July 4, 1881, as the day for the opening of the school in the little shanty and church which had been secured for its accommodation. The white people, as well as the coloured, were greatly interested in the starting of the new school, and the opening day was looked forward to with much earnest discussion. There were not a few white people in the vicinity of Tuskegee who looked with some disfavour upon the project. They questioned its value to the coloured people, and had a fear that it might result in bringing about trouble between the races. Some had the feeling that in proportion as the Negro received education, in the same proportion would his value decrease as an economic factor in the state. These people feared the result of education would be that the Negroes would leave the farms, and that it would be difficult to secure them for domestic service.

The white people who questioned the wisdom of starting this new school had in their minds pictures of what was called an educated Negro, with a high hat, imitation gold eye-glasses, a showy walking-stick, kid gloves, fancy boots, and what not—in a word, a man who was determined to live by his wits. It was difficult for these people to see how education would produce any other kind of a coloured man. . . .

On the morning that the school opened, thirty students reported for admission. I was the only teacher. The students were about equally divided between the sexes. Most of them lived in Macon County, the county in which Tuskegee is situated and of which it is the county-seat. A great many more students wanted to enter the school, but it had been decided to receive only those who were above fifteen years of age, and who had previously received some education. The greater part of the thirty were public-school teachers, and some of them were nearly forty years of age. With the teachers came some of their former pupils, and when they were examined it was amusing to note that in several cases the pupil entered a higher class than did his former teacher. It was also interesting to note how many big books some of them had studied, and how many high-sounding subjects some of them claimed to have mastered. The bigger the book and the longer the name of the subject, the prouder they felt of their accomplishment. Some had studied Latin, and one or two Greek. This they thought entitled them to special distinction.

In fact, one of the saddest things I saw during the month of travel which I have described was a young man, who had attended some high school, sitting down in a one-room cabin, with grease on his clothing, filth all around him, and weeds in the yard and garden, engaged in studying French grammar.

The students who came first seemed to be fond of memorizing long and complicated "rules" in grammar and mathematics, but had little thought or knowledge of applying these rules to the everyday affairs of their life. One subject which they liked to talk about, and tell me that they had mastered, in arithmetic, was "banking and discount," but I soon found out that neither they nor almost any one in the neighbourhood in which they lived had ever had a bank account. In registering the names of the students, I found that almost every one of them had one or more middle initials. When I asked what the "J" stood for, in the name of John J. Jones, it was explained to me that this was a part of his "entitles." Most of the students wanted to get an education because they thought it would enable them to earn more money as school-teachers.

Notwithstanding what I had said about them in these respects, I have never seen a more earnest and willing company of young men and women than these students were. They were all willing to learn the right things as soon as it was shown them what was right. I was determined to start them off on a solid and thorough foundation, so far as their books were concerned. I soon learned that most of them had the merest smattering of the high-sounding things that they had studied. While they could locate the Desert of Sahara or the capital of China on an artificial globe, I found out that the girls could not locate the proper places for the knives and forks on an actual dinner-table, or the places on which the bread and meat should be set.

I had to summon a good deal of courage to take a student who had been studying cube root and "banking and discount," and explain to him that the wisest thing for him to do first was thoroughly to master the multiplication table.

The number of pupils increased each week, until by the end of the first month there were nearly fifty. Many of them, however, said that, as they could remain only for two or three months, they wanted to enter a high class and get a diploma the first year if possible.

At the end of the first six weeks a new and rare face entered the school as a co-teacher. This was Miss Olivia A. Davidson, who later became my wife. Miss Davidson was born in Ohio, and received her preparatory education in the public schools of that state. When little more than a girl, she heard of the need of teachers in the South. She went to the state of Mississippi and began teaching there. Later she taught in the city of Memphis. While teaching in Mississippi, one of her pupils became ill with smallpox. Every one in the community was so frightened that no one would nurse the boy. Miss Davidson closed her school and remained by the bedside of the boy night and day until he recovered. While she was at her Ohio home on her vacation, the worst epidemic of yellow fever broke out in Memphis, Tenn., that perhaps has ever occurred in the South. When she heard of this, she at once telegraphed the Mayor of Memphis, offering her services as a yellow-fever nurse, although she had never had the disease.

Miss Davidson's experience in the South showed her that the people needed something more than mere book-learning. She heard of the Hampton system of education, and decided that this was what she wanted in order to prepare herself for better work in the South. The attention of Mrs. Mary Hemenway, of Boston, was attracted to her rare ability. Through Mrs. Hemenway's kindness and generosity, Miss Davidson, after graduating at Hampton, received an opportunity to complete a two years' course of training at the Massachusetts State Normal School at Framingham.

Before she went to Framingham, some one suggested to Miss Davidson that, since she was so very light in colour, she might find it more comfortable not to be known as a coloured woman in this school in Massachusetts. She at once replied that under no circumstances and for no considerations would she consent to deceive any one in regard to her racial identity.

Soon after her graduation from the Framingham institution, Miss Davidson came to Tuskegee, bringing into the school many valuable and fresh ideas as to the best methods of teaching, as well as a rare moral character and a life of unselfishness that I think has seldom been equalled. No single individual did more toward laying the foundations of the Tuskegee Institute so as to insure the successful work that has been done there than Olivia A. Davidson.

Miss Davidson and I began consulting as to the future of the school from the first. The students were making progress in learning books and in developing their minds; but it became apparent at once that; if we were to make any permanent impression upon those who had come to us for training, we must do something besides teach them mere books. The students had come from homes where they had had no opportunities for lessons which would teach them how to care for their bodies. With few exceptions, the homes in Tuskegee in which the students boarded were but little improvement upon those from which they had come. We wanted to teach the students how to bathe; how to care for their teeth and clothing. We wanted to teach them what to eat, and how to eat it properly, and how to care for their rooms. Aside from this, we wanted to give them such a practical knowledge of some one industry, together with the spirit of industry, thrift, and economy, that they would be sure of knowing how to make a living after they had left us. We wanted to teach them to study actual things instead of mere books alone. . . .

[Washington borrowed $500 and purchased an old plantation on which to relocate Tuskegee Institute.]

During the summer of 1882, at the end of the first year's work of the school, I was married to Miss Fannie N. Smith, of Walden, W. Va. We began keeping house in Tuskegee early in the fall. This made a home for our teachers, who now had been increased to four in number. My wife was also a graduate of the Hampton Institute. After earnest and constant work in the interests of the school, together with her housekeeping duties, my wife passed away in May, 1884. One child, Portia M. Washington, was born during our marriage.

From the first, my wife most earnestly devoted her thoughts and time to the work of the school, and was completely one with me in every interest and ambition. She passed away, however, before she had an opportunity of seeing what the school was designed to be.

From the very beginning, at Tuskegee, I was determined to have the students do not only the agricultural and domestic work, but to have them erect their own buildings. My plan was to have them, while performing this service, taught the latest and best methods of labour, so that the school would not only get the benefit of their efforts, but the students themselves would be taught to see not only utility in labour, but beauty and dignity, would be taught, in fact, how to lift labour up from mere drudgery and toil, and would learn to love work for its own sake. My plan was not to teach them to work in the old way but to show them how to make the forces of nature—air, water, steam, electricity, horse-power—assist them in their labour.

At first many advised against the experiment of having the buildings erected by the labour of the students, but I was determined to stick to it. I told those who doubted the wisdom of the plan that I knew that our first buildings would not be so comfortable or so complete in their finish as buildings erected by the experienced hands of outside workmen, but that in the teaching of civilization, self-help, and self-reliance, the erection of the buildings by the students themselves would more than compensate for any lack of comfort or fine finish.

I further told those who doubted the wisdom of this plan, that the majority of our students came to us in poverty, from the cabins of the cotton, sugar, and rice plantations of the South, and that while I knew it would please the students very much to place them at once in finely constructed buildings I felt that it would be following out a more natural process of development to teach them how to construct their own buildings. Mistakes I knew would be made, but these mistakes would teach us valuable lessons for the future.

During the now nineteen years' existence of the Tuskegee school, the plan of having the buildings erected by student labour has been adhered to. In this time forty buildings, counting small and large, have been built, and all except four are almost wholly the product of student labour. As an additional result, hundreds of men are now scattered throughout the South who received their knowledge of mechanics while being taught how to erect these buildings. Skill and knowledge are now handed down from one set of students to another in this way, until at the present time a building of any description or size can be constructed wholly by our instructors and students, from the drawing of the plans to the putting in of the electric fixtures without going off the grounds for a single workman.

Not a few times, when a new student has been led into the temptation of marring the looks of some building by leadpencil marks or by the cuts of a jack-knife, I have heard an old student remind him: "Don't do that. That is our building. I helped put it up."

In the early days of the school I think my most trying experience was in the matter of brickmaking. As soon as we got the farm work reasonably well started, we directed our next efforts toward the industry of making bricks. We needed these for use in connection with the erection of our own buildings; but there was also another reason for establishing this industry. There was no brickyard in the town, and in addition to our own needs there was a demand for bricks in the general market.

I had always sympathized with the "Children of Israel," in their task of "making bricks without straw," but ours was the task of making bricks with no money and no experience.

In the first place, the work was hard and dirty, and it was difficult to get the students to help. When it came to brickmaking, their distaste for manual labour in connection with book education became especially manifest. It was not a pleasant task for one to stand in the mud-pit for hours, with the mud up to his knees. More than one man became disgusted and left the school.

We tried several locations before we opened up a pit that furnished brick clay. I had always supposed that brickmaking was very simple, but I soon found out by bitter experience that it required special skill and knowledge, particularly in the burning of the bricks. After a good deal of effort we moulded about twenty-five thousand bricks, and put them into a kiln to be burned. This kiln turned out to be a failure, because it was not properly constructed or properly burned. We began at once, however, on a second kiln. This, for some reason, also proved a failure. The failure of this kiln made it still more difficult to get the students to take any part in the work. Several of the teachers, however, who had been trained in the industries at Hampton, volunteered their services, and in some way we succeeded in getting a third kiln ready for burning. The burning of the kiln required about a week. Toward the latter part of the week, when it seemed as if we were going to have a good many thousand bricks in a few hours, in the middle of the night the kiln fell. For the third time we had failed.

The failure of this last kiln left me without a single dollar with which to make another experiment. Most of the teachers advised the abandoning of the effort to make bricks. In the midst of my troubles I thought of a watch which had come into my possession years before. I took this watch to the city of Montgomery, which was not far distant, and placed it in a pawn-shop. I secured cash upon it to the amount of fifteen dollars, with which to renew the brickmaking experiment. I returned to Tuskegee, and, with the help of the fifteen dollars, rallied our rather demoralized and discouraged forces and began a fourth attempt to make bricks. This time, I am glad to say, we were successful. Before I got hold of any money, the time-limit on my watch had expired, and I have never seen it since; but I have never regretted the loss of it.

Brickmaking has now become such an important industry at the school that last season our students manufactured twelve hundred thousand of first-class bricks, of a quality suitable to be sold to any market. Aside from this, scores of young men have mastered the brickmaking trade—both the making of bricks by hand and by machinery—and are now engaged in this industry in many parts of the South.

The making of these bricks taught me an important lesson in regard to the relations of the two races in the South. Many white people who had had no contact with the school, and perhaps no sympathy with it, came to us to buy bricks because they found out that ours were good bricks. They discovered that we were supplying a real want in the community. The making of these bricks caused many of the white residents of the neighbourhood to begin to feel that the education of the Negro was not making him worthless, but that in educating our students we were adding something to the wealth and comfort of the community. As the people of the neighborhood came to us to buy bricks, we got acquainted with them; they traded with us and we with them. Our business interests became intermingled. We had something which they wanted; they had something which we wanted. . . .

[The students themselves constructed all the new buildings with money Washington raised from local people and from Northern industrialists. John D. Rockefeller and Andrew Carnegie contributed heavily to keep the school afloat.]

While a great deal of stress is laid upon the industrial side of the work at Tuskegee, we do not neglect or overlook in any degree the religious and spiritual side. The school is strictly undenominational, but it is thoroughly Christian, and the spiritual training of the students is not neglected. Our preaching service, prayer-meetings, Sunday-school, Christian Endeavour Society, Young Men's Christian Association, and various missionary organizations, testify to this.

In 1885, Miss Olivia Davidson, to whom I have already referred as being largely responsible for the success of the school during its early history, and I were married. During our married life she continued to divide her time and strength between our home and the work for the school. She not only continued to work in the school at Tuskegee, but also kept up her habit of going North to secure funds. In 1889 she died, after four years of happy married life and eight years of hard and happy work for the school. She literally wore herself out in her never ceasing efforts in behalf of the work that she so dearly loved. During our married life there were born to us two bright, beautiful boys, Booker Taliaferro and Ernest Davidson. The older of these, Booker, has already mastered the brick-maker's trade at Tuskegee.

I have often been asked how I began the practice of public speaking. In answer I would say that I never planned to give any large part of my life to speaking in public. I have always had more of an ambition to *do* things than merely to talk *about* doing them. It seems that when I went North with General Armstrong to speak at the series of public meetings to which I have referred, the President of the National Educational Association, the Hon. Thomas W. Bicknell, was present at one of those meetings and heard me speak. A few days afterward he sent me an invitation to deliver an address at the next meeting of the Educational Association. This meeting was to be held in Madison, Wis. I accepted the invitation. This was, in a sense, the beginning of my public-speaking career.

On the evening that I spoke before the Association there must have been not far from four thousand persons present. Without my knowing it, there were a large number of people present from Alabama, and some from the town of Tuskegee. These white people afterward frankly told me that they went to this meeting expecting to hear the South roundly abused, but were pleasantly surprised to find that there was no word of abuse in my address. On the contrary, the South was given credit for all the praiseworthy things that it had done. A white lady who was teacher in a college in Tuskegee wrote back to the local paper that she was gratified, as well as surprised, to note the credit which I gave the white people of Tuskegee for their help in getting the school started. This address at Madison was the first that I had delivered that in any large measure dealt with the general problem of the races. Those who heard it seemed to be pleased with what I said and with the general position that I took.

When I first came to Tuskegee, I determined that I would make it my home, that I would take as much pride in the right actions of the people of the town as any white man could do, and that I would, at the same time, deplore the wrong-doing of the people as much as any white man. I determined never to say anything in a public address in the North that I would not be willing to say in the South. I early learned that it is a hard matter to convert an individual by abusing him, and that this is more often accomplished by giving credit for all the praiseworthy actions performed than by calling attention alone to all the evil done.

While pursuing this policy I have not failed, at the proper time and in the proper manner, to call attention, in no uncertain terms, to the wrongs which any part of the South has been guilty of. I have found that there is a large element in the South that is quick to respond to straightforward, honest criticism of any wrong policy. As a rule, the place to criticise the South, when criticism is necessary, is in the South—not in Boston. A Boston man who came to Alabama to criticise Boston would not effect so much good, I think, as one who had his word of criticism to say in Boston.

In this address at Madison I took the ground that the policy to be pursued with reference to the races was, by every honourable means, to bring them together and to encourage the cultivation of friendly relations, instead of doing that which would embitter. I further contended that, in relation to his vote, the Negro should more and more consider the interests of the community in which he lived, rather than seek alone to please some one who lived a thousand miles away from him and from his interests.

In this address I said that the whole future of the Negro rested largely upon the question as to whether or not he should make himself, through his skill, intelligence, and character, of such undeniable value to the community in which he lived that the community could not dispense with his presence. I said that any individual who learned to do something better than anybody else—learned to do a common thing in an uncommon manner—had solved his problem, regardless of the colour of his skin, and that in proportion as the Negro learned to produce what other people wanted and must have, in the same proportion would he be respected. . . .

I now come to that one of the incidents in my life which seems to have excited the greatest amount of interest, and which perhaps went farther than anything else in giving me a reputation that in a sense might be called National. I refer to the address which I delivered at the opening of the Atlanta Cotton states and International Exposition, at Atlanta, Ga., September, 18, 1895. . . .

The receiving of this invitation brought to me a sense of responsibility that it would be hard for any one not placed in my position to appreciate. What were my feelings when this invitation came to me? I remembered that I had been a slave; that my early years had been spent in the lowest depths of poverty and ignorance, and that I had had little opportunity to prepare me for such a responsibility as this. It was only a few years before that time that any white man in the audience might have claimed me as his slave; and it was easily possible that some of my former owners might be present to hear me speak.

I knew, too, that this was the first time in the entire history of the Negro that a member of my race had been asked to speak from the same platform with white Southern men and women on any important National occasion. I was asked now to speak to an audience composed of the wealth and culture of the white South, the representatives of my former masters. I knew, too, that while the greater part of my audience would be composed of Southern people, yet there would be present a large number of Northern whites, as well as a great many men and women of my own race.

I was determined to say nothing that I did not feel from the bottom of my heart to be true and right. When the invitation came to me, there was not one word of intimation as to what I should say or as to what I should omit. In this I felt that the Board of Directors had paid a tribute to me. They knew that by one sentence I could have blasted, in a large degree, the success of the Exposition. I was also painfully conscious of the fact that, while I must be true to my own race in my utterances, I had it in my power to make such an ill-timed address as would result in preventing any similar invitation being extended to a black man again for years to come. I was equally determined to be true to the North, as well as to the best element of the white South, in what I had to say. . . .

When I arose to speak, there was considerable cheering, especially from the coloured people. As I remember it now, the thing that was uppermost in my mind was the desire to say something that would cement the friendship of the races and bring about hearty cooperation between them. So far as my outward surroundings were concerned, the only thing that I recall distinctly now is that when I got up, I saw thousands of eyes looking intently into my face. The following is the address which I delivered:—

Mr. President and Gentlemen of the Board of Directors and Citizens.

One-third of the population of the South is of the Negro race. No enterprise seeking the material, civil, or moral welfare of this section can disregard this element of our population and reach the highest success. I but convey to you, Mr. President and Directors, the sentiment of the masses of my race when I say that in no way have the value and manhood of the American Negro been more fittingly and generously recognized than by the managers of this magnificent Exposition at every stage of its progress. It is a recognition that will do more to cement the friendship of the two races than any occurrence since the dawn of our freedom.

Not only this, but the opportunity here afforded will awaken among us a new era of industrial progress. Ignorant and inexperienced, it is not strange that in the first years of our new life we began at the top instead of at the bottom; that a seat in Congress or the state legislature was more sought than real estate or industrial skill; that the political convention of stump speaking had more attractions than starting a dairy farm or truck garden.

A ship lost at sea for many days suddenly sighted a friendly vessel. From the mast of the unfortunate vessel was seen a signal, "Water, water; we die of thirst!"

The answer from the friendly vessel at once came back, "Cast down your bucket where you are." A second time the signal, "Water, water; send us water!" ran up from the distressed vessel, and was answered, "Cast down your bucket where you are." And a third and fourth signal for water was answered, "Cast down your bucket where you are." The captain of the distressed vessel, at last heeding the injunction, cast down his bucket, and it came up full of fresh, sparkling water from the mouth of the Amazon River. To those of my race who depend on bettering their condition in a foreign land or who underestimate the importance of cultivating friendly relations with the Southern white man, who is their next-door neighbour, I would say: "Cast down your bucket where you are"—cast it down in making friends in every manly way of the people of all races by whom we are surrounded.

Cast it down in agriculture, mechanics, in commerce, in domestic service, and in the professions. And in this connection it is well to bear in mind that whatever other sins the South may be called to bear, when it comes to business, pure and simple, it is in the South that the Negro is given a man's chance in the commercial world, and in nothing is this Exposition more eloquent than in emphasizing this chance. Our greatest danger is that in the great leap from slavery to freedom we may overlook the fact that the masses of us are to live by the productions of our hands, and fail to keep in mind that we shall prosper in proportion as we learn to dignify and glorify common labour and put brains and skill into the common occupations of life; shall prosper in proportion as we learn to draw the line between the superficial and the substantial, the ornamental gewgaws of life and the useful. No race can prosper till it learns that there is as much dignity in tilling a field as in writing a poem. It is at the bottom of life we must begin, and not at the top. Nor should we permit our grievances to overshadow our opportunities.

To those of the white race who look to the incoming of those of foreign birth and strange tongue and habits for the prosperity of the South, were I permitted I would repeat what I say to my own race, "Cast down your bucket where you are." Cast it down among the eight millions of Negroes whose habits you know, whose fidelity and love you have tested in days when to have proved treacherous meant the ruin of your firesides. Cast down your bucket among these people who have, without strikes and labour wars, tilled your fields, cleared your forests, builded your railroads and cities, and brought forth treasures from the bowels of the earth, and helped make possible this magnificent representation of the progress of the South. Casting down your bucket among my people, helping and encouraging them as you are doing on these grounds, and to education of head, hand, and heart, you will find that they will buy your surplus land, make blossom the waste places in your fields, and run your factories. While doing this, you can be sure in the future, as in the past, that you and your families will be surrounded by the most patient, faithful, law-abiding, and unresentful people that the world has seen. As we have proved our loyalty to you in the past, in nursing your children, watching by the sickbed of your mothers and fathers, and often following them with tear-dimmed eyes to their graves, so in the future, in our humble way, we shall stand by you with a devotion that no foreigner can approach, ready to lay down our lives, if need be, in defence of yours, interlacing our industrial, commercial, civil, and religious life with yours in a way that shall make the interests of both races one. In all things that are purely social we can be as separate as the fingers, yet one as the hand in all things essential to mutual progress.

There is no defence or security for any of us except in the highest intelligence and development of all. If anywhere there are efforts tending to curtail the fullest growth of the Negro, let these efforts be turned into stimulating, encouraging, and making him the most useful and intelligent citizen. Effort or means so invested will pay a thousand per cent interest. These efforts will be twice blessed— "blessing him that gives and him that takes."

There is no escape through law of man or God from the inevitable:—

> The laws of changeless justice bind
>   Oppressor with oppressed;
> And close as sin and suffering joined
>   We march to fate abreast.

Nearly sixteen millions of hands will aid you in pulling the load upward, or they will pull against you the load downward. We shall constitute one-third and more of the ignorance and crime of the South, or one-third its intelligence and progress; we shall contribute one-third to the business and industrial prosperity of the South, or we shall prove a veritable body of death, stagnating, depressing, retarding every effort to advance the body politic.

Gentlemen of the Exposition, as we present to you our humble effort at an exhibition of our progress, you must not expect overmuch. Starting thirty years ago with ownership here and there in a few quilts and pumpkins and chickens (gathered from miscellaneous sources), remember the path that has led from these to the inventions and production of agricultural implements, buggies, steam-engines, newspapers, books, statuary, carving, paintings, the management of drug-stores and banks, has not been trodden without contact with thorns and thistles. While we take pride in what we exhibit as a result of our independent efforts, we do not for a moment forget that our part in this exhibition would fall far short of your expectations but for the constant help that has come to our educational life, not only from the Southern states, but especially from Northern philanthropists, who have made their gifts a constant stream of blessing and encouragement.

The wisest among my race understand that the agitation of questions of social equality is the extremest folly, and that progress in the enjoyment of all the privileges that will come to us must be the result of severe and constant struggle rather than of artificial forcing. No race that has anything to contribute to the markets of the world is long in any degree ostracized. It is important and right that all privileges of the law be ours, but it is vastly more important that we be prepared for the exercises of these privileges. The opportunity to earn a dollar in a factory just now is worth infinitely more than the opportunity to spend a dollar in an opera-house.

In conclusion, may I repeat that nothing in thirty years has given us more hope and encouragement, and drawn us so near to you of the white race, as this opportunity offered by the Exposition; and here bending, as it were, over the altar that represents the results of the struggles of your race and mine, both starting practically empty-handed three decades ago. I pledged that in your effort to work out the great and intricate problem which God has laid at the doors of the South, you shall have at all times the patient, sympathetic help of my race; only let this be constantly in mind, that, while from representations in these buildings of the product of field, of forest, of mine, of factory, letters, and art, much good will come, yet far above and beyond material benefits will be that higher good, that, let us pray God, will come, in a blotting out of sectional differences and racial animosities and suspicions, in a determination to administer absolute justice, in a willing obedience among all classes to the mandates of law. This, then, coupled with our material prosperity, will bring into our beloved South a new heaven and a new earth.

The first thing that I remember, after I had finished speaking, was that Governor Bullock rushed across the platform and took me by the hand, and that others did the same. I received so many and such hearty congratulations that I found it difficult to get out of the building. I did not appreciate to any degree, however, the impression which my address seemed to have made, until the next morning, when I went into the business part of the city. As soon as I was recognized, I was surprised to find myself pointed out and surrounded by a crowd of men who wished to shake hands with me. This was kept up on every street on to which I went, to an extent which embarrassed me so much that I went back to my boarding-place. The next morning I returned to Tuskegee. At the station in Atlanta, and at almost all of the stations at which the train stopped between that city and Tuskegee, I found a crowd of people anxious to shake hands with me.

The papers in all parts of the United States published the address in full, and for months afterward there were complimentary editorial references to it. Mr. Clark Howell, the editor of the Atlanta *Constitution,* telegraphed to a New York paper, among other words, the following, "I do not exaggerate when I say that Professor Booker T. Washington's address yesterday was one of the most notable speeches, both as to character and as to the warmth of its reception, ever delivered to a Southern audience. The address was a revelation. The whole speech is a platform upon which blacks and whites can stand with full justice to each other."

The Boston *Transcript* said editorially: "The speech of Booker T. Washington at the Atlanta Exposition, this week, seems to have dwarfed all the other proceedings and the Exposition itself. The sensation that it has caused in the press has never been equalled."

I very soon began receiving all kinds of propositions from lecture bureaus, and editors of magazines and papers, to take the lecture platform, and to write articles. One lecture bureau offered me fifty thousand dollars, or two hundred dollars a night and expenses, if I would place my services at its disposal for a given period. To all these communications I replied that my life-work was at Tuskegee; and that whenever I spoke it must be in the interests of the Tuskegee school and my race, and that I would enter into no arrangements that seemed to place a mere commercial value upon my services. . . .

The coloured people and the coloured newspapers at first seemed to be greatly pleased with the character of my Atlanta address, as well as with its reception. But after the first burst of enthusiasm began to die away, and the coloured people began reading the speech in cold type, some of them seemed to feel that they had been hypnotized. They seemed to feel that I had been too liberal in my remarks toward the Southern whites, and that I had not spoken out strongly enough for what they termed the "rights" of the race. . . .

I am often asked to express myself more freely than I do upon the political condition and the political future of my race. These recollections of my experience in Atlanta give me the opportunity to do so briefly. My own belief is, although I have never before said so in so many words, that the time will come when the Negro in the South will be accorded all the political rights which his ability, character, and material possessions entitle him to. I think, though, that the opportunity to freely exercise such political rights will not come in any large degree through outside or artificial forcing, but will be accorded to the Negro by the Southern white people themselves, and that they will protect him in the exercise of those rights. Just as soon as the South gets over the old feeling that it is being forced by "foreigners," or "aliens," to do something which it does not want to do, I believe that the change in the direction that I have indicated is going to begin. In fact, there are indications that it is already beginning in a slight degree.

Let me illustrate my meaning. Suppose that some months before the opening of the Atlanta Exposition there had been a general demand from the press and public platform outside the South that a Negro be given a place on the opening programme, and that a Negro be placed upon the board of jurors of award. Would any such recognition of the race have taken place? I do not think so. The Atlanta officials went as far as they did because they felt it to be a pleasure, as well as a duty, to reward what they considered merit in the Negro race. Say what we will, there is something in human nature which we cannot blot out, which makes one man, in the end, recognize and reward merit in another, regardless of colour or race.

I believe it is the duty of the Negro—as the greater part of the race is already doing—to deport himself modestly in regard to political claims, depending upon the slow but sure influences that proceed from the possession of property, intelligence, and high character for the full recognition of his political rights. I think that the according of the full exercise of political rights is going to be a matter of natural, slow growth, not an over-night, gourd-vine affair. I do not believe that the Negro should cease voting, for a man cannot learn the exercise of self-government by ceasing to vote any more than a boy can learn to swim by keeping out of the water, but I do believe that in his voting he should more and more be influenced by those of intelligence and character who are his next-door neighbours.

I know coloured men who, through the encouragement, help, and advice of Southern white people, have accumulated thousands of dollars' worth of property, but who, at the same time, would never think of going to those same persons for advice concerning the casting of their ballots. This, it seems to me, is unwise and unreasonable, and should cease. In saying this I do not mean that the Negro should truckle, or not vote from principle, for the instant he ceases to vote from principle he loses the confidence and respect of the Southern white man even.

I do not believe that any state should make a law that permits an ignorant and poverty-stricken white man to vote, and prevents a black man in the same condition from voting. Such a law is not only unjust, but it will react, as all unjust laws do, in time; for the effect of such a law is to encourage the Negro to secure education and property, and at the same time it encourages the white man to remain in ignorance and poverty. I believe that in time, through the operation of intelligence and friendly race relations, all cheating at the ballot box in the South will cease. It will become apparent that the white man who begins by cheating a Negro out of his ballot soon learns to cheat a white man out of his, and that the man who does this ends his career of dishonesty by the theft of property or by some equally serious crime. In my opinion, the time will come when the South will encourage all of its citizens to vote. It will see that it pays better, from every standpoint, to have healthy, vigorous life than to have that political stagnation which always results when one-half of the population has no share and no interest in the Government.

As a rule, I believe in universal, free suffrage, but I believe that in the South we are confronted with peculiar conditions that justify the protection of the ballot in many of the states, for a while at least, either by an educational test, a property test, or by both combined; but whatever tests are required, they should be made to apply with equal and exact justice to both races.

MARY ANTIN
1881–1949

For Mary Antin, as for fellow immigrant Andrew Carnegie, the United States was the promised land. Both wrote success stories but defined success very differently.

Mary Antin, a Jew, was born in tsarist Russia, where economic and political persecution of Jews was vicious and commonplace. Her father was educated to become a rabbi but instead went into business. Ill health, ill luck, and endless repression persuaded him to emigrate to the United States in 1891. A year later his family joined him. Prosperity continued to elude them, even in the land of opportunity, and the family moved from one Boston tenement to another.

Her autobiography, therefore, measured success not by wealth but by academic and intellectual achievement. She was a brilliant student, graduating from eighth grade only four years after her arrival in the United States, and she began to publish her poetry even before her graduation. Antin was awarded a scholarship to an elite private high school for girls, where she won social acceptance and more honors. Because she was living out the life of an intellectual to which he had aspired, her father allowed her to continue her education instead of going to work and earning the money that her family still desperately needed.

Mary Antin turned down a scholarship to Radcliffe College in order to marry a geologist and moved to New York, where she attended Barnard College and Columbia University. In 1911 the Atlantic Monthly *serialized* The Promised Land, *her best-known work.*

The popularity of this immigrant autobiography was due in part to its unflagging praise of American life, explicitly and implicitly compared with tsarist Russia. Here, Jews could worship—or not worship—as they pleased; here, Jewish women could receive an education, the privilege reserved to Jewish men in the Old World.

The Promised Land *in many ways resembles Japanese-American Monica Sone's* Nisei Daughter. *Both autobiographies describe hardships, especially painful disruptions of family life, but both are relentlessly optimistic as the authors tried to persuade their readers that persons like themselves—Russian Jews and Japanese-Americans—were grateful to be in the United States and had much to contribute to American life.*

Like the stories of Anne Moody and Frederic C. Howe, Mary Antin's is a spiritual autobiography about intellectual growth and emotional development. She intended to contrast the Russian Jewish child of the Old

World with the assimilated American adult of the New. As is often the case in autobiography, however, the adult present is foreshadowed in the recounting of the past.

The Promised Land, *1912. Reprint, Boston: Houghton Mifflin, 1969.*

When I was a little girl, the world was divided into two parts; namely, Polotzk, the place where I lived, and a strange land called Russia. All the little girls I knew lived in Polotzk, with their fathers and mothers and friends. Russia was the place where one's father went on business. It was so far off, and so many bad things happened there, that one's mother and grandmother and grown-up aunts cried at the railroad station, and one was expected to be sad and quiet for the rest of the day, when the father departed for Russia. . . .

It was very strange that the Czar and the police should want all Russia for themselves. It was a very big country; it took many days for a letter to reach one's father in Russia. Why might not everybody be there who wanted to?

I do not know when I became old enough to understand. The truth was borne in on me a dozen times a day, from the time I began to distinguish words from empty noises. My grandmother told me about it, when she put me to bed at night. My parents told me about it, when they gave me presents on holidays. My playmates told me, when they drew me back into a corner of the gateway, to let a policeman pass. Vanka, the little white-haired boy, told me all about it, when he ran out of his mother's laundry on purpose to throw mud after me when I happened to pass. I heard about it during prayers, and when women quarrelled in the market place; and sometimes, waking in the night, I heard my parents whisper it in the dark. There was no time in my life when I did not hear and see and feel the truth—the reason why Polotzk was cut off from the rest of Russia. It was the first lesson a little girl in Polotzk had to learn. But for a long while I did not understand. Then there came a time when I knew that Polotzk and Vitebsk and Vilna and some other places were grouped together as the "Pale of Settlement," and within this area the Czar commanded me to stay, with my father and mother and friends, and all other people like us. We must not be found outside the Pale, because we were Jews.

So there was a fence around Polotzk, after all. The world was divided into Jews and Gentiles. This knowledge came so gradually that it could not shock me. It trickled into my consciousness drop by drop. By the time I fully understood that I was a prisoner, the shackles had grown familiar to my flesh. . . .

The Gentiles were always crossing themselves; when they went into a church, and when they came out, when they met a priest, or passed an image in the street. The dirty beggars on the church steps never stopped crossing themselves; and even when they stood on the corner of a Jewish street, and received alms from Jewish people, they crossed themselves and mumbled Christian prayers. In every Gentile house there was what they called an "icon," which was an image or picture of the Christian god, hung up in a corner, with a light always burning before it. In front of the icon the Gentiles said their prayers, on their knees, crossing themselves all the time.

I tried not to look in the corner where the icon was, when I came into a Gentile house. I was afraid of the cross. Everybody was, in Polotzk—all the Jews, I mean. For it was the cross that made the priests, and the priests made our troubles, as

MARY ANTIN

even some Christians admitted. The Gentiles said that we had killed their God, which was absurd, as they never had a God—nothing but images. Besides, what they accused us of had happened so long ago; the Gentiles themselves said it was long ago. Everybody had been dead for ages who could have had anything to do with it. Yet they put up crosses everywhere, and wore them on their necks, on purpose to remind themselves of these false things; and they considered it pious to hate and abuse us, insisting that we had killed their God. To worship the cross and to torment a Jew was the same thing to them. That is why we feared the cross.

Another thing the Gentiles said about us was that we used the blood of murdered Christian children at the Passover festival. Of course that was a wicked lie. It made me sick to think of such a thing. I knew everything that was done for Passover, from the time I was a very little girl. The house was made clean and shining and holy, even in the corners where nobody ever looked. Vessels and dishes that were used all the year round were put away in the garret, and special vessels were brought out for the Passover week. I used to help unpack the new dishes, and find my own blue mug. When the fresh curtains were put up, and the white floors were uncovered, and everybody in the house put on new clothes, and I sat down to the feast in my new dress, I felt clean inside and out. And when I asked the Four Questions, about the unleavened bread and the bitter herbs and the other things, and the family, reading from their books, answered me, did I not know all about Passover, and what was on the table, and why? It was wicked of the Gentiles to tell lies about us. The youngest child in the house knew how Passover was kept.

The Passover season, when we celebrated our deliverance from the land of Egypt, and felt so glad and thankful, as if it had only just happened, was the time our Gentile neighbors chose to remind us that Russia was another Egypt. That is what I heard people say, and it was true. It was not so bad in Polotzk, within the Pale; but in Russian cities, and even more in the country districts, where Jewish families lived scattered, by special permission of the police, who were always changing their minds about letting them stay, the Gentiles made the Passover a time of horror for the Jews. Somebody would start up that lie about murdering Christian children, and the stupid peasants would get mad about it, and fill themselves with vodka, and set out to kill the Jews. They attacked them with knives and clubs and scythes and axes, killed them or tortured them, and burned their houses. This was called a "pogrom." Jews who escaped the pogroms came to Polotzk with wounds on them, and horrible, horrible stories, of little babies torn limb from limb before their mothers' eyes. Only to hear these things made one sob and sob and choke with pain. People who saw such things never smiled any more, no matter how long they lived; and sometimes their hair turned white in a day, and some people became insane on the spot.

Often we heard that the pogrom was led by a priest carrying a cross before the mob. Our enemies always held up the cross as the excuse of their cruelty to us. I never was in an actual pogrom, but there were times when it threatened us, even in Polotzk; and in all my fearful imaginings, as I hid in dark corners, thinking of the horrible things the Gentiles were going to do to me, I saw the cross, the cruel cross. . . .

There was no free school for girls, and even if your parents were rich enough to send you to a private school, you could not go very far. At the high school, which was under government control, Jewish children were admitted in limited numbers,—only ten to every hundred,—and even if you were among the lucky ones, you had your troubles. The tutor who prepared you talked all the time about the examinations you would have to pass, till you were scared. You heard on all sides that the brightest Jewish children were turned down if the examining officers did not like the turn of their noses. You went up to be examined with the other Jewish children, your heart heavy about the matter of your nose. There was a special examination for the Jewish candidates, of course; a nine-year-old Jewish child had to answer questions that a thirteen-year-old Gentile was hardly expected to understand. But that did not matter so much. You had been prepared for the thirteen-year-old test; you found the questions quite easy. You wrote your answers triumphantly—and you received a low rating, and there was no appeal. . . .

Not every man could hope to be a rev [rabbi], but no Jewish boy was allowed to grow up without at least a rudimentary knowledge of Hebrew. The scantiest income had to be divided so as to provide for the boys' tuition. To leave a boy without a teacher was a disgrace upon the whole family, to the remotest relative. For the children of the destitute there was a free school, supported by the charity of the pious. And so every boy was sent to heder (Hebrew school) almost as soon as he could speak; and usually he continued to study until his confirmation, at thirteen years of age, or as much longer as his talent and ambition carried him. My brother was five years old when he entered on his studies. He was carried to the heder, on the first day, covered over with a praying-shawl, so that nothing unholy should look on him; and he was presented with a bun, on which were traced, in honey, these words: "The Torah left by Moses is the heritage of the children of Jacob."

After a boy entered heder, he was the hero of the family. He was served before the other children at table, and nothing was too good for him. If the family were very poor, all the girls might go barefoot, but the heder boy must have shoes, he must have a plate of hot soup, though the others ate dry bread. When the rebbe (teacher) came on Sabbath afternoon, to examine the boy in the hearing of the family, everybody sat around the table and nodded with satisfaction, if he read his portion well; and he was given a great saucerful of preserves, and was praised, and blessed, and made much of. No wonder he said, in his morning prayer, "I thank Thee, Lord, for not having created me a female." It was not much to be a girl, you see. Girls could not be scholars and rabbonim. . . .

A girl's real schoolroom was her mother's kitchen. There she learned to bake and cook and manage, to knit, sew, and embroider; also to spin and weave, in country places. And while her hands were busy, her mother instructed her in the laws regulating a pious Jewish household and in the conduct proper for a Jewish wife; for, of course, every girl hoped to be a wife. A girl was born for no other purpose.

How soon it came, the pious burden of wifehood! One day the girl is playing forfeits with her laughing friends, the next day she is missed from the circle. She has been summoned to a conference with the shadchan (marriage broker), who has been for months past advertising her housewifely talents, her piety, her good looks, and her marriage portion, among families with marriageable sons. Her parents are pleased with the son-in-law proposed by the shadchan, and now, at the last, the girl is brought in, to be examined and appraised by the prospective parents-in-law. If the negotiations go off smoothly, the marriage contract is written, presents are exchanged between the engaged couple, through their respective parents, and all that is left the girl of her maidenhood is a period of busy preparation for the wedding. . . .

[Antin's father aspired to provide an education for his daughters, but both her parents became ill, and the family's fortunes declined rapidly.]

Just at this time occurred one of the periodic anti-Semitic movements whereby government officials were wont to clear the forbidden cities of Jews, whom, in the intervals of slack administration of the law, they allowed to maintain an illegal residence in places outside the Pale, on payment of enormous bribes and at the cost of nameless risks and indignities.

It was a little before Passover that the cry of the hunted thrilled the Jewish world with the familiar fear. The wholesale expulsion of Jews from Moscow and its surrounding district at cruelly short notice was the name of this latest disaster. Where would the doom strike next? The Jews who lived illegally without the Pale turned their possessions into cash and slept in their clothes, ready for immediate flight. Those who lived in the comparative security of the Pale trembled for their brothers and sisters without, and opened wide their doors to afford the fugitives refuge. And hundreds of fugitives, preceded by a wail of distress, flocked into the open district, bringing their trouble where trouble was never absent, mingling their tears with the tears that never dried.

The open cities becoming thus suddenly crowded, every man's chance of making a living was diminished in proportion to the number of additional competitors. Hardship, acute distress, ruin for many: thus spread the disaster, ring beyond ring, from the stone thrown by a despotic official into the ever-full river of Jewish persecution.

Passover was celebrated in tears that year. In the story of the Exodus we would have read a chapter of current history, only for us there was no deliverer and no promised land.

But what said some of us at the end of the long service? Not "May we be next year in Jerusalem," but "Next year—in America!" So there was our promised land, and many faces were turned towards the West. And if the waters of the Atlantic did not part for them, the wanderers rode its bitter flood by a miracle as great as any the rod of Moses ever wrought.

My father was carried away by the westward movement, glad of his own deliverance, but sore at heart for us whom he left behind. It was the last chance for all of us. . . .

[Her mother sold tea and spices and barely kept the family from starvation until her father could borrow the money to bring them to the United States.]

And so suffering, fearing, brooding, rejoicing, we crept nearer and nearer to the coveted shore, until, on a glorious May morning, six weeks after our departure from Polotzk, our eyes beheld the Promised Land, and my father received us in his arms. . . .

Our initiation into American ways began with the first step on the new soil. My father found occasion to instruct or correct us even on the way from the pier to Wall Street, which journey we made crowded together in a rickety cab. He told us not to lean out of the windows, not to point, and explained the word "green-horn." We did not want to be "greenhorns," and gave the strictest attention to my father's instructions. I do not know when my parents found opportunity to review together the history of Polotzk in the three years past, for we children had no patience with the subject; my mother's narrative was constantly interrupted by irrelevant questions, interjections, and explanations.

The first meal was an object lesson of much variety. My father produced several kinds of food, ready to eat, without any cooking, from little tin cans that had printing all over them. He attempted to introduce us to a queer, slippery kind of fruit, which he called "banana," but had to give it up for the time being. After the meal, he had better luck with a curious piece of furniture on runners, which he called "rocking-chair." There were five of us newcomers, and we found five different ways of getting into the American machine of perpetual motion, and as many ways of getting out of it. One born and bred to the use of a rocking-chair cannot imagine how ludicrous people can make themselves when attempting to use it for the first time. We laughed immoderately over our various experiments with the novelty, which was a wholesome way of letting off steam after the unusual excitement of the day.

In our flat we did not think of such a thing as storing the coal in the bathtub. There was no bathtub. So in the evening of the first day my father conducted us to the public baths. As we moved along in a little procession, I was delighted with the illumination of the streets. So many lamps, and they burned until morning, my father said, and so people did not need to carry lanterns. In America, then, every-thing was free, as we had heard in Russia. Light was free; the streets were as bright as a synagogue on a holy day. Music was free; we had been serenaded, to our gaping delight, by a brass band of many pieces, soon after our installation on Union Place.

Education was free. That subject my father had written about repeatedly, as comprising his chief hope for us children, the essence of American opportunity, the treasure that no thief could touch, not even misfortune or poverty. It was the one thing that he was able to promise us when he sent for us; surer, safer than bread or shelter. On our second day I was thrilled with the realization of what this freedom of education meant. A little girl from across the alley came and offered to conduct us to school. My father was out, but we five between us had a few words of English by this time. We knew the word school. We understood. This child, who had never seen us till yesterday, who could not pronounce our names, who was not much better dressed than we, was able to offer us the freedom of the schools of Boston! No application made, no questions asked, no examinations, rulings, exclusions; no machinations, no fees. The doors stood open for every one of us. The smallest child could show us the way.

This incident impressed me more than anything I had heard in advance of the freedom of education in America. It was a concrete proof—almost the thing itself. One had to experience it to understand it.

It was a great disappointment to be told by my father that we were not to enter upon our school career at once. It was too near the end of the term, he said, and we were going to move to Crescent Beach in a week or so. We had to wait until the opening of the schools in September. What a loss of precious time—from May till September!

Not that the time was really lost. Even the interval on Union Place was crowded with lessons and experiences. We had to visit the stores and be dressed from head to foot in American clothing; we had to learn the mysteries of the iron stove, the washboard, and the speaking-tube; we had to learn to trade with the fruit peddler through the window, and not to be afraid of the policeman; and, above all, we had to learn English.

The kind people who assisted us in these important matters form a group by themselves in the gallery of my friends. If I had never seen them from those early days till now, I should still have remembered them with gratitude. When I enumerate the long list of my American teachers, I must begin with those who came to us on Wall Street and taught us our first steps. To my mother, in her perplexity over the cookstove, the woman who showed her how to make the fire was an angel of deliverance. A fairy godmother to us children was she who led us to a wonderful country called "uptown," where, in a dazzlingly beautiful palace called a "department store," we exchanged our hateful homemade European costumes, which pointed us out as "greenhorns" to the children on the street, for real American machine-made garments, and issued forth glorified in each other's eyes.

With our despised immigrant clothing we shed also our impossible Hebrew names. A committee of our friends, several years ahead of us in American experience, put their heads together and concocted American names for us all. Those of our real names that had no pleasing American equivalents they ruthlessly discarded, content if they retained the initials. My mother, possessing a name that was not easily translatable, was punished with the undignified nickname of Annie. Fetchke, Joseph, and Deborah issued as Frieda, Joseph, and Dora, respectively. As for poor me, I was simply cheated. The name they gave me was hardly new. My Hebrew name being Maryashe in full, Mashke for short, Russianized into Marya *(Mar-ya),* my friends said that it would hold good in English as *Mary;* which was very disappointing, as I longed to possess a strange-sounding American name like the others.

I am forgetting the consolation I had, in this matter of names, from the use of my surname, which I have had no occasion to mention until now. I found on my arrival that my father was "Mr. Antin" on the slightest provocation, and not, as in Polotzk, on state occasions alone. And so I was "Mary Antin," and I felt very important to answer to such a dignified title. It was just like America that even plain people should wear their surnames on week days. . . .

[W]e made our stand in the wrong end of the town. Arlington Street was inhabited by poor Jews, poor Negroes, and a sprinkling of poor Irish. The side streets leading from it were occupied by more poor Jews and Negroes. It was a proper locality for a man without capital to do business. My father rented a tenement with a store in the basement. He put in a few barrels of flour and of sugar, a few boxes of crackers, a few gallons of kerosene, an assortment of soap of the "save the coupon" brands; in the cellar, a few barrels of potatoes, and a pyramid of kindling-wood; in the showcase, an alluring display of penny candy. He put out his sign, with a gilt-lettered warning of "Strictly Cash," and proceeded to give credit indiscriminately. That was the regular way to do business on Arlington Street. My father, in his three years' apprenticeship, had learned the tricks of many trades. He knew when and how to "bluff." The legend of "Strictly Cash" was a protection against notoriously irresponsible customers; while none of the "good" customers, who had a record for paying regularly on Saturday, hesitated to enter the store with empty purses.

If my father knew the tricks of the trade, my mother could be counted on to throw all her talent and tact into the business. Of course she had no English yet, but as she could perform the acts of weighing, measuring, and mental computation of fractions mechanically, she was able to give her whole attention to the dark mysteries of the language, as intercourse with her customers gave her opportunity. In this she made such rapid progress that she soon lost all sense of disadvantage, and conducted herself behind the counter very much as if she were back in her old store in Polotzk. It was far more cosey than Polotzk—at least, so it seemed to me; for behind the store was the kitchen, where, in the intervals of slack trade, she did her cooking and washing. Arlington Street customers were used to waiting while the storekeeper salted the soup or rescued a loaf from the oven. . . .

Father himself conducted us to school. He would not have delegated that mission to the President of the United States. He had awaited the day with impatience equal to mine, and the visions he saw as he hurried us over the sun-flecked pavements transcended all my dreams. Almost his first act on landing on American soil, three years before, had been his application for naturalization. He had taken the remaining steps in the process with eager promptness, and at the earliest moment allowed by the law, he became a citizen of the United States. It is true that he had left home in search of bread for his hungry family, but he went blessing the necessity that drove him to America. The boasted freedom of the New World meant to him far more than the right to reside, travel, and work wherever he pleased; it meant the freedom to speak his thoughts, to throw off the shackles of superstition, to test his own fate, unhindered by political or religious tyranny. He was only a young man when he landed—thirty-two; and most of his life he had been held in leading-strings. He was hungry for his untasted manhood.

Three years passed in sordid struggle and disappointment. He was not prepared to make a living even in America, where the day laborer eats wheat instead of rye. Apparently the American flag could not protect him against the pursuing Nemesis of his limitations; he must expiate the sins of his fathers who slept across the seas. He had been endowed at birth with a poor constitution, a nervous, restless temperament, and an abundance of hindering prejudices. In his boyhood his body was starved, that his mind might be stuffed with useless learning. In his youth this dearly gotten learning was sold, and the price was the bread and salt which he had not been trained to earn for himself. Under the wedding canopy he was bound for life to a girl whose features were still strange to him; and he was bidden to multiply himself, that sacred learning might be perpetuated in his sons, to the glory of the God of his fathers. All this while he had been led about as a creature without a will, a chattel, an instrument. In his maturity he awoke, and found himself poor in health, poor in purse, poor in useful knowledge, and hampered on all sides. At the first nod of opportunity he broke away from his prison, and strove to atone for his wasted youth by a life of useful labor; while at the same time he sought to lighten the gloom of his narrow scholarship by freely partaking of modern ideas. But his utmost endeavor still left him far from his goal. In business, nothing prospered with him. Some fault of hand or mind or temperament led him to failure where other men found success. Wherever the blame for his disabilities be placed, he reaped their bitter fruit. "Give me bread!" he cried to America. "What will you do to earn it?" the challenge came back. And he found that he was master of no art, of no trade; that even his precious learning was of no avail, because he had only the most antiquated methods of communicating it.

So in his primary quest he had failed. There was left him the compensation of intellectual freedom. That he sought to realize in every possible way. He had very little opportunity to prosecute his education, which, in truth, had never been begun. His struggle for a bare living left him no time to take advantage of the public evening school; but he lost nothing of what was to be learned through reading, through attendance at public meetings, through exercising the rights of citizenship. Even here he was hindered by a natural inability to acquire the English language. In time, indeed, he learned to read, to follow a conversation or lecture; but he never learned to write correctly, and his pronunciation remains extremely foreign to this day.

If education, culture, the higher life were shining things to be worshipped from afar, he had still a means left whereby he could draw one step nearer to them. He could send his children to school, to learn all those things that he knew by fame to be desirable. The common school, at least, perhaps high school; for one or two, perhaps even college! His children should be students, should fill his house with books and intellectual company; and thus he would walk by proxy in the Elysian Fields of liberal learning. As for the children themselves, he knew no surer way to their advancement and happiness.

So it was with a heart full of longing and hope that my father led us to school on that first day. He took long strides in his eagerness, the rest of us running and hopping to keep up.

At last the four of us stood around the teacher's desk; and my father, in his impossible English, gave us over in her charge, with some broken word of his hopes for us that his swelling heart could no longer contain. I venture to say that Miss Nixon was struck by something uncommon in the group we made, something outside of Semitic features and the abashed manner of the alien. My little sister was as pretty as a doll, with her clear pink-and-white face, short golden curls, and eyes like blue violets when you caught them looking up. My brother might have been a girl, too, with his cherubic contours of face, rich red color, glossy black hair, and fine eyebrows. Whatever secret fears were in his heart, remembering his former teachers, who had taught with the rod, he stood up straight and uncringing before the American teacher, his cap respectfully doffed. Next to him stood a starved-looking girl with eyes ready to pop out, and short dark curls that would not have made much of a wig for a Jewish bride.

All three children carried themselves rather better than the common run of "green" pupils that were brought to Miss Nixon. But the figure that challenged attention to the group was the tall, straight father, with his earnest face and fine forehead, nervous hands eloquent in gesture, and a voice full of feeling. This foreigner, who brought his children to school as if it were an act of consecration, who regarded the teacher of the primer class with reverence, who spoke of visions, like a man inspired, in a common schoolroom, was not like other aliens, who brought their children in dull obedience to the law; was not like the native fathers, who brought their unmanageable boys, glad to be relieved of their care. I think Miss Nixon guessed what my father's best English could not convey. I think she divined that by the simple act of delivering our school certificates to her he took possession of America. . . .

I was not a bit too large for my little chair and desk in the baby class, but my mind, of course, was too mature by six or seven years for the work. So as soon as I could understand what the teacher said in class, I was advanced to the second grade. This was within a week after Miss Nixon took me in hand. But I do not mean to give my dear teacher all the credit for my rapid progress, nor even half the credit. I shall divide it with her on behalf of my race and my family. I was Jew enough to have an aptitude for language in general, and to bend my mind earnestly to my task; I was Antin enough to read each lesson with my heart, which gave me an inkling of what was coming next, and so carried me along by leaps and bounds. As for the teacher, she could best explain what theory she followed in teaching us foreigners to read. I can only describe the method, which was so simple that I wish holiness could be taught in the same way.

There were about half a dozen of us beginners in English, in age from six to fifteen. Miss Nixon made a special class of us, and aided us so skilfully and earnestly in our endeavors to "see-a-cat," and "hear-a-dog-bark," and "look-at-the-hen," that we turned over page after page of the ravishing history, eager to find out how the common world looked, smelled, and tasted in the strange speech. The teacher knew just when to let us help each other out with a word in our own tongue,—it happened that we were all Jews,—and so, working all together, we actually covered more ground in a lesson than the native classes, composed entirely of the little tots. . . .

How long would you say, wise reader, it takes to make an American? By the middle of my second year in school I had reached the sixth grade. When, after the Christmas holidays, we began to study the life of Washington, running through a summary of the Revolution, and the early days of the Republic, it seemed to me that all my reading and study had been idle until then. The reader, the arithmetic, the song book, that had so fascinated me until now, became suddenly sober exercise books, tools wherewith to hew a way to the source of inspiration. When the teacher read to us out of a big book with many bookmarks in it, I sat rigid with attention in my little chair, my hands tightly clasped on the edge of my desk; and I painfully held my breath, to prevent sighs of disappointment escaping, as I saw the teacher skip the parts between bookmarks. When the class read, and it came my turn, my voice shook and the book trembled in my hands. I could not pronounce the name of George Washington without a pause. Never had I prayed, never had I chanted the songs of David, never had I called upon the Most Holy, in such utter reverence and worship as I repeated the simple sentences of my child's story of the patriot. I gazed with adoration at the portraits of George and Martha Washington, till I could see them with my eyes shut. And whereas formerly my self-consciousness had bordered on conceit, and I thought myself an uncommon person, parading my schoolbooks through the streets, and swelling with pride when a teacher detained me in conversation, now I grew humble all at once, seeing how insignificant I was beside the Great.

As I read about the noble boy who would not tell a lie to save himself from punishment, I was for the first time truly repentant of my sins. Formerly I had fasted and prayed and made sacrifice on the Day of Atonement, but it was more than half play, in mimicry of my elders. I had no real horror of sin, and I knew so many ways of escaping punishment. I am sure my family, my neighbors, my teachers in Polotzk—all my world, in fact—strove together, by example and precept, to teach me goodness. Saintliness had a new incarnation in about every third person I knew. I did respect the saints, but I could not help seeing that most of them were a little bit stupid, and that mischief was much more fun than piety. Goodness, as I had known it, was respectable, but not necessarily admirable. The people I really admired, like my Uncle Solomon, and Cousin Rachel, were those who preached the least and laughed the most. My sister Frieda was perfectly good, but she did not think the less of me because I played tricks. What I loved in my friends was not inimitable. One could be downright good if one really wanted to. One could be learned if one had books and teachers. One could sing funny songs and tell anecdotes if one travelled about and picked up such things, like one's uncles and cousins. But a human being strictly good, perfectly wise, and unfailingly valiant, all at the same time, I had never heard or dreamed of. This wonderful George Washington was as inimitable as he was irreproachable. Even if I had never, never told a lie, I could not compare myself to George Washington; for I was not brave—I was afraid to go out when snowballs whizzed—and I could never be the First President of the United States.

So I was forced to revise my own estimate of myself. But the twin of my new-born humility, paradoxical as it may seem, was a sense of dignity I had never known before. For if I found that I was a person of small consequence, I discovered at the same time that I was more nobly related than I had ever supposed. I had relatives and friends who were notable people by the old standards,—I had never been ashamed of my family,—but this George Washington, who died long before I was born, was like a king in greatness, and he and I were Fellow Citizens. There was a great deal about Fellow Citizens in the patriotic literature we read at this time; and I knew from my father how he was a Citizen, through the process of naturalization, and how I also was a citizen by virtue of my relation to him. Undoubtedly I was a Fellow Citizen, and George Washington was another. It thrilled me to realize what sudden greatness had fallen on me; and at the same time it sobered me, as with a sense of responsibility. I strove to conduct myself as befitted a Fellow Citizen. . . .

Where had been my country until now? What flag had I loved? What heroes had I worshipped? The very names of these things had been unknown to me. Well I knew that Polotzk was not my country. It was *goluth*—exile. On many occasions in the year we prayed to God to lead us out of exile. The beautiful Passover service closed with the words, "Next year, may we be in Jerusalem." On childish lips, indeed, those words were no conscious aspiration; we repeated the Hebrew syllables after our elders, but without their hope and longing. Still not a child among us was too young to feel in his own flesh the lash of the oppressor. We knew what it was to be Jews in exile, from the spiteful treatment we suffered at the hands of the smallest urchin who crossed himself; and thence we knew that Israel had good reason to pray for deliverance. But the story of Exodus was not history to me in the sense that the story of the American Revolution was. It was more like a glorious myth, a belief in which had the effect of cutting me off from the actual world, by linking me with a world of phantoms. Those moments of exaltation which the contemplation of the Biblical past afforded us, allowing us to call ourselves the children of princes, served but to tinge with a more poignant sense of disinheritance the long humdrum stretches of our life. In very truth we were a people without a country. Surrounded by mocking foes and detractors, it was difficult for me to realize the persons of my people's heroes or the events in which they moved. Except in moments of abstraction from the world around me, I scarcely understood that Jerusalem was an actual spot on the earth, where once the Kings of the Bible, real people, like my neighbors in Polotzk, ruled in puissant majesty. For the conditions of our civil life did not permit us to cultivate a spirit of nationalism. The freedom of worship that was grudgingly granted within the narrow limits of the Pale by no means included the right to set up openly any ideal of a Hebrew State, any hero other than the Czar. What we children picked up of our ancient political history was confused with the miraculous story of the

Creation, with the supernatural legends and hazy associations of Bible lore. As to our future, we Jews in Polotzk had no national expectations; only a life-worn dreamer here and there hoped to die in Palestine. . . .

[Antin composed a poem about George Washington so precocious and patriotic that it was published in a Boston newspaper, making her celebrated in her school and family and beginning her career as a professional writer.]

My father gave my mother very little time to adjust herself. He was only three years from the Old World with its settled prejudices. Considering his education, he had thought out a good deal for himself, but his line of thinking had not as yet brought him to include woman in the intellectual emancipation for which he himself had been so eager even in Russia. This was still in the day when he was astonished to learn that women had written books—had used their minds, their imaginations, unaided. He still rated the mental capacity of the average woman as only a little above that of the cattle she tended. He held it to be a wife's duty to follow her husband in all things. He could do all the thinking for the family, he believed; and being convinced that to hold to the outward forms of orthodox Judaism was to be hampered in the race for Americanization, he did not hesitate to order our family life on unorthodox lines. There was no conscious despotism in this; it was only making manly haste to realize an ideal the nobility of which there was no one to dispute.

My mother, as we know, had not the initial impulse to depart from ancient usage that my father had in his habitual scepticism. He had always been a nonconformist in his heart; she bore lovingly the yoke of prescribed conduct. Individual freedom, to him, was the only tolerable condition of life; to her it was confusion. My mother, therefore, gradually divested herself, at my father's bidding, of the mantle of orthodox observance; but the process cost her many a pang, because the fabric of that venerable garment was interwoven with the fabric of her soul.

My father did not attempt to touch the fundamentals of her faith. He certainly did not forbid her to honor God by loving her neighbor, which is perhaps not far from being the whole of Judaism. If his loud denials of the existence of God influenced her to reconsider her creed, it was merely an incidental result of the freedom of expression he was so eager to practise, after his life of enforced hypocrisy. As the opinions of a mere woman on matters so abstract as religion did not interest him in the least, he counted it no particular triumph if he observed that my mother weakened in her faith as the years went by. He allowed her to keep a Jewish kitchen as long as she pleased, but he did not want us children to refuse invitations to the table of our Gentile neighbors. He would have no bar to our social intercourse with the world around us, for only by freely sharing the life of our neighbors could we come into our full inheritance of American freedom and opportunity. On the holy days he bought my mother a ticket for the synagogue, but the children he sent to school. On Sabbath eve my mother might light the consecrated candles, but he kept the store open until Sunday morning. My mother might believe and worship as she pleased, up to the point where her orthodoxy began to interfere with the American progress of the family.

The price that all of us paid for this disorganization of our family life has been levied on every immigrant Jewish household where the first generation clings to the traditions of the Old World, while the second generation leads the life of the New. Nothing more pitiful could be written in the annals of the Jews; nothing more inevitable; nothing more hopeful. Hopeful, yes; alike for the Jew and for the country that has given him shelter. For Israel is not the only party that has put up a forfeit in this contest. The nations may well sit by and watch the struggle, for humanity has a stake in it. I say this, whose life has borne witness, whose heart is heavy with revelations it has not made. And I speak for thousands; oh, for thousands! . . . .

The stretch of weeks from June to September, when the schools were closed, would have been hard to fill in had it not been for the public library. At first I made myself a calendar of the vacation months, and every morning I tore off a day, and comforted myself with the decreasing number of vacation days. But after I discovered the public library I was not impatient for the reopening of school. The library did not open till one o'clock in the afternoon, and each reader was allowed to take out only one book at a time. Long before one o'clock I was to be seen on the library steps, waiting for the door of paradise to open. I spent hours in the reading-room, pleased with the atmosphere of books, with the order and quiet of the place, so unlike anything on Arlington Street. The sense of these things permeated my consciousness even when I was absorbed in a book, just as the rustle of pages turned and the tiptoe tread of the librarian reached my ear, without distracting my attention. Anything so wonderful as a library had never been in my life. It was even better than school in some ways. One could read and read, and learn and learn, as fast as one knew how, without being obliged to stop for stupid little girls and inattentive little boys to catch up with the lesson. When I went home from the library I had a book under my arm; and I would finish it before the library opened next day, no matter till what hours of the night I burned my little lamp. . . .

[Four years after her arrival in Boston, Antin graduated from grammar school with honors. Her academic promise meant that she did not go to work, like many young women of her age, but instead continued her education at the elite Girls's Latin School, despite her family's poverty.]

A new life began for me when I entered the Latin School in September. Until then I had gone to school with my equals, and as a matter of course. Now it was distinctly a feat for me to keep in school, and my schoolmates were socially so far superior to me that my poverty became conspicuous. The pupils of the Latin School, from the nature of the institution, are an aristocratic set. They come from refined homes, dress well, and spend the recess hour talking about parties, beaux, and the matinée. As students they are either very quick or very hard-working; for the course of study, in the lingo of the school world, is considered "stiff." The girl with half her brain asleep, or with too many beaux, drops out by the end of the first year; or a one and only beau may be the fatal element. At the end of the course the weeding process has reduced the once numerous tribe of academic candidates to a cosey little family.

By all these tokens I should have had serious business on my hands as a pupil in the Latin School, but I did not find it hard. To make myself letter-perfect in my lessons required long hours of study, but that was my delight. To make myself at home in an alien world was also within my talents; I had been practising it day and night for the past four years. To remain unconscious of my shabby and ill-fitting clothes when the rustle of silk petticoats in the schoolroom protested against them was a matter still within my moral reach. Half a dress a year had been my allowance for many seasons; even less, for as I did not grow much I could wear my dresses as long as they lasted. And I had stood before editors, and exchanged polite calls with school-teachers, untroubled by the detestable colors and archaic design of my garments. To stand up and recite Latin declensions without trembling from hunger was something more of a feat, because I sometimes went to school with little or no breakfast; but even that required no special heroism— at most it was a matter of self-control. I had the advantage of a poor appetite, too; I really did not need much breakfast. Or if I was hungry it would hardly show; I coughed so much that my unsteadiness was self-explained.

Everything helped, you see. My schoolmates helped. Aristocrats though they were, they did not hold themselves aloof from me. Some of the girls who came to school in carriages were especially cordial. They rated me by my scholarship, and not by my father's occupation. They teased and admired me by turns for learning the footnotes in the Latin grammar by heart; they never reproached me for my ignorance of the latest comic opera. And it was more than good breeding that made them seem unaware of the incongruity of my presence. It was a generous appreciation of what it meant for a girl from the slums to be in the Latin School, on the way to college. If our intimacy ended on the steps of the school-house, it was more my fault than theirs. Most of the girls were democratic enough to have invited me to their homes, although to some, of course, I was "impossible." But I had no time for visiting; school work and reading and family affairs occupied all the daytime, and much of the night time. I did not "go with" any of the girls, in the school-girl sense of the phrase. I admired some of them, either for good looks, or beautiful manners, or more subtle attributes; but always at a distance. I discovered something inimitable in the way the Back Bay girls carried themselves; and I should have been the first to perceive the incongruity of Commonwealth Avenue entwining arms with Dover Street. Some day, perhaps, when I should be famous and rich; but not just then. So my companions and I parted on the steps of the school-house, in mutual respect; they guiltless of snobbishness, I innocent of envy. It was a graciously American relation, and I am happy to this day to recall it. . . .

> **[Antin discovered the settlement, Hale House, which further encouraged her Americanization and her interest in natural history. She found in the theory of evolution the answer to her own religious doubts.]**

Hale House is situated in the midst of the labyrinth of narrow streets and alleys that constitutes the slum of which Harrison Avenue is the backbone, and of which Dover Street is a member.

Bearing in mind the fact that there are almost no playgrounds in all this congested district, you will understand that Hale House has plenty of work on its hands to carry a little sunshine into the grimy tenement homes. The beautiful story of how that is done cannot be told here, but what Hale House did for me I may not omit to mention. . . .

Some of my friends in the Natural History Club were deeply versed in the principles of evolutionary science, and were able to guide me in my impetuous rush to learn everything in a day. I was in a hurry to deduce, from the conglomeration of isolated facts that I picked up in the lectures, the final solution of all my problems. It took both patience and wisdom to check me and at the same time satisfy me, I have no doubt; but then I was always fortunate in my friends. Wisdom and patience in plenty were spent on me, and I was instructed and inspired and comforted. Of course my wisest teacher was not able to tell me how the original spark of life was kindled, nor to point out, on the starry map of heaven, my future abode. The bread of absolute knowledge I do not hope to taste in this life. But all creation was remodelled on a grander scale by the utterances of my teachers; and my problems, though they deepened with the expansion of all namable phenomena, were carried up to the heights of the impersonal, and ceased to torment me. . . .

I liked to remind myself of Polotzk, the better to bring out the wonder of my life. That I who was born in the prison of the Pale should roam at will in the land of freedom was a marvel that it did me good to realize. That I who was brought up to my teens almost without a book should be set down in the midst of all the books that ever were written was a miracle as great as any on record. That an outcast should become a privileged citizen, that a beggar should dwell in a palace—this was a romance more thrilling than poet ever sung. Surely I was rocked in an enchanted cradle. . . .

MARY JONES
1830?–1930

While Booker T. Washington preached accommodation, Mary Jones preached confrontation. The ally of American workers, she describes in vivid detail some of the pivotal events of American labor history: the Haymarket riot of 1886, the 1902 coal strike, the Ludlow massacre of 1914, the 1919 steel strike. With broad, colorful strokes she paints a portrait of union militance; the exploitation of men, women, and children, and the political and economic tyranny of organized capital.

Mary Jones began her own long career as a union organizer and labor agitator during the bloody and destructive railway strike of 1877, the first coast-to-coast strike in American history. She became a paid organizer for the United Mine Workers of America, founded in 1890 and the first industrial union to affiliate with the American Federation of Labor. Her work for the UMWA and other unions took her to mines, mills, and company towns from Pennsylvania to Colorado. She rallied men and women to fight back against their employers and marched children across the country to dramatize the evils of child labor. Not formally affiliated with any left-wing political organization, she was on friendly terms with Socialists like Eugene Debs, and in 1905 she attended the founding convention of the Industrial Workers of the World, a radical labor union. She was often arrested, occasionally jailed, but never silenced. In 1915 she took her protests on behalf of labor to the United States Congress. The red scare that followed World War I injured labor's cause, linking strikes with the Bolshevik Revolution. In a decade of unrestrained confidence in business, organized labor lost membership and legitimacy. In 1924 Mother Jones fought her last battle, a strike lost by dressmakers in Chicago.

Both the story and its central character, Mother Jones, were the creations of this energetic individual. Her uncertain and selective memory— she wrote the book when she was quite old—allowed her to make some factual errors: she was probably born in 1836 or 1839, not in 1830, and she was probably not a member of the Knights of Labor in the 1870s, as she states, although she was a good friend of its leader Terence V. Powderly. She rejected her early conventional jobs of teacher and seamstress, and the death of her husband and children cut short a socially sanctioned career of wife and mother. Instead, she invented an alternative role for herself in her life and in the autobiography, mother to her "boys," the coal miners. She liked to dress the part, appearing in a demure black dress with a lace collar, be-spectacled and grey-haired. This disguise gained her necessary respect-

ability and permitted her to do wildly unrespectable things such as tramp over mountains, carry a gun, and use profane and earthy language.

Mother Jones was a doer and a talker, not a writer. Her story has no clear narrative direction, and the chapters are sometimes out of sequence. Yet there is no doubt about where her life journey was headed, or which side of the fight for economic justice she was on.

The Autobiography of Mother Jones, *1925. Reprint, Chicago: Charles H. Kerr Publishing Co., 1980. (Reprinted with permission.)*

I was born in the city of Cork, Ireland, in 1830. My people were poor. For generations they had fought for Ireland's freedom. Many of my folks have died in that struggle. My father, Richard Harris, came to America in 1835, and as soon as he had become an American citizen he sent for his family. His work as a laborer with railway construction crews took him to Toronto, Canada. Here I was brought up but always as the child of an American citizen. Of that citizenship I have ever been proud.

After finishing the common schools, I attended the Normal school with the intention of becoming a teacher. Dress-making too, I learned proficiently. My first position was teaching in a convent in Monroe, Michigan. Later, I came to Chicago and opened a dressmaking establishment. I preferred sewing to bossing little children.

However, I went back to teaching again, this time in Memphis, Tennessee. Here I was married in 1861. My husband was an iron moulder and a staunch member of the Iron Moulders' Union.

In 1867, a yellow fever epidemic swept Memphis. Its victims were mainly among the poor and the workers. The rich and the well-to-do fled the city. Schools and churches were closed. People were not permitted to enter the house of a yellow fever victim without permits. The poor could not afford nurses. Across the street from me, ten persons lay dead from the plague. The dead surrounded us. They were buried at night quickly and without ceremony. All about my house I could hear weeping and the cries of delirium. One by one, my four little children sickened and died. I washed their little bodies and got them ready for burial. My husband caught the fever and died. I sat alone through nights of grief. No one came to me. No one could. Other homes were as stricken as was mine. All day long, all night long, I heard the grating of the wheels of the death cart.

After the union had buried my husband, I got a permit to nurse the sufferers. This I did until the plague was stamped out.

I returned to Chicago and went again into the dressmaking business with a partner. We were located on Washington Street near the lake. We worked for the aristocrats of Chicago, and I had ample opportunity to observe the luxury and extravagance of their lives. Often while sewing for the lords and barons who lived in magnificent houses on the Lake Shore Drive, I would look out of the plate glass windows and see the poor, shivering wretches, jobless and hungry, walking along the frozen lake front. The contrast of their condition with that of the tropical comfort of the people for whom I sewed was painful to me. My employers seemed neither to notice nor to care.

Summers, too, from the windows of the rich, I used to watch the mothers come from the west side slums, lugging babies and little children, hoping for a

MARY JONES

breath of cool, fresh air from the lake. At night, when the tenements were stifling hot, men, women and little children slept in the parks. But the rich, having donated to the charity ice fund, had, by the time it was hot in the city, gone to seaside and mountains.

In October, 1871, the great Chicago fire burned up our establishment and everything that we had. The fire made thousands homeless. We stayed all night and the next day without food on the lake front, often going into the lake to keep cool. Old St. Mary's church at Wabash Avenue and Peck Court was thrown open to the refugees and there I camped until I could find a place to go.

Near by in an old, tumbled down, fire scorched building the Knights of Labor held meetings. The Knights of Labor was the labor organization of those days. I used to spend my evenings at their meetings, listening to splendid speakers. Sundays we went out into the woods and held meetings.

Those were the days of sacrifice for the cause of labor. Those were the days when we had no halls, when there were no high salaried officers, no feasting with the enemies of labor. Those were the days of the martyrs and the saints.

I became acquainted with the labor movement. I learned that in 1865, after the close of the Civil War, a group of men met in Louisville, Kentucky. They came from the North and from the South; they were the "blues" and the "greys" who a year or two before had been fighting each other over the question of chattel slavery. They decided that the time had come to formulate a program to fight another brutal form of slavery—industrial slavery. Out of this decision had come the Knights of Labor.

From the time of the Chicago fire I became more and more engrossed in the labor struggle and I decided to take an active part in the efforts of the working people to better the conditions under which they worked and lived. I became a member of the Knights of Labor.

One of the first strikes that I remember occurred in the Seventies. The Baltimore and Ohio Railroad employees went on strike and they sent for me to come help them. I went. The mayor of Pittsburgh swore in as deputy sheriffs a lawless, reckless bunch of fellows who had drifted into that city during the panic of 1873. They pillaged and burned and rioted and looted. Their acts were charged up to the striking workingmen. The governor sent the militia.

The Railroads had succeeded in getting a law passed that in case of a strike, the train-crew should bring in the locomotive to the roundhouse before striking. This law the strikers faithfully obeyed. Scores of locomotives were housed in Pittsburgh.

One night a riot occurred. Hundreds of box cars standing on the tracks were soaked with oil and set on fire and sent down the tracks to the roundhouse. The roundhouse caught fire. Over one hundred locomotives, belonging to the Pennsylvania Railroad Company were destroyed. It was a wild night. The flames lighted the sky and turned to fiery flames the steel bayonettes of the soldiers.

The strikers were charged with the crimes of arson and rioting, although it was common knowledge that it was not they who instigated the fire; that it was started by hoodlums backed by the business men of Pittsburgh who for a long time had felt that the Railroad Company discriminated against their city in the matter of rates.

I knew the strikers personally. I knew that it was they who had tried to enforce orderly law. I knew they disciplined their members when they did violence. I knew, as everybody knew, who really perpetrated the crime of burning the railroad's property. Then and there I learned in the early part of my career that labor must bear the cross for others' sins, must be the vicarious sufferer for the wrongs that others do.

These early years saw the beginning of America's industrial life. Hand and hand with the growth of factories and the expansion of railroads, with the accumulation of capital and the rise of banks, came anti-labor legislation. Came strikes. Came violence. Came the belief in the hearts and minds of the workers that legislatures but carry out the will of the industrialists.

From 1880 on, I became wholly engrossed in the labor movement. In all the great industrial centers the working class was in rebellion. The enormous immigration from Europe crowded the slums, forced down wages and threatened to destroy the standard of living fought for by American working men. Throughout the country there was business depression and much unemployment. In the cities there was hunger and rags and despair.

Foreign agitators who had suffered under European despots preached various schemes of economic salvation to the workers. The workers asked only for bread and a shortening of the long hours of toil. The agitators gave them visions. The police gave them clubs.

Particularly the city of Chicago was the scene of strike after strike, followed by boycotts and riots. The years preceeding 1886 had witnessed strikes of the lake seamen, of dock laborers and street railway workers. These strikes had been brutally suppressed by policemen's clubs and by hired gunmen. The grievance on the part of the workers was given no heed. John Bonfield, inspector of police, was particularly cruel in the suppression of meetings where men peacefully assembled to discuss matters of wages and of hours. Employers were defiant and open in the expression of their fears and hatreds. The Chicago Tribune, the organ of the employers, suggested ironically that the farmers of Illinois treat the tramps that poured out of the great industrial centers as they did other pests, by putting strychnine in the food.

The workers started an agitation for an eight-hour day. The trades unions and the Knights of Labor endorsed the movement but because many of the leaders of the agitation were foreigners, the movement itself was regarded as "foreign" and as "un-American." Then the anarchists of Chicago, a very small group, espoused the cause of the eight-hour day. From then on the people of Chicago seemed incapable of discussing a purely economic question without getting excited about anarchism.

The employers used the cry of anarchism to kill the movement. A person who believed in an eight-hour working day was, they said, an enemy to his country, a traitor, an anarchist. The foundations of government were being gnawed away by the anarchist rats. Feeling was bitter. The city was divided into two angry camps. The working people on one side—hungry, cold, jobless, fighting gunmen and police clubs with bare hands. On the other side the employers, knowing neither hunger nor cold, supported by the newspapers, by the police, by all the power of the great state itself.

The anarchists took advantage of the wide-spread discontent to preach their doctrines. Orators used to address huge crowds on the windy, barren shore of Lake Michigan. Although I never endorsed the philosophy of anarchism, I often attended the meetings on the lake shore, listening to what these teachers of a new order had to say to the workers.

Meanwhile the employers were meeting. They met in the mansion of George

M. Pullman on Prairie Avenue or in the residence of Wirt Dexter, an able corporation lawyer. They discussed means of killing the eight-hour movement which was to be ushered in by a general strike. They discussed methods of dispersing the meetings of the anarchists.

A bitterly cold winter set in. Long unemployment resulted in terrible suffering. Bread lines increased. Soup kitchens could not handle the applicants. Thousands knew actual misery.

On Christmas day, hundreds of poverty stricken people in rags and tatters, in thin clothes, in wretched shoes paraded on fashionable Prairie Avenue before the mansions of the rich, before their employers, carrying the black flag. I thought the parade an insane move on the part of the anarchists, as it only served to make feeling more bitter. As a matter of fact, it had no educational value whatever and only served to increase the employers' fear, to make the police more savage, and the public less sympathetic to the real distress of the workers.

The first of May, which was to usher in the eight-hour day uprising, came. The newspapers had done everything to alarm the people. All over the city there were strikes and walkouts. Employers quaked in their boots. They saw revolution. The workers in the McCormick Harvester Works gathered outside the factory. Those inside who did not join the strikers were called scabs. Bricks were thrown. Windows were broken. The scabs were threatened. Some one turned in a riot call.

The police without warning charged down upon the workers, shooting into their midst, clubbing right and left. Many were trampled under horses' feet. Numbers were shot dead. Skulls were broken. Young men and young girls were clubbed to death.

The Pinkerton agency formed armed bands of ex-convicts and hoodlums and hired them to capitalists at eight dollars a day, to picket the factories and incite trouble.

On the evening of May 4th, the anarchists held a meeting in the shabby, dirty district known to later history as Haymarket Square. All about were railway tracks, dingy saloons and the dirty tenements of the poor. A half a block away was the Desplaines Street Police Station presided over by John Bonfield, a man without tact or discretion or sympathy, a most brutal believer in suppression as the method to settle industrial unrest.

Carter Harrison, the mayor of Chicago, attended the meeting of the anarchists and moved in and about the crowds in the square. After leaving, he went to the Chief of Police and instructed him to send no mounted police to the meeting, as it was being peacefully conducted and the presence of mounted police would only add fuel to fires already burning red in the workers' hearts. But orders perhaps came from other quarters, for disregarding the report of the mayor, the chief of police sent mounted policemen in large numbers to the meeting.

One of the anarchist speakers was addressing the crowd. A bomb was dropped from a window overlooking the square. A number of the police were killed in the explosion that followed.

The city went insane and the newspapers did everything to keep it like a madhouse. The workers' cry for justice was drowned in the shriek for revenge. Bombs were "found" every five minutes. Men went armed and gun stores kept open nights. Hundreds were arrested. Only those who had agitated for an eight-hour day, however, were brought to trial and a few months later hanged. But the man, Schnaubelt, who actually threw the bomb was never brought into the case, nor was his part in the terrible drama ever officially made clear.

The leaders in the eight hour day movement were hanged Friday, November the 11th. That day Chicago's rich had chills and fever. Ropes stretched in all directions from the jail. Policemen were stationed along the ropes armed with riot rifles. Special patrols watched all approaches to the jail. The roofs about the grim stone building were black with police. The newspapers fed the public imagination with stories of uprisings and jail deliveries.

But there were no uprisings, no jail deliveries, except that of Louis Lingg, the only real preacher of violence among all the condemned men. He outwitted the gallows by biting a percussion cap and blowing off his head.

The Sunday following the executions, the funerals were held. Thousands of workers marched behind the black hearses, not because they were anarchists but they felt that these men, whatever their theories, were martyrs to the workers' struggle. The procession wound through miles and miles of streets densely packed with silent people.

In the cemetery of Waldheim, the dead were buried. But with them was not buried their cause. The struggle for the eight hour day, for more human conditions and relations between man and man lived on, and still lives on.

Seven years later, Governor Altgeld, after reading all the evidence in the case, pardoned the three anarchists who had escaped the gallows and were serving life sentences in jail. He said the verdict was unjustifiable, as had William Dean Howells and William Morris at the time of its execution. Governor Altgeld committed political suicide by his brave action but he is remembered by all those who love truth and those who have the courage to confess it. . . .

It was about 1891 when I was down in Virginia. There was a strike in the Dietz mines and the boys had sent for me. When I got off the train at Norton a fellow walked up to me and asked me if I were Mother Jones.

"Yes, I am Mother Jones."

He looked terribly frightened. "The superintendent told me that if you came down here he would blow out your brains. He said he didn't want to see you 'round these parts."

"You tell the superintendent that I am not coming to see him anyway. I am coming to see the miners."

As we stood talking a poor fellow, all skin and bones, joined us.

"Do you see those cars over there, Mother, on the siding?" He pointed to cars filled with coal.

"Well, we made a contract with the coal company to fill those cars for so much, and after we had made the contract, they put lower bottoms in the cars, so that they would hold another ton or so. I have worked for this company all my life and all I have now is this old worn-out frame."

We couldn't get a hall to hold a meeting. Every one was afraid to rent to us. Finally the colored people consented to give us their church for our meeting. Just as we were about to start the colored chairman came to me and said: "Mother, the coal company gave us this ground that the church is on. They have sent word that they will take it from us if we let you speak here."

I would not let those poor souls lose their ground so I adjourned the meeting to the four corners of the public roads. When the meeting was over and the people had dispersed, I asked my co-worker, Dud Hado, a fellow from Iowa, if he would go with me up to the post office. He was a kindly soul but easily frightened.

As we were going along the road, I said, "Have you got a pistol on you?"

"Yes," said he, "I'm not going to let any one blow your brains out."

"My boy," said I, "it is against the law in this county to carry concealed weapons. I want you to take that pistol out and expose a couple of inches of it."

As he did so about eight or ten gunmen jumped out from behind an old barn beside the road, jumped on him and said, "Now we've got you, you dirty organizer." They bullied us along the road to the town and we were taken to an office where they had a notary public and we were tried. All those blood-thirsty murderers were there and the general manager came in.

"Mother Jones, I am astonished," said he.

"What is your astonishment about?" said I.

"That you should go into the house of God with anyone who carries a gun."

"Oh that wasn't God's house," said I. "That is the coal company's house. Don't you know that God Almighty never comes around to a place like this!"

He laughed and of course, the dogs laughed, for he was the general manager.

They dismissed any charges against me and they fined poor Dud twenty-five dollars and costs. They seemed surprised when I said I would pay it. I had the money in my petticoat.

I went over to a miner's shack and asked his wife for a cup of tea. Often in these company-owned towns the inn-keepers were afraid to let me have food. The poor soul was so happy to have me there that she excused herself to "dress for company." She came out of the bedroom with a white apron on over her cheap cotton wrapper.

One of the men who was present at Dud's trial followed me up to the miner's house. At first the miner's wife would not admit him but he said he wanted to speak privately to Mother Jones. So she let him in.

"Mother," he said, "I am glad you paid that bill so quickly. They thought you'd appeal the case. Then they were going to lock you both up and burn you in the coke ovens at night and then say that you had both been turned loose in the morning and they didn't know where you had gone."

Whether they really would have carried out their plans I do not know. But I do know that there are no limits to which powers of privilege will not go to keep the workers in slavery. . . .

Before 1899 the coal fields of Pennsylvania were not organized. Immigrants poured into the country and they worked cheap. There was always a surplus of immigrant labor, solicited in Europe by the coal companies, so as to keep wages down to barest living. Hours of work down under ground were cruelly long. Fourteen hours a day was not uncommon, thirteen, twelve. The life or limb of the miner was unprotected by any laws. Families lived in company owned shacks that were not fit for their pigs. Children died by the hundreds due to the ignorance and poverty of their parents.

Often I have helped lay out for burial the babies of the miners, and the mothers could scarce conceal their relief at the little ones' deaths. Another was already on its way, destined, if a boy, for the breakers; if a girl, for the silk mills where the other brothers and sisters already worked.

The United Mine Workers decided to organize these fields and work for human conditions for human beings. Organizers were put to work. Whenever the spirit of the men in the mines grew strong enough a strike was called.

In Arnot, Pennsylvania, a strike had been going on four or five months. The men were becoming discouraged. The coal company sent the doctors, the school teachers, the preachers and their wives to the homes of the miners to get them to sign a document that they would go back to work.

The president of the district, Mr. Wilson, and an organizer, Tom Haggerty, got despondent. The signatures were overwhelmingly in favor of returning on Monday.

Haggerty suggested that they send for me. Saturday morning they telephoned to Barnesboro, where I was organizing, for me to come at once or they would lose the strike.

"Oh Mother," Haggerty said, "Come over quick and help us! The boys are that despondent! They are going back Monday."

I told him that I was holding a meeting that night but that I would leave early Sunday morning.

I started at daybreak. At Roaring Branch, the nearest train connection with Arnot, the secretary of the Arnot Union, a young boy, William Bouncer, met me with a horse and buggy. We drove sixteen miles over rough mountain roads. It was biting cold. We got into Arnot Sunday noon and I was placed in the coal company's hotel, the only hotel in town. I made some objections but Bouncer said, "Mother, we have engaged this room for you and if it is not occupied, they will never rent us another."

Sunday afternoon I held a meeting. It was not as large a gathering as those we had later but I stirred up the poor wretches that did come.

"You've got to take the pledge," I said. "Rise and pledge to stick to your brothers and the union till the strike's won!"

The men shuffled their feet but the women rose, their babies in their arms, and pledged themselves to see that no one went to work in the morning.

"The meeting stands adjourned till ten o'clock tomorrow morning," I said. "Everyone come and see that the slaves that think to go back to their masters come along with you."

I returned to my room at the hotel. I wasn't called down to supper but after the general manager of the mines and all of the other guests had gone to church, the housekeeper stole up to my room and asked me to come down and get a cup of tea.

At eleven o'clock that night the housekeeper again knocked at my door and told me that I had to give up my room; that she was told it belonged to a teacher. "It's a shame, mother," she whispered, as she helped me into my coat.

I found little Bouncer sitting on guard down in the lobby. He took me up the mountain to a miner's house. A cold wind almost blew the bonnet from my head. At the miner's shack I knocked.

A man's voice shouted, "Who is there?"

"Mother Jones," said I.

A light came in the tiny window. The door opened.

"And did they put you out, Mother?"

"They did that."

"I told Mary they might do that," said the miner. He held the oil lamp with the thumb and his little finger and I could see that the others were off. His face was young but his body was bent over.

He insisted on my sleeping in the only bed, with his wife. He slept with his head on his arms on the kitchen table. Early in the morning his wife rose to keep the children quiet, so that I might sleep a little later as I was very tired.

At eight o'clock she came into my room, crying.

"Mother, are you awake?"

"Yes, I am awake."

"Well, you must get up. The sheriff is here to put us out for keeping you. This house belongs to the Company."

The family gathered up all their earthly belongings, which weren't much, took down all the holy pictures, and put them in a wagon, and they with all their neighbors went to the meeting. The sight of that wagon with the sticks of furniture and the holy pictures and the children, with the father and mother and myself walking along through the streets turned the tide. It made the men so angry that they decided not to go back that morning to the mines. Instead they came to the meeting where they determined not to give up the strike until they had won the victory.

Then the company tried to bring in scabs. I told the men to stay home with the children for a change and let the women attend to the scabs. I organized an army of women housekeepers. On a given day they were to bring their mops and brooms and "the army" would charge the scabs up at the mines. The general manager, the sheriff and the corporation hirelings heard of our plans and were on hand. The day came and the women came with the mops and brooms and pails of water.

I decided not to go up to the Drip Mouth myself, for I knew they would arrest me and that might rout the army. I selected as leader an Irish woman who had a most picturesque appearance. She had slept late and her husband had told her to hurry up and get into the army. She had grabbed a red petticoat and slipped it over a thick cotton night gown. She wore a black stocking and a white one. She had tied a little red fringed shawl over her wild red hair. Her face was red and her eyes were mad. I looked at her and felt that she could raise a rumpus.

I said, "You lead the army up to the Drip Mouth. Take that tin dishpan you have with you and your hammer, and when the scabs and the mules come up, begin to hammer and howl. Then all of you hammer and howl and be ready to chase the scabs with your mops and brooms. Don't be afraid of anyone."

Up the mountain side, yelling and hollering, she led the women, and when the mules came up with the scabs and the coal, she began beating on the dishpan and hollering and all the army joined in with her. The sheriff tapped her on the shoulder.

"My dear lady," said he, "remember, the mules. Don't frighten them."

She took the old tin pan and she hit him with it and she hollered, "To hell with you and the mules!"

He fell over and dropped into the creek. Then the mules began to rebel against scabbing. They bucked and kicked the scab drivers and started off for the barn. The scabs started running down hill, followed by the army of women with their mops and pails and brooms.

A poll parrot in a near by shack screamed at the superintendent, "Got hell, did you? Got hell?"

There was a great big doctor in the crowd, a company lap dog. He had a little satchel in his hand and he said to me, impudent like, "Mrs. Jones, I have a warrant for you."

"All right," said I. "Keep it in your pill bag until I come for it. I am going to hold a meeting now."

From that day on the women kept continual watch of the mines to see that the company did not bring in scabs. Every day women with brooms or mops in one hand and babies in the other arm wrapped in little blankets, went to the mines and watched that no one went in. And all night long they kept watch. They were heroic women. In the long years to come the nation will pay them high tribute for they were fighting for the advancement of a great country. . . .

One night [in 1902] I went with an organizer named Scott to a mining town in the Fairmont district where the miners had asked me to hold a meeting. When we got off the car I asked Scott where I was to speak and he pointed to a frame building. We walked in. There were lighted candles on an altar. I looked around in the dim light. We were in a church and the benches were filled with miners.

Outside the railing of the altar was a table. At one end sat the priest with the money of the union in his hands. The president of the local union sat at the other end of the table. I marched down the aisle.

"What's going on?" I asked.

"Holding a meeting," said the president.

"What for?"

"For the union, Mother. We rented the church for our meetings."

I reached over and took the money from the priest. Then I turned to the miners.

"Boys," I said, "this is a praying institution. You should not commercialize it. Get up, every one of you and go out in the open fields."

They got up and went out and sat around in a field while I spoke to them. The sheriff was there and he did not allow any traffic to go along the road while I was speaking. In front of us was a school house. I pointed to it and I said, "Your ancestors fought for you to have a share in that institution over there. It's yours. See the school board, and every Friday night hold your meetings there. Have your wives clean it up Saturday morning for the children to enter Monday. Your organization is not a praying institution. It's a fighting institution. It's an educational institution along industrial lines. Pray for the dead and fight like hell for the living!" . . .

In the spring of 1903 I went to Kensington, Pennsylvania, where seventy-five thousand textile workers were on strike. Of this number at least ten thousand were little children. The workers were striking for more pay and shorter hours. Every day little children came into Union Headquarters, some with their hands off, some with the thumb missing, some with their fingers off at the knuckle. They were stooped little things, round shouldered and skinny. Many of them were not over ten years of age, although the state law prohibited their working before they were twelve years of age.

The law was poorly enforced and the mothers of these children often swore falsely as to their children's age. In a single block in Kensington, fourteen women, mothers of twenty-two children all under twelve, explained it was a question of starvation or perjury. That the fathers had been killed or maimed at the mines.

I asked the newspaper men why they didn't publish the facts about child labor in Pennsylvania. They said they couldn't because the mill owners had stock in the papers.

"Well, I've got stock in these little children," said I, "and I'll arrange a little publicity."

We assembled a number of boys and girls one morning in Independence Park and from there we arranged to parade with banners to the court house where we would hold a meeting.

A great crowd gathered in the public square in front of the city hall. I put the little boys with their fingers off and hands crushed and maimed on a platform. I held up their mutilated hands and showed them to the crowd and made the statement that Philadelphia's mansions were built on the broken bones, the quivering hearts and drooping heads of these children. That their little lives went out to make wealth for others. That neither state or city officials paid any attention to these wrongs. That they did not care that these children were to be the future citizens of the nation.

The officials of the city hall were standing in the open windows. I held the little ones of the mills high up above the heads of the crowd and pointed to their puny arms and legs and hollow chests. They were light to lift.

I called upon the millionaire manufacturers to cease their moral murders, and I cried to the officials in the open windows opposite, "Some day the workers will take possession of your city hall, and when we do, no child will be sacrificed on the altar of profit."

The officials quickly closed the windows, just as they had closed their eyes and hearts.

The reporters quoted my statement that Philadelphia mansions were built on the broken bones and quivering hearts of children. The Philadelphia papers and the New York papers got into a squabble with each other over the question. The universities discussed it. Preachers began talking. That was what I wanted. Public attention on the subject of child labor.

The matter quieted down for a while and I concluded the people needed stirring up again. The Liberty Bell that a century ago rang out for freedom against tyranny was touring the country and crowds were coming to see it everywhere. That gave me an idea. These little children were striking for some of the freedom that childhood ought to have, and I decided that the children and I would go on a tour.

I asked some of the parents if they would let me have their little boys and girls for a week or ten days, promising to bring them back safe and sound. They consented. A man named Sweeny was marshal for our "army." A few men and women went with me to help with the children. They were on strike and I thought they might as well have a little recreation.

The children carried knapsacks on their backs in which was a knife and fork, a tin cup and plate. We took along a wash boiler in which to cook the food on the road. One little fellow had a drum and another had a fife. That was our band. We carried banners that said, "We want more schools and less hospitals." "We want time to play." "Prosperity is here. Where is ours?"

We started from Philadelphia where we held a great mass meeting. I decided to go with the children to see President Roosevelt to ask him to have Congress pass a law prohibiting the exploitation of childhood. I thought that President Roosevelt might see these mill children and compare them with his own little ones who were spending the summer on the seashore at Oyster Bay. I thought, too, out of politeness, we might call on Morgan in Wall Street who owned the mines where many of these children's fathers worked.

The children were very happy, having plenty to eat, taking baths in the brooks and rivers every day. I thought when the strike is over and they go back to the mills, they will never have another holiday like this. All along the line of march the farmers drove out to meet us with wagon loads of fruit and vegetables. Their wives brought the children clothes and money. The interurban trainmen would stop their trains and give us free rides.

Marshal Sweeny and I would go ahead to the towns and arrange sleeping quarters for the children, and secure meeting halls. As we marched on, it grew terribly hot. There was no rain and the roads were heavy with dust. From time to time we had to send some of the children back to their homes. They were too weak to stand the march.

We were on the outskirts of New Trenton, New Jersey, cooking our lunch in the wash boiler, when the conductor on the interurban car stopped and told us the police were coming down to notify us that we could not enter the town. There were mills in the town and the mill owners didn't like our coming.

I said, "All right, the police will be just in time for lunch."

Sure enough, the police came and we invited them to dine with us. They looked at the little gathering of children with their tin plates and cups around the wash boiler. They just smiled and spoke kindly to the children, and said nothing at all about not going into the city.

We went in, held our meeting, and it was the wives of the police who took the little children and cared for them that night, sending them back in the morning with a nice lunch rolled up in paper napkins.

Everywhere we had meetings, showing up with living children, the horrors of child labor.

At one town the mayor said we could not hold a meeting because he did not have sufficient police protection. "These little children have never known any sort of protection, your honor," I said, "and they are used to going without it." He let us have our meeting.

One night in Princeton, New Jersey, we slept in the big cool barn on Grover Cleveland's great estate. The heat became intense. There was much suffering in our ranks, for our little ones were not robust. The proprietor of the leading hotel sent for me. "Mother," he said, "order what you want and all you want for your army, and there's nothing to pay."

I called on the mayor of Princeton and asked for permission to speak opposite the campus of the University. I said I wanted to speak on higher education. The mayor gave me permission. A great crowd gathered, professors and students and the people; and I told them that the rich robbed these little children of any education of the lowest order that they might send their sons and daughters to places of higher education. That they used the hands and feet of little children that they might buy automobiles for their wives and police dogs for their daughters to talk French to. I said the mill owners take babies almost from the cradle. And I showed those professors children in our army who could scarcely read or write because they were working ten hours a day in the silk mills of Pennsylvania.

"Here's a text book on economics," I said, pointing to a little chap, James Ashworth, who was ten years old and who was stooped over like an old man from carrying bundles of yarn that weighed seventy-five pounds. "He gets three dollars a week and his sister who is fourteen gets six dollars. They work in a carpet factory ten hours a day while the children of the rich are getting their higher education."

That night we camped on the banks of Stony Brook where years and years before the ragged Revolutionary Army camped, Washington's brave soldiers that made their fight for freedom.

From Jersey City we marched to Hoboken. I sent a committee over to the New York Chief of Police, Ebstein, asking for permission to march up Fourth Avenue to Madison Square where I wanted to hold a meeting. The chief refused and forbade our entrance to the city.

I went over myself to New York and saw Mayor Seth Low. The mayor was most courteous but he said he would have to support the police commissioner. I asked him what the reason was for refusing us entrance to the city and he said that we were not citizens of New York.

"Oh, I think we will clear that up, Mr. Mayor," I said. "Permit me to call your attention to an incident which took place in this nation just a year ago. A piece of rotten royalty came over here from Germany, called Prince Henry. The Congress of the United States voted $45,000 to fill that fellow's stomach for three weeks and to entertain him. His brother was getting $4,000,000 dividends out of the blood of the workers in this country. Was he a citizen of this land?"

"And it was reported, Mr. Mayor, that you and all the officials of New York and the University Club entertained that chap." And I repeated, "Was he a citizen of New York?"

"No, Mother," said the mayor, "he was not."

"And a Chinaman called Lee Woo was also entertained by the officials of New York. Was he a citizen of New York?"

"No, Mother, he was not."

"Did they ever create any wealth for our nation?"

"No, Mother, they did not," said he.

"Well, Mr. Mayor, these are the little citizens of the nation and they also produce its wealth. Aren't we entitled to enter your city?"

"Just wait," says he, and he called the commissioner of police over to his office.

Well, finally they decided to let the army come in. We marched up Fourth Avenue to Madison Square and police officers, captains, sergeants, roundsmen and reserves from three precincts accompanied us. But the police would not let us hold a meeting in Madison Square. They insisted that the meeting be held in Twentieth Street.

I pointed out to the captain that the single taxers were allowed to hold meetings in the square. "Yes," he said, "but they won't have twenty people and you might have twenty thousand."

We marched to Twentieth Street. I told an immense crowd of the horrors of child labor in the mills around the anthracite region and I showed them some of the children. I showed them Eddie Dunphy, a little fellow of twelve, whose job it was to sit all day on a high stool, handing in the right thread to another worker. Eleven hours a day he sat on the high stool with dangerous machinery all about him. All day long, winter and summer, spring and fall, for three dollars a week.

And then I showed them Gussie Rangnew, a little girl from whom all the childhood had gone. Her face was like an old woman's. Gussie packed stockings in a factory, eleven hours a day for a few cents a day.

We raised a lot of money for the strikers and hundreds of friends offered their homes to the little ones while we were in the city.

The next day we went to Coney Island at the invitation of Mr. Bostick who owned the wild animal show. The children had a wonderful day such as they never had in all their lives. After the exhibition of the trained animals, Mr. Bostick let me speak to the audience. There was a back drop to the tiny stage of the Roman Colosseum with the audience painted in and two Roman emperors down in front with their thumbs down. Right in front of the emperors were the empty iron cages of the animals. I put my little children in the cages and they clung to the iron bars while I talked.

I told the crowd that the scene was typical of the aristocracy of employers with their thumbs down to the little ones of the mills and factories, and people sitting dumbly by.

"We want President Roosevelt to hear the wail of the children who never have a chance to go to school but work eleven and twelve hours a day in the textile mills of Pennsylvania; who weave the carpets that he and you walk upon; and the lace curtains in your windows, and the clothes of the people. Fifty years ago there was a cry against slavery and men gave up their lives to stop the selling of black children on the block. Today the white child is sold for two dollars a week to the manufacturers. Fifty years ago the black babies were sold C.O.D. Today the white baby is sold on the installment plan.

"In Georgia where children work day and night in the cotton mills they have just passed a bill to protect song birds. What about the little children from whom all song is gone?

"I shall ask the president in the name of the aching hearts of these little ones that he emancipate them from slavery. I will tell the president that the prosperity he boasts of is the prosperity of the rich wrung from the poor and the helpless.

"The trouble is that no one in Washington cares. I saw our legislators in one hour pass three bills for the relief of the railways but when labor cries for aid for the children they will not listen.

"I asked a man in prison once how he happened to be there and he said he had stolen a pair of shoes. I told him if he had stolen a railroad he would be a United States Senator.

"We are told that every American boy has the chance of being president. I tell you that these little boys in the iron cages would sell their chance any day for good square meals and a chance to play. These little toilers whom I have taken from the mills—deformed, dwarfed in body and soul, with nothing but toil before them—have never heard that they have a chance, the chance of every American male citizen, to become the president.

"You see those monkeys in those cages over there." I pointed to a side cage. "The professors are trying to teach them to talk. The monkeys are too wise for they fear that the manufacturers would buy them for slaves in their factories."

I saw a stylishly dressed young man down in the front of the audience. Several times he grinned. I stopped speaking and pointing to him I said, "Stop your smiling, young man! Leave this place! Go home and beg the mother who bore you in pain, as the mothers of these little children bore them, go home and beg her to give you brains and a heart."

He rose and slunk out, followed by the eyes of the children in the cage. The people sat stone still and out in the rear a lion roared.

The next day we left Coney Island for Manhattan Beach to visit Senator Platt, who had made an appointment to see me at nine o'clock in the morning. The children got stuck in the sand banks and I had a time cleaning the sand off the littlest ones. So we started to walk on the railroad track. I was told it was private property and we had to get off. Finally a saloon keeper showed us a short cut into the sacred grounds of the hotel and suddenly the army appeared in the lobby. The little fellows played "Hail, hail, the gang's all here" on their fifes and drums, and Senator Platt when he saw the little army ran away through the back door to New York.

I asked the manager if he would give the children breakfast and charge it up to the Senator as we had an invitation to breakfast that morning with him. He gave us a private room and he gave those children such a breakfast as they had never had in all their lives. I had breakfast too, and a reporter from one of the Hearst papers and I charged it all up to Senator Platt.

We marched down to Oyster Bay but the president refused to see us and he would not answer my letters. But our march had done its work. We had drawn the attention of the nation to the crime of child labor. And while the strike of the textile workers in Kensington was lost and the children driven back to work, not long afterward the Pennsylvania legislature passed a child labor law that sent thousands of children home from the mills, and kept thousands of others from entering the factory until they were fourteen years of age. . . .

I went down to Cottondale [Alabama] to get a job in the cotton mills. I wanted to see for myself if the grewsome stories of little children working in the mills were true.

I applied for a job but the manager told me he had nothing for me unless I had a family that would work also. I told the manager I was going to move my family to Cottondale but I had come on ahead to see what chances there were for getting work.

"Have you children?"

"Yes, there are six of us."

"Fine," he said. He was so enthusiastic that he went with me to find a house to rent.

"Here's a house that will do plenty," said he. The house he brought me to was a sort of two-story plank shanty. The windows were broken and the door sagged open. Its latch was broken. It had one room down stairs and unfinished loft upstairs. Through the cracks in the roof the rain had come in and rotted the flooring. Downstairs there was a big old open fireplace in front of which were holes big enough to drop a brick through.

The manager was delighted with the house.

"The wind and the cold will come through these holes," I said.

He laughed. "Oh, it will be summer soon and you will need all the air you can get."

"I don't know that this house is big enough for six of us."

"Not big enough?" he stared at me. "What you all want, a hotel?"

I took the house, promising to send for my family by the end of the month when they could get things wound up on the farm. I was given work in the factory, and there I saw the children, little children working, the most heart-rending spectacle in all life. Sometimes it seemed to me I could not look at those silent little figures; that I must go north, to the grim coal fields, to the Rocky Mountain camps, where the labor fight is at least fought by grown men.

Little girls and boys, barefooted, walked up and down between the endless rows of spindles, reaching thin little hands into the machinery to repair snapped threads. They crawled under machinery to oil it. They replaced spindles all day long, all day long; night through, night through. Tiny babies of six years old with faces of sixty did an eight-hour shift for ten cents a day. If they fell asleep, cold water was dashed in their faces, and the voice of the manager yelled above the ceaseless racket and whir of the machines.

Toddling chaps of four years old were brought to the mills to "help" the older sister or brother of ten years but their labor was not paid.

The machines, built in the north, were built low for the hands of little children.

At five-thirty in the morning, long lines of little grey children came out of the early dawn into the factory, into the maddening noise, into the lint filled rooms. Outside the birds sang and the blue sky shone. At the lunch half-hour, the children would fall to sleep over their lunch of cornbread and fat pork. They would lie on the bare floor and sleep. Sleep was their recreation, their release, as play is to the free child. The boss would come along and shake them awake. After the lunch period, the hour-in grind, the ceaseless running up and down between the whirring spindles. Babies, tiny children!

Often the little ones were afraid to go home alone in the night. Then they would sleep till sunrise on the floor. That was when the mills were running a bit slack and the all-night shift worked shorter hours. I often went home with the little ones after the day's work was done, or the night shift went off duty. They were too tired to eat. With their clothes on, they dropped on the bed . . . to sleep, to sleep . . . the one happiness these children know.

But they had Sundays, for the mill owners, and the mill folks themselves were pious. To Sunday School went the babies of the mills, there to hear how God had inspired the mill owner to come down and build the mill, so as to give His little ones work that they might develop into industrious, patriotic citizens and earn money to give to the missionaries to convert the poor unfortunate heathen Chinese. . . .

[In 1913 Jones was arrested in West Virginia and jailed for the murder of a mine guard during a strike. She was released after national publicity generated a federal Senate investigation of the strike. In January 1914 she traveled to Colorado where miners were on strike in the Rockefeller-owned mines.]

From January on until the final brutal outrage—the burning of the tent colony in Ludlow—my ears wearied with the stories of brutality and suffering. My eyes ached with the misery I witnessed. My brain sickened with the knowledge of man's inhumanity to man.

It was, "Oh, Mother, my daughter has been assaulted by the soldiers—such a little girl!"

"Oh, Mother, did you hear how the soldiers entered Mrs. Hall's house, how they terrified the little children, wrecked the home, and did worse—terrible things—and just because Mr. Hall, the undertaker, had buried two miners whom the militia had killed!"

"And, Oh Mother, did you hear how they are arresting miners for vagrancy, for loafing, and making them work in company ditches without pay, making them haul coal and clear snow up to the mines for nothing!"

"Mother, Mother, listen! A Polish fellow arrived as a strike breaker. He didn't know there was a strike. He was a big, strapping fellow. They gave him a star and a gun and told him to shoot strikers!"

"Oh, Mother, they've brought in a shipment of guns and machine guns— what's to happen to us!"

A frantic mother clutched me. "Mother Jones," she screamed, "Mother Jones, my little boy's all swollen up with the kicking and beating he got from a soldier because he said, 'Howdy, John D. feller!' 'Twas just a kid teasing, and now he's lying like dead!"

"Mother, 'tis an outrage for an adjutant general of the state to shake his fist and holler in the face of a grey-haired widow for singing a union song in her own kitchen while she washes the dishes!"

"It is all an outrage," said I. " 'Tis an outrage indeed that Rockefeller should own the coal that God put in the earth for all the people. 'Tis an outrage that gunmen and soldiers are here protecting mines against workmen who ask a bit more than a crust, a bit more than bondage! 'Tis an ocean of outrage!"

"Mother, did you hear of poor, old Colner? He was going to the postoffice and was arrested by the militia. They marched him down the hill, making him carry a shovel and a pick on his back. They told him he was to die and he must dig his own grave. He stumbled and fell on the road. They kicked him and he staggered up. He begged to be allowed to go home and kiss his wife and children goodbye.

"We'll do the kissing," laughed the soldiers.

At the place they picked out for his grave, they measured him, and then they ordered him to dig—two feet deeper, they told him. Old Colner began digging while the soldiers stood around laughing and cursing and playing craps for his tin watch. Then Colner fell fainting into the grave. The soldiers left him there till he recovered by himself. There he was alone—and he staggered back to camp, Mother, and he isn't quite right in the head!"

I sat through long nights with sobbing widows, watching the candles about the corpse of the husband burn down to their sockets.

"Get out and fight," I told those women. "Fight like hell till you go to Heaven!" That was the only way I knew to comfort them.

I nursed men back to sanity who were driven to despair. I solicited clothes for the ragged children, for the desperate mothers. I laid out the dead, the martyrs of the strike. I kept the men away from the saloons, whose licenses as well as those of the brothels, were held by the Rockefeller interests.

The miners armed, armed as it is permitted every American citizen to do in defense of his home, his family; as he is permitted to do against invasion. The smoke of armed battle rose from the arroyos and ravines of the Rocky Mountains.

No one listened. No one cared. The tickers in the offices of 26 Broadway sounded louder than the sobs of women and children. Men in the steam heated luxury of Broadway offices could not feel the stinging cold of Colorado hillsides where families lived in tents.

Then came Ludlow and the nation heard. Little children roasted alive make a front page story. Dying by inches of starvation and exposure does not.

On the 19th of April, 1914, machine guns, used on the strikers in the Paint Creek strike, were placed in position above the tent colony of Ludlow. Major Pat Hamrock and Lieutenant K. E. Linderfelt were in charge of the militia, the majority of whom were company gunmen sworn in as soldiers.

Early in the morning soldiers approached the colony with a demand from headquarters that Louis Tikas, leader of the Greeks, surrender two Italians. Tikas demanded a warrant for their arrest. They had none. Tikas refused to surrender them. The soldiers returned to headquarters. A signal bomb was fired. Then another. Immediately the machine guns began spraying the flimsy tent colony, the only home the wretched families of the miners had, spraying it with bullets. Like iron rain, bullets fell upon men, women and children.

The women and children fled to the hills. Others tarried. The men defended their homes with their guns. All day long the firing continued. Men fell dead, their faces to the ground. Women dropped. The little Snyder boy was shot through the head, trying to save his kitten. A child carrying water to his dying mother was killed.

By five o'clock in the afternoon, the miners had no more food, nor water, nor ammunition. They had to retreat with their wives and little ones into the hills. Louis Tikas was riddled with shots while he tried to lead women and children to safety. They perished with him.

Night came. A raw wind blew down the canyons where men, women and children shivered and wept. Then a blaze lighted the sky. The soldiers, drunk with blood and with the liquor they had looted from the saloon, set fire to the tents of Ludlow with oil-soaked torches. The tents, all the poor furnishings, the clothes and bedding of the miners' families burned. Coils of barbed wire were stuffed into the well, the miners' only water supply.

After it was over, the wretched people crept back to bury their dead. In a dugout under a burned tent, the charred bodies of eleven little children and two women were found—unrecognizable. Everything lay in ruins. The wires of bed springs writhed on the ground as if they, too, had tried to flee the horror. Oil and fire and guns had robbed men and women and children of their homes and slaughtered tiny babies and defenseless women. Done by order of Lieutenant Linderfelt, a savage, brutal executor of the will of the Colorado Fuel and Iron Company.

The strikers issued a general call to arms: every able bodied man must shoulder a gun to protect himself and his family from assassins, from arson and plunder. From jungle days to our own so-named civilization, this is a man's inherent right. To a man they armed, throughout the whole strike district. Ludlow went on burning in their hearts.

Everybody got busy. A delegation from Ludlow went to see President Wilson. Among them was Mrs. Petrucci whose three tiny babies were crisped to death in the black hole of Ludlow. She had something to say to her President.

Immediately he sent the United States cavalry to quell the gunmen. He studied the situation, and drew up proposals for a three-year truce, binding upon miner and operator. The operators scornfully refused.

A mass meeting was called in Denver. Judge Lindsey spoke. He demanded that the operators be made to respect the laws of Colorado. That something be done immediately. It was. The Denver Real Estate Exchange appointed a committee to spit on Judge Lindsey for his espousal of the cause of the miners.

Rockefeller got busy. Writers were hired to write pamphlets which were sent broadcast to every editor in the country, bulletins. In these leaflets, it was shown how perfectly happy was the life of the miner until the agitators came; how joyous he was with the company's saloon, the company's pigstys for homes, the company's teachers and preachers and coroners. How the miners hated the state law of an eight-hour working day, begging to be allowed to work ten, twelve. How they hated the state law that they should have their own check weighman to see that they were not cheated at the tipple.

And all the while the mothers of the children who died in Ludlow were mourning their dead. . . .

Five hundred women got up a dinner and asked me to speak. Most of the women were crazy about women suffrage. They thought that Kingdom-come would follow the enfranchisement of women.

"You must stand for free speech in the streets," I told them.

"How can we," piped a woman, "when we haven't a vote?"

"I have never had a vote," said I, "and I have raised hell all over this country! You don't need a vote to raise hell! You need convictions and a voice!"

Some one meowed, "You're an anti!"

"I am not an anti to anything which will bring freedom to my class," said I. "But I am going to be honest with you sincere women who are working for votes for women. The women of Colorado have had the vote for two generations and the working men and women are in slavery. The state is in slavery, vassal to the Colorado Iron and Fuel Company and its subsidiary interests. A man who was present at a meeting of mine owners told me that when the trouble started in the mines, one operator proposed that women be disfranchised because here and there some woman had raised her voice in behalf of the miners. Another operator jumped to his feet and shouted, 'For God's sake! What are you talking about! If it had not been for the women's vote the miners would have beaten us long ago!' "

Some of the women gasped with horror. One or two left the room. I told the women I did not believe in women's rights nor in men's rights but in human rights. "No matter what your fight," I said, "don't be ladylike! God Almighty made women and the Rockefeller gang of thieves made the ladies. I have just fought through sixteen months of bitter warfare in Colorado. I have been up against armed mercenaries but this old woman, without a vote, and with nothing but a hatpin has scared them.

"Organized labor should organize its women along industrial lines. Politics is only the servant of industry. The plutocrats have organized their women. They keep them busy with suffrage and prohibition and charity." . . .

Many of our modern leaders of labor have wandered far from the thorny path of these early crusaders. Never in the early days of the labor struggle would you find leaders wining and dining with the aristocracy; nor did their wives strut about like diamond-bedecked peacocks; nor were they attended by humiliated, cringing colored servants.

The wives of these early leaders took in washing to make ends meet. Their children picked and sold berries. The women shared the heroism, the privation of their husbands.

In those days labor's representatives did not sit on velvet chairs in conference with labor's oppressors; they did not dine in fashionable hotels with the representatives of the top capitalists, such as the Civic Federation. They did not ride in Pullmans nor make trips to Europe.

The rank and file have let their servants become their masters and dictators. The workers have now to fight not alone their exploiters but likewise their own leaders, who often betray them, who sell them out, who put their own advancement ahead of that of the working masses, who make of the rank and file political pawns.

Provision should be made in all union constitutions for the recall of leaders. Big salaries should not be paid. Career hunters should be driven out, as well as leaders who use labor for political ends. These types are menaces to the advancement of labor.

In big strikes I have known, the men lay in prison while the leaders got out on bail and drew high salaries all the time. The leaders did not suffer. They never missed a meal. Some men make a profession out of labor and get rich thereby. John Mitchell [leader of the United Mine Workers] left to his heirs a fortune, and his political friends are using the labor movement to gather funds to erect a monument to his memory, to a name that should be forgotten.

In spite of oppressors, in spite of false leaders, in spite of labor's own lack of understanding of its needs, the cause of the worker continues onward. Slowly his hours are shortened, giving him leisure to read and to think. Slowly his standard of living rises to include some of the good and beautiful things of the world. Slowly the cause of his children becomes the cause of all. His boy is taken from the breaker, his girl from the mill. Slowly those who create the wealth of the world are permitted to share it. The future is in labor's strong, rough hands.

FREDERIC C. HOWE
1867–1940

Frederic C. Howe's career epitomizes the political reformism of the Progressive period. As journalist, author, and public servant, he engaged in its ambitious efforts to reform the American city as well as its efforts to win a war, which brought the defeat of Progressive ideals.

Howe's Confessions of a Reformer *is a story of his public life to the mid-1920s. His optimistic belief that human beings could shape and improve their world was born at Johns Hopkins University, where one of his teachers was Woodrow Wilson, "our greatest lecturer." Howe's reforming ambitions were later fired by his close political and emotional links to Tom L. Johnson, mayor of Cleveland from 1901 to 1909. A member of the Johnson administration, Howe became converted to Johnson's favorite causes: the municipal ownership of utilities, especially the street railway system, and the single tax. After Johnson's defeat, Howe left Cleveland and—briefly—politics. He soon returned, however, as commissioner of immigration of the port of New York, seeking to humanize Ellis Island, which sheltered thousands upon thousands of immigrants every year. In 1919 as delegate to the Paris Peace Conference at the conclusion of World War I, Howe hoped to reshape the post-war world.*

Despite the political conservatism of the 1920s, Howe became active in the Conference on Progressive Political Action, an organization of unions and agrarian radicals that in 1924 initiated the presidential candidacy of Wisconsin Senator Robert M. LaFollette on the Progressive Party ticket. When liberal reformism resurfaced during the presidency of Franklin D. Roosevelt, Howe re-entered public service, working in the Agricultural Adjustment Administration from 1933 to 1937. He also wrote several books on urban reform, including The City: The Hope of Democracy *(1905) and* The British City: The Beginnings of Democracy *(1907).*

Howe's autobiography is also an intensely personal story about his search for a calling and a usable philosophy. Each major event in his life led him to re-think his principles, to jettison outmoded ideas and formulate new ones. He even admits to re-assessing his ideas about women's proper role—or trying to. Confessions of a Reformer *is a spiritual as well as a political odyssey.*

Howe's public and private lives were full of trials and disappointments. His optimism was constantly shaken. His mentors, Johnson and Wilson, died defeated men; their dreams—and Howe's—went unrealized. Howe

had good reason for claiming to be disillusioned. Yet he remained a re-
former, dedicated, despite the odds, to making the world a better place.

Confessions of a Reformer, *1925. Reprint, Kent, Ohio: Kent State*
University Press, 1988.

There was nothing in my inheritance to make me want the world any different. None of my ancestors ever crusaded. They took no part in the Revolutionary War; they were not Abolitionists; they escaped service in the Civil War. My mother's people were Quakers in a direct line of descent from the little band of settlers which Gustavus Adolphus sent out from Sweden in the early days of the seventeenth century to build a Swedish colony on the shores of Delaware Bay. There was no meeting-house in Meadville, and, like many Quakers, my mother's family had joined the Methodist church. Her grandparents were farmers who had drifted west till they came to rest in the very centre of what was later the town of Meadville, Pa. There my grandfather laid off a big city block and settled his five children around him.

My paternal ancestors came from the north of Ireland in the eighteenth century. They were what is known as Scotch-Irish, which means that they were Scotch Presbyterians who went over to Ireland and took the land away from the Irish and gave them their Scotch brand of religion in exchange. Like my mother's people, they came to this country poor, to get a new start in life. Only those who had little to lose came to America in those days, in sailing-ships which often took months in the crossing. They settled in northeastern Pennsylvania, and when other settlers trod on their heels they packed up their few possessions and trekked to the western part of the State. My father came to Meadville as a young man and there he married my mother. There I was born and lived to my twenty-fifth year.

Neither of my parents had any interest in reform. They did not want the world changed. It was a comfortable little world, Republican in politics, careful in conduct, Methodist in religion. . . .

When my sisters and I finished high school we went to Allegheny College, not because we had any love of learning but because it was the proper thing to do. The income from my father's business was somehow stretched to suffice for all of us. Allegheny was one of the two colleges in Meadville that gave to the town the modest name of the "Athens of the West." Allegheny was thoroughly sectarian. Progress toward a degree was made easy for men who said they were going into the church or into foreign missions. Many of our professors were retired ministers or missionaries, who knew none too much about their subjects. Professions of faith were rather more important than scholarship, and revival meetings were the great events of the winter. I found study a bore. None of the subjects stirred in me the least enthusiasm and I cut classes as often as I dared. I was never able to make head or tail of the sciences, mathematics, Latin, and Greek. As far as I can recall, I went through college without having an enthusiasm awakened, yet I wanted to know things, to be admitted to the secrets of life. My classmates seemed to get as little out of the course as I did. Because the college failed to satisfy us, we created activities of our own. Mine were in college journalism. I planned in class and fraternity politics to get the posts I wanted. The first thrill of my academic life came from getting out the commencement edition of the college weekly. I worked on it day and night. I could hardly wait for the summer vacation to end to take up the work again. The furtive and forbidden amusements of theatre-going, card-playing, and dancing were but slightly diverting as compared with the joy of working over an editorial column.

The winter revival meetings at the college found me inwardly rebellious, outwardly passive. They were thoroughly organized. Freshmen and sophomores were allotted to the seniors, who took us on long walks, during which they inquired about our souls. Night after night they herded us into the Stone church. There revivalists prayed, worked on our fears, made us feel that we were eternally damned if we went without their particular brand of religion. Under the influence of Moody and Sankey hymns I went to the mourners' bench the second winter. I crept forward to be prayed for by strangers for sins of which I was ignorant and for a salvation that seemed at best dreary. I did what relatives, friends, and older college students expected me to do. I had no conviction of sin, no sense of guilt, or of being abandoned. And nothing happened. The great change that was promised did not come over me. Convinced of my own callousness, and rather sick at heart because of it, I found myself hating every one engaged in the proceedings and wishing heartily to escape. I had gone through the ordeal of being prayed for, of confessing a desire for regeneration, and had found no relief; no heavenly manna had fallen my way. I was resentful of religion, and deliberately refused from that time on to attend revival meetings, scandalizing and grieving my teachers and friends.

Physical escape from the embraces of evangelical religion did not mean moral escape. From that religion my reason was never emancipated. By it I was conformed to my generation and made to share its moral standards and ideals. . . .

[Howe decided to become an editorial writer for a newspaper. After hearing a lecture by economist Richard T. Ely, then a professor at Johns Hopkins University, Howe enrolled in 1889 in a doctoral program at the university, which he thought would help him land a newspaper job. Howe helped to pay his expenses by free-lance writing for magazines and newspapers.]

From many of the evils of American education Johns Hopkins was conspicuously free. Censorship of thought, mental docility, waste of enthusiasms, of adventure, of individuality—all were foreign to it. It was free from fear. It was as unlike the timid small college from which I came as it is unlike the universities of to-day, which seek their presidents from among business men, lawyers, good money-getters, and in which freedom of teaching is being subordinated to the desire for a big endowment. The teachers, not the trustees, determined what was to be taught and how they should teach it. There was no placating of possible donors, no mirroring of the views of an economic class. In the nineties at Johns Hopkins I had the good fortune to be born into the world of thought, to be associated with men to whom honesty was a matter of course, and to whom courage was the first essential of a gentleman and a scholar.

Johns Hopkins freed me from many small-town limitations. It gave me new authorities, but they were still authorities outside of myself. I continued to think as others thought, only now I was thinking as did wise men, men who paid little attention to the church, but who had a worshipful veneration for some scientist or teacher under whose influence they had fallen. I accepted these new authorities as

FREDERIC C. HOWE

quite natural. Acceptance fell in with my earlier assumption that authority was proper, necessary, probably the first of the moralities. Not till years after did I come consciously to believe that I had a right to be my own authority. And not until I had made serious mistakes did I awaken to the belief that I had some rights of my own in the world, the right to pursue my own enthusiasms, to choose what was agreeable rather than what was not. Duty was always first; happiness was to be scrutinized. . . .

When I descended from the platform on Commemoration Day in May, 1892, with a certificate conferring on me a doctor's degree, I felt assured that it, if not my abilities, would be recognized as a matter of course. I had great confidence in that certificate of scholarship, but I wondered a little that it had been conferred on me; I did not feel scholarly, I had not been able to master the abstractions of political economy, I was not soaked in history as were some of my associates. And I had never had any great enthusiasm for any of my subjects. But that the degree was an invaluable possession I had no doubt. It would open doors, command friends, assure a job; of that there was no question. Only a few men had taken advanced degrees at that time. Johns Hopkins was the first and almost the only American university that emphasized postgraduate work. A Hopkins Ph.D. was a distinction of which I was infinitely proud. I should have no difficulty in finding a position. Journalism was my goal. . . .

I determined first to try the New York *Times*. I should have preferred to go to *The Nation* and *The Evening Post,* then edited by Lawrence Godkin, Horace White, and a group of other intellectual liberals, but that was far above me. *The Times* appealed to me as a free-trade paper.

After many days I managed to see the city editor.

I told him who I was and my unusual preparation for editorial work. I had studied history and political economy. I was familiar with historical jurisprudence. I had travelled abroad; had been editor of several college publications. Very few men were as well equipped as I was. We should have a new deal in politics. Trusts and monopolies should be destroyed. Possibly the railroads should be owned by the government. Labor must be treated with more consideration. Most important of all, a new type of men should be drawn into politics. I had prepared my creed of service for the interview. *The Times* seemed the best of all mediums for the propagation of my ideas, and I was eager to begin.

The city editor—I think his name was McGuire—listened tolerantly. He told me one did not begin as an editorial writer; one had to work his way up; one must be familiar with the traditions of the paper, with the city of New York. He was rather sharp in his comments on my contempt of reportorial work. That was the only way to begin, he said. Moreover, many men were out of work. The industrial depression had hit the newspapers as it had everything else. Finally he said:

"You may sit around here if you want to. I will send you on any assignment that cannot be covered by our regular staff."

I sat around for days. I was there on time. I read the files of *The Times*. I was faithful in small things. Nobody paid any attention to me, and finally I began to think I had been forgotten. I could not afford to be forgotten. My board bill was five dollars a week, and pretty soon I should be unwelcome at West Tenth Street.

I ventured to call the attention of the city editor to the fact that I was there and wanted to earn my salary.

He smiled at the word salary. I was working on space. "Here," he said, "is a call for an up-town fire. Beat it and get back as quick as you can."

That fire story was a remarkable bit of literature. It was at least a column long. That meant four dollars. I lingered in the hope that the city editor would notice it; possibly I might be permitted to see the proofs; but that was denied me. I went to bed happy and was up in the morning earlier than the milkman. The story was not on the front page; it was not on the second page. I finally found a few lines hidden in an obscure corner. Not a word of my fine writing did it contain.

I ate little breakfast. I hated McGuire; felt that he should be fired. Some weeks later I resigned—rather I just stayed at home. My weekly earnings scarcely paid car-fare.

I tried other papers without success. I was not known anywhere. My doctor's degree seemed a liability; soon I ceased to mention it. I was willing to begin anywhere if I could be assured a wage sufficient to live on. But New York was filled with discharged newspaper men, and those whom I came to know seemed to be very capable. . . . .

[Discouraged with journalism, Howe enrolled at New York Law School and finished the two-year course in one year. He returned to Meadville and passed the Pennsylvania state bar exams. He also met his wife-to-be, Marie Jenney, who became an active suffragist and feminist.]

One afternoon I was walking out into the country and passed a girl whom I had never seen before. I watched her until she disappeared. There was something about her that held me. I wanted to follow and speak with her. She did not live in Meadville. Perhaps she belonged to a theatrical company. She wore a wide, sweeping hat, her feet were unusually small, and her ankles were in keeping with her trim body. It was her eyes that held me. They were big and brown and warm.

That evening I asked my sisters about a strange girl I had seen. They identified her at once. Everybody in town knew and wondered about her. She was Miss Marie Jenney, of Syracuse, and was attending the Unitarian Theological Seminary. There were other women studying at the school, but Miss Jenney was different. She was too beautiful to be a minister. People insisted that she could not be serious. They argued that there was probably a man at the seminary who had brought her there. Only a man could explain such a beautiful girl, with good clothes and evidences of wealth, at a theological seminary. Women did not go in for careers thirty years ago, and saving souls was a man's job.

A few days later I saw an announcement that the seminary students were to give a theatrical performance at the Unitarian church, and her name was in the cast. I slipped off to the church after supper and secured a front seat. There were three men in the play and I hated every one of them. Miss Jenney took the leading role. Her acting was extraordinary. As people passed out of the church they spoke about it, and said how strange it was that with such talent she was not on the stage. It seemed absurd for her to go into the ministry.

Nothing mattered but to find some way of meeting her. College would soon be over and she would probably not return. I waited about the Unitarian church the following Sunday and spoke with the people with whom she lived. They asked me to dinner. Miss Jenney came in late with her arms filled with flowers. I fell quite dumb at the introduction. But she scarcely noticed me. She ignored me during dinner. Why should such a woman want to be a minister, I thought; why should she be studying Hebrew, Greek, and the early church fathers? It was all very stupid. I had never heard of such a thing. She could not be serious. All girls got married if they could; certainly all good-looking girls did. I quoted a remark of Heine that every woman who did anything in the world had one eye on her work and the other eye on a man. The only exception was Countess Somebody or Other, but then she only had one eye. The joke failed miserably. I endeavored to bolster it up by saying that Johns Hopkins did not admit women and that I hoped it never would.

After dinner I tried to square myself. We talked about political economy, and I found she was interested, especially in Socialism and advanced ideas. Here was something I knew about and I tried to show my wisdom. But the afternoon was a dismal failure. She seemed quite willing to see me go.

There were some weeks left and I made the most of them. I arranged walks and picnics to the lake. I brought books on economics and we read together. But much of the time I was preoccupied and silent.

Books had taught me new things about economics and politics; they had taught me nothing about women. My beliefs about women were far deeper hidden in my mind than were even the moralities of the church. I had gotten them as a child, had taken them in from relatives, neighbors, family. Men and women fell in love, they married, had children; the wife cooked the meals, kept the house clean, entertained relatives and friends, spent as little as possible, asked for what she got on Saturday evening with the weekly expense-account in her hands. She cared for the family when sick, got the children ready for school and church, arranged the men's clothes, on Sundays went on a buggy ride, and during the winter made cakes and pies for the church sociables. She did not offend the opinions of neighbors or of her husband, she was careful of her conduct, and only had an opinion of her own in a whisper. In so far as I thought of it at all women were conveniences of men. Mothers were, sisters were, wives would be. Men were kind to them; they did not swear in their presence, they cleaned their boots before entering the house, gave them as good a home as they could, and were true to their marital vows. That was the most binding obligation of all. Men who failed in the latter regard were quite beyond the pale of the people I knew. Men whom I had discovered on questionable streets or who had been seen with women of doubtful morality I avoided; anything could be believed about them.

Some day I undoubtedly would have that kind of a wife. I had thought very little about it at college, for I had been completely absorbed in other things. At Johns Hopkins I had danced, gone to teas and dinners, had looked at girls from a distance, but they had not gotten in the way of my studies. In fact, I had never taken thought of my opinions about women; they had scarcely existed for me. I had a kind of fear of them; certainly a bashfulness that I had never outgrown. They were outside of my life, but when they entered they would enter on my terms, the terms of my boyhood conceptions as to the proprieties of things.

Miss Jenney was different from this picture. And I did not like to have my picture disturbed, especially as I was so greatly attracted to the disturber. I expected women to agree; she had ideas of her own; they were better than my own, more logical, more consistent too with my democratic ideas on other things. She believed that women should vote for the same reasons that men voted. I snorted at the idea. Women should go to college as did men and find their work in the world. This shattered my picture of her convenience in the home. Women, to her, should be economically independent, they should not be compelled to ask for money, they should have an allowance; they did their share of the common work, and marriage was a partnership. This destroyed my sense of masculine power, of noblesse oblige, of generosity. To her, life was not a man's thing, it was a human thing. It was to be enjoyed by women as it was by men; there should be equality in all things, not in the ballot alone but in the mind, in work, in a career. Men and women were different in some ways, they were alike in more.

Unlearning economics and politics had been an easy matter. I had given up a small-town authority for a more distinguished one. Giving up my masculine authority meant giving up of one eminence I felt sure of. We did not state these things; they broke into our talks about life, about ourselves. I tried to avoid them. They were disagreeable; when we were married there would be time enough to discuss such questions. But this independence of mind was one of the things that made me want this new woman who had come across my path and gripped me in a way that left no doubt in my mind as to what I desired. While she weakened my masculine authority, she gave me strength in other ways. I would get courage from a woman who saw things as she saw them; could rely on a woman who faced me when other women would have smiled assent.

She has courage as well as beauty, I thought. And we will have fine talks, endless discussions, for she was interested in all of the things that I had studied. And her mind assimilated them far more readily than my own had done. But I was never able to square my ideas of marriage with hers; I could not give up the belief that a woman's place was where other women were. . . .

[Howe moved to Cleveland in 1894 and joined the law firm of Harry and James R. Garfield, sons of the late President.]

For two years I worked listlessly at the law during the day and played cards in the evenings. Never skilful at cards, and unable to see our drinking-parties to a finish without paying for it the following day, I sought escape by climbing nine flights of stairs to our law offices, where, high above the city, I sat looking out over Lake Erie far into the night. There I could be by myself. So far as I could see, my life was a failure. I disliked the law, had a fear of the judges, and most of all shrank from the experienced practitioners with whom I felt I could never cope. My university training gave me little comfort, it made me no friends, it did not aid me in trial work. At times it impeded me. . . .

In the spring of 1901 . . . rumors began to circulate that Tom L. Johnson planned to return to Cleveland from New York to run for mayor on the Democratic ticket. I had heard about Tom Johnson ever since I had been in the city. He was a dramatic personality; every one had a story about him. I knew about his life what every one knew: that he had come to Cleveland as a young man with no capital and had bought out an old horse-car line of no particular value on the west side, thereby coming into conflict with Mark Hanna [wealthy industrialist and Republican Party kingmaker], who looked upon the west side of the city as his own. He and his brother Albert had driven their own cars and collected fares. When he wanted to extend his car-line into the public square, he went before a Republican council and promised to carry passengers over his entire system for a single fare. The extension was granted in the teeth of Mark Hanna's opposition. In time he was recognized by other street-railway magnates; and he induced them to form a consolidation, capitalized far in excess of the capitalization of the constituent companies. Then he sold out his holdings and went to Brooklyn, where he repeated the operation. He repeated it again in Detroit and Philadelphia. He acquired steel-mills in Johnstown, Pa., and Lorain, Ohio, and sold them out to the Street Trust. He had made most of his money by stock manipulations of this kind and was reputed to be many times a millionaire. He had a palatial home on Euclid Avenue, where he entertained generously. Although he was an intimate friend of many of the rich people of Cleveland, he was distrusted because of his unusual opinions and the apparent discrepancy between his social position and the things he advocated. He was a Democrat and an absolute free-trader. He had been elected to Congress by advocating free trade in a city in the heart of the iron and steel district. He had advocated it in Congress, protesting against a protective tariff on iron and steel, which he said would add new millions to his wealth for which others would have to pay. He advocated the public ownership of street railways, although he had made most of his fortune out of them. He had a devoted following wherever he went; many people loved him. Among the poor he was known for his generosity. Waiters, doorkeepers, cab-drivers knew him as the man whose smallest change was a dollar bill. . . .

[Johnson] would go to a Republican meeting and ask permission to talk from the same platform with the Republican candidate for mayor. When permission was denied him, the crowd followed him out into the street, almost emptying the hall. One night he talked about poverty, about how to be rid of it. He said that society should be changed not by getting good men into office, but by making it possible for all men to be good. He said that most men would be reasonably good if they had a chance. We had evil in the world because people were poor. The trouble was not with people, it was with poverty. Poverty was the cause of vice and crime. It was social conditions that were bad rather than people. These conditions could be changed only through politics.

This bothered me, as did most of his speeches. Surely some people were good, while others were bad. My classifications were simple. Roughly, the members of the University Club and the Chamber of Commerce were good; McKisson, Bernstein, and the politician were bad. The bad were commonly in power; they held offices and controlled elections. They did not do their work well and were paid very much more than they should receive. At the primaries they elected their own kind to office. The way to change this vicious circle, I thought, was to get the good people to form committees in each ward as had been done in my own. If these committees nominated men who would go out and fight the politicians, if we gave enough thought to politics—as we were under a moral obligation to do—we should drive out the spoilsmen. It was all quite clear to me and very simple. It was the choice between the good and the bad.

But here was a man who said that bad people were not bad; they were merely poor and had to fight for a living. They got an easier living out of politics than they did working twelve hours a day in the steel-mills. So they went into politics. And being in the majority, they won out. . . .

Tom Johnson was elected mayor on the issue of municipal ownership and a three-cent fare on the street-railways. Along with a number of other men indorsed by the Municipal Association, I was returned to the council, which had enough independent members to be organized on a non-partisan basis. The beginning of the political renaissance had come. Spoilsmen, bosses, grafters would be driven out. Cleveland was to be America's pace-maker. . . .

[Although a Republican, Howe soon became Johnson's close friend and political ally in the mayor's fight for public ownership of utilities and the single tax.]

[T]hrough the activity of Mr. Johnson, Cleveland acquired a city-wide system of parks, playgrounds, and public baths. On Saturday and Sunday the whole population played baseball in hundreds of parks laid out for that purpose. Cleveland became a play city, and this generous provision for play has declared dividends. Workmen like to live in Cleveland. Workmen are followed by factory-owners. The growth of Cleveland in the last decade is partly traceable to the policy of making the city an attractive place in which to live.

In spite of its initial confusion and in spite of disappointments my term on the city council was one of happy activity. I grew to love the city and the big problems it presented. I visited other cities to study police administration, methods of street-cleaning, the grouping of public buildings. The city appealed to me as a social agency of great possibilities; at an insignificant cost it could fill the lives of people with pleasure. It could protect the poor by more intelligent use of the police force. It could provide things at wholesale; could open playgrounds and public baths. It could develop the lake front into a beautiful, long esplanade. It could take over the charities and run them as public agencies. I no longer believed in private charity. It seemed unfair that men and women who had given their lives to industry should have to rely upon private benevolence when in need. I saw endless possibilities of beauty in Cleveland. . . .

[Changing his party affiliation, Howe was appointed chairman of the finance commission of Cleveland.]

Mr. Johnson called his ten years' fight against privilege a war for "A City on a Hill." To the young men in the movement, and to tens of thousands of the poor who gave it their support, it was a moral crusade rarely paralleled in American politics. The struggle involved the banks, the press, the Chamber of Commerce, the clubs, and the social life of the city. It divided families and destroyed friendships. You were either for Tom Johnson or against him. If for him, you were a disturber of business, a Socialist, to some an anarchist. Had the term "Red" been in vogue, you would have been called a communist in the pay of Soviet Russia. Every other political issue and almost every topic of conversation was subordinated to the struggle. . . .

The immediate struggle revolved about two main issues: the public ownership of public utilities, especially the street-railways and electric-lighting service, and the reduction of street-railway fares to three cents. Neither of them seemed adequate to explain the bitterness of the conflict and the power which reaction was able to organize to obstruct the movement. These issues mobilized the conservative forces of the city—banks, the Chamber of Commerce, lawyers, doctors, clubs, and churches. The press was partly owned by Mark Hanna, while advertisers were organized to bring pressure on editors and owners. Instinct held the propertied classes together no matter how detached they might be from the interests that were directly menaced. Before the expiration of the first two years of Mr. Johnson's term of mayoralty the city was divided into two camps along clearly defined economic lines. There was bitterness, hatred, abuse. Also social ostracism and business boycott. The press was unscrupulous in its attacks. On the one side were men of property and influence; on the other the politicians, immigrants, workers, and persons of small means. This line of cleavage continued to the end. . . .

After his death admirers of Mr. Johnson erected a statue of him on this spot on the public square that had been dedicated to free speech. There are rostrums at the four corners of the monument where speakers stand. To the north is the group of public buildings which began to take form during his administration and which was largely carried through by his insistence. Tom Johnson's belief in freedom is finely symbolized in this memorial. . . .

With three other men from Cleveland I was elected to the State Senate on the reform wave. The Democratic platform was clear-cut. It gave home rule to cities, gave them power to own and operate public-utility corporations, and do practically anything else that the people desired. It taxed railroads and public-utility corporations the same as other property. It committed us to a simple direct-primary law, to the initiative and referendum, and the recall.

I believed fervently in this platform. We would have great cities—the city was always my passion—in America if the people were given power. They had shown in Cleveland their willingness to follow a leader. But we had been thwarted by bad laws, an inflexible constitution, by out-of-date charters. We had failed because we were manacled by laws. Our first task was to get freed from the legislature. And I fully expected that we should succeed. . . .

I came away from the legislature with scant respect for the laws of the land. I had seen how they were made. Some were frankly bought and paid for. Many were passed the last day. Only occasionally were bills in the public interest forced through by the pressure of public opinion. And these were so crippled with amendments that they were of little value. A great part of the laws was so much rubbish. . . .

[In 1910 Howe served on a Cleveland tax commission which imposed more equitable taxes on industrial and commercial properties. In 1911 he and his wife moved to Greenwich Village in New York City, where he became director of the People's Institute of the Cooper Union, a forum for public discussion and debates.]

The years from 1911 to 1914 were a happy interim for me. Working with college men and women who were convinced that the old order was breaking up, living in a world that had confidence in literature and in the power of ideas, it seemed to me that a new dispensation was about to be ushered in. A half-dozen monthly magazines had built up their circulation on disclosures of corruption and economic wrong; Lincoln Steffens, Ida M. Tarbell, Ray Stannard Baker, Charles Edward Russell had the attention of America; forums were being opened in the churches, city reformers were springing up all over the country. A dozen insurgents had been elected to Congress; direct primaries, the direct election of United States senators, the initiative and referendum were being adopted, while municipal ownership, labor legislation, woman suffrage, and the single tax seemed but a short way off. It was good form to be a liberal. Conservative lawyers, bankers, and men of affairs stepped out from their offices and lent their names to radical movements. They presided at meetings and contributed to causes. Branches of the Intercollegiate Socialist League were being organized in the colleges, woman suffrage was enlisting the most prominent women of the country, President Roosevelt was providing catchwords for radicals to conjure with, while Woodrow Wilson was taken from the cloisters of Princeton to be made governor of New Jersey, to be later elected to the presidency.

"The new freedom" was to replace the old serfdom of bosses, the younger generation was to achieve the things that had been denied my own—a generation ignorant of the old Egypt of small capitalism, aware of the cruel feudalism of the new. The political renaissance was now surely coming. It would not stop with economic reform; it would bring in a rebirth of literature, art, music, and spirit, not unlike that which came to Italy in the thirteenth century after the *popolo grasso* had made their pile and then turned to finer things. The colleges were to lead it; it was to have the support of the more enlightened business men; it would call forth the impoverished talents of the immigrant and the poor. The spirit of this young America was generous, hospitable, brilliant; it was care-free and full of variety. The young people in whom it leaped to expression hated injustice. They had no questions about the soundness of American democracy. They had supreme confidence in the mind. They believed, not less than I had always believed, that the truth would make us free. . . .

[In 1914 his former Johns Hopkins professor, President Woodrow Wilson, appointed Howe commissioner of immigration of the port of New York, responsible for the administration of Ellis Island.]

I set myself to changing the reputation of the island. I meant that it should be a kindly place to the million-odd people who in normal times passed through its gates each year. Instead of a prison, it should become a place of temporary detention. Aliens were allowed a great deal of freedom. For the first time men and women were permitted to be together in the detention rooms. The war lengthened the period of detention into months, so I opened a school for children. Outside playgrounds were equipped, and the immigrants were permitted to go on the lawns. This aroused an indignant protest. The lawns had been made at great expense, the officials said. They made a beautiful approach to the island. I replied that live babies were more precious than live grass, and took a great deal of satisfaction in seeing the lawns trampled under foot. On Sunday concerts were given by immigrant groups, which readily co-operated with me in caring for their nationals. The Italians arranged to have Caruso sing on Italian day. . . .

[After the United States entrance into World War I in April 1917, Howe's efforts to reform Ellis Island came to a halt.]

The three islands, isolated in New York harbor and capable of accommodating several thousand people, were demanded by the War Department and the Navy Department for emergency purposes. They were admirably situated as a place of detention for war suspects. The Department of Justice and hastily organized espionage agencies made them a dumping-ground of aliens under suspicion, while the Bureau of Immigration launched a crusade against one type of immigrant after another, and brought them to Ellis Island for deportation. No one was concerned over our facilities for caring for the warring groups deposited upon us. The buildings were unsuited for permanent residence; the floors were of cement, the corridors were chill, the islands were storm-swept, and soon the ordinary functions of the island became submerged in war activities. Eighteen hundred Germans were dumped on us at three o'clock one morning, following the sequestration of the German ships lying in New York harbor. The sailors had been promised certain privileges, including their beer, which was forbidden by law on the Island. Several hundred nurses were detained for their training prior to embarkation; each day brought a contingent of German, Hungarian, Austrian suspects, while incoming trains from the West added quotas of immoral men and women, prostitutes, procurers, and alleged white-slavers arrested under the hue and cry started early in the war, with the passage of the Mann White Slave Act and the hysterical propaganda that was carried on by moralistic agencies all over the country.

I was the custodian of all these groups. Each group had to be isolated. I became a jailer instead of a commissioner of immigration; a jailer not of convicted offenders but of suspected persons who had been arrested and railroaded to Ellis Island as the most available dumping-ground under the successive waves of hysteria which swept the country. . . .

The final outbreak of hysteria was directed against the "Reds" the winter of 1918–19. It started in the State of Washington in the lumber camps, and was directed against members of the I. W. W. [Industrial Workers of the World] organization which had superseded the more conservative craft unions affiliated with the American Federation of Labor. There was a concerted determination on the part of employers to bring wages back to pre-war conditions and to break the power of organized labor. This movement against alien labor leaders had the support of the Department of Justice. Private detective agencies and strike-breakers acted with assurance that in any outrages they would be supported by the government itself. The press joined in the cry of "Red revolution," and frightened the country with scare head-lines of an army of organized terrorists who were determined to usher in revolution by force. The government borrowed the agent provocateur from old Russia; it turned loose innumerable private spies. For two years we were in a panic of fear over the Red revolutionists, anarchists, and enemies of the Republic who were said to be ready to overthrow the government. . . .

As I look back over these years, my outstanding memories are not of the immigrant. They are rather of my own people. Things that were done forced one almost to despair of the mind, to distrust the political state. Shreds were left of our courage, our reverence. The Department of Justice, the Department of Labor, and Congress not only failed to protest against hysteria, they encouraged these excesses; the state not only abandoned the liberty which it should have protected, it lent itself to the stamping out of individualism and freedom. It used the agent provocateur, it permitted private agencies to usurp government powers, turned over the administration of justice to detective agencies, card-indexed liberals and progressives. It became frankly an agency of employing and business interests at a time when humanity—the masses, the poor—were making the supreme sacrifice of their lives.

I had fondly imagined that we prized individual liberty; I had believed that to Anglo-Saxons human rights were sacred and they would be protected at any cost.

Latin peoples might be temperamental, given to hysteria; but we were hard-headed, we stood for individuality. But I found that we were lawless, emotional, given to mob action. We cared little for freedom of conscience, for the rights of men to their opinions. Government was a convenience of business. Discussion of war profiteers was not to be permitted. The Department of Justice lent itself to the suppression of those who felt that war should involve equal sacrifice. Civil liberties were under the ban. Their subversion was not, however, an isolated thing; it was an incident in the ascendancy of business privileges and profits acquired during the war—an ascendancy that could not bear scrutiny or brook the free discussion which is the only safe basis of orderly popular government. . . .

My attitude toward the state was changed as a result of these experiences. I have never been able to bring it back. I became distrustful of the state. It seemed to want to hurt people; it showed no concern for innocence; it aggrandized itself and protected its power by unscrupulous means. It was not my America, it was something else. And I think I lost interest in it, just as did thousands of other persons, whose love of country was questioned, and who were turned from love into fear of the state and all that it signified. Possibly the falling off in the number of voters, numbered by millions, is in some way related to this disillusionment, this fear of the state which came into existence during these hysterical years. . . .

[Howe resigned his post at Ellis Island and went with President Wilson to the Paris Peace Conference, at which the terms for ending the war were framed.]

When the armistice was signed I felt that the international millennium was at hand. The President's idealism had carried the world; his Fourteen Points had been accepted; armies were to be disbanded, armaments scrapped, imperialism ended. Self-determination was to be extended to all peoples, hates were to be assuaged, and peace to reign.

I was ready to embrace a league of nations, even a league to enforce peace. Any international arrangement that would prevent war was worth while. I believed that the negotiators at Paris wanted peace and were willing to make any sacrifices for it; that war was going to be forever ended on the earth. . . .

[T]he League of Nations, which issued like the Treaty of Versailles, was a league of conquest rather than a covenant of freedom. It was an international sanction of servitude to make permanent the conquests of the war. Like the Treaty of Versailles, it provided a moral approval of economic and imperialistic exploitation. . . .

At fifty I saw myself as I saw the political state. I had lost the illusions I had spent a lifetime in hoarding. I had lost illusions of myself. Much of my intellectual capital had flown. Drafts on my mind came back indorsed: "No funds." But I was still not bankrupt. The new truth that a free world would only come through labor was forced on me. I did not seek it; did not welcome it. But it crowded into mind and demanded tenancy as the old occupants gave notice to leave. . . .

[In 1922 in response to pro-business, anti-union policies, a new liberal organization, the Conference on Progressive Political Action, was formed to further the political cause of labor and farmers.]

I became secretary of the organization, which carried on a vigorous fight in the congressional elections of 1922. We prepared political instructions for primaries and elections; unions were circularized; the labor executives sent their best men into strategic States—Wisconsin, Minnesota, Iowa, Montana. They demonstrated real political ability. As a result, a half-dozen men were elected to the United States Senate, and nearly fifty to the Lower House. It was my conviction that labor should begin at the bottom, in city and State elections; that in national affairs it should concentrate its power on congressmen and build up a labor-farmer bloc in Congress. I urged the nomination of dirt farmers, actual workers rather than liberals outside of the ranks. Preliminary training was essential; it would be gained in city, State, and congressional elections. Gains of this kind would not be lost. In time we would have the group system in Congress; ultimately workers and farmers, being in the majority, would control it. Then a third party would come. . . .

[T]he movement has started. It has a following of nearly five millions; it will require me to overcome inertia. No man can call into being a new party; it will come from economic and biological forces. The people will have to learn to use the ballot as they use their hands and their brains to satisfy their wants. Morality does not change men's politics; my class cannot be brought to do justice; justice will come through the efforts of those to whom it is now denied. Justice has never been given to people; they have had to take it for themselves. From the beginning men have had to fight for equality of opportunity; they will have to fight for it, I believe, to the end.

ANNA HOWARD SHAW
1847–1919

Anna Howard Shaw pioneered in the ministry and medicine, as did Mary Jones in union organizing. Mother Jones believed that women did not need the vote "to raise hell"; Anna Howard Shaw found her life's work in woman suffrage.

Like Andrew Carnegie and Mary Antin, Anna Howard Shaw was an immigrant. Her parents were Scotch-English. Business reverses persuaded her father to emigrate from England to the United States. In 1851 her mother and six small children, including Anna, followed.

Anna Howard Shaw's trail-blazing began in the woods of Michigan. Her father, having staked a claim and built a cabin, returned to the East, leaving his family to cope alone in the wilderness for 18 months. When her father and brother joined the Union Army, Anna Howard Shaw became a chief sustainer of her mother and sisters. Freed from family responsibilities after their return, Anna Howard Shaw, eighteen years old and fired by energy and ambition, attended high school and college, graduated from divinity and medical schools, and became a successful preacher and lecturer. As a full-time suffrage activist, she served as vice-president of the National American Woman Suffrage Association from 1892 to 1904 and president from 1904 to 1915. During World War I, Shaw served as chairman of the Woman's Committee of the United States Council of National Defense and at the war's end, undertook a speaking tour on behalf of Woodrow Wilson's proposed League of Nations. Anna Howard Shaw died in 1919, knowing that Congress had finally passed the Nineteenth Amendment to enfranchise all American women.

The autobiography reveals both the best and the worst sides of the suffrage movement as it approached this final victory. Shaw described the courage, stamina, perseverance, and sense of humor which had sustained activists for women's rights through the decades after the 1848 Seneca Falls convention. At that convention, the vote was only one of many demands intended to guarantee women equality in all areas of life. The suffragists of Anna Howard Shaw's generation, however, had narrowed their focus: the vote had become the single most important goal. Her story also reveals the high moral price of success: to win support from Southern women, suffragists abandoned the commitment to racial justice out of which the first woman's movement had been born. As a child, Anna Howard Shaw herself had supported abolition.

The Story of A Pioneer *is aptly titled, for it suggests two significant, related themes of the book. It was hard to be a pioneer, to be the first to settle in the Michigan woods, to study at the theological school of Boston University, to stump for woman suffrage in South Dakota. It was hard also to be an intelligent, ambitious woman. The book makes clear connections between the author's personal life and her public advocacies. Relating her own hardships, injustices, and indignities, and those of her mother, and other women, was intended to explain her own thirty years of devotion to the suffrage movement and to advance what Anna Howard Shaw believed was "the great cause" of suffrage.*

The Story of A Pioneer. *New York and London: Harper and Brothers Publishers, 1915.*

[M]y father began to dream the great dream of those days. He would go to America. Surely, he felt, in that land of infinite promise all would be well with him and his. He waited for the final payment of his debts and for my younger sister's birth. Then he bade us good-by and sailed away to make an American home for us; and in the spring of 1851 my mother followed him with her six children, starting from Liverpool in a sailing-vessel, the *John Jacob Westervelt....*

We went to New Bedford with father, who had found work there at his old trade; and here I laid the foundations of my first childhood friendship, not with another child, but with my next-door neighbor, a ship-builder. Morning after morning this man swung me on his big shoulder and took me to his shipyard, where my hatchet and saw had violent exercise as I imitated the workers around me. Discovering that my tiny petticoats were in my way, my new friend had a little boy's suit made for me; and thus emancipated, at this tender age, I worked unwearyingly at his side all day long and day after day. No doubt it was due to him that I did not casually saw off a few of my toes and fingers. Certainly I smashed them often enough with blows of my dull but active hatchet. I was very, very busy; and I have always maintained that I began to earn my share of the family's living at the age of five—for in return for the delights of my society, which seemed never to pall upon him, my new friend allowed my brothers to carry home from the shipyard all the wood my mother could use.

We remained in New Bedford less than a year, for in the spring of 1852 my father made another change, taking his family to Lawrence, Massachusetts, where we lived until 1859. The years in Lawrence were interesting and formative ones. At the tender age of nine and ten I became interested in the Abolition movement....

[Her father decided to move the family to Michigan to establish a settlement and take up farming.]

Father preceded us to the Michigan woods, and there, with his oldest son, James, took up a claim. They cleared a space in the wilderness just large enough for a log cabin, and put up the bare walls of the cabin itself. Then father returned to Lawrence and his work, leaving James behind. A few months later (this was in 1859), my mother, my two sisters, Eleanor and Mary, my youngest brother,

ANNA HOWARD SHAW

Henry, eight years of age, and I, then twelve, went to Michigan to work on and hold down the claim while father, for eighteen months longer, stayed on in Lawrence, sending us such remittances as he could. His second and third sons, John and Thomas, remained in the East with him. . . .

We all had an idea that we were going to a farm, and we expected some resemblance at least to the prosperous farms we had seen in New England. My mother's mental picture was, naturally, of an English farm. Possibly she had visions of red barns and deep meadows, sunny skies and daisies. What we found awaiting us were the four walls and the roof of a good-sized log-house, standing in a small cleared strip of the wilderness, its doors and windows represented by square holes, its floor also a thing of the future, its whole effect achingly forlorn and desolate. It was late in the afternoon when we drove up to the opening that was its front entrance, and I shall never forget the look my mother turned upon the place. Without a word she crossed its threshold, and, standing very still, looked slowly around her. Then something within her seemed to give way, and she sank upon the ground. She could not realize even then, I think, that this was really the place father had prepared for us, that here he expected us to live. When she finally took it in she buried her face in her hands, and in that way she sat for hours without moving or speaking. For the first time in her life she had forgotten us; and we, for our part, dared not speak to her. We stood around her in a frightened group, talking to one another in whispers. Our little world had crumbled under our feet. Never before had we seen our mother give way to despair.

Night began to fall. The woods became alive with night creatures, and the most harmless made the most noise. The owls began to hoot, and soon we heard the wildcat, whose cry—a screech like that of a lost and panic-stricken child—is one of the most appalling sounds of the forest. Later the wolves added their howls to the uproar, but though darkness came and we children whimpered around her, our mother still sat in her strange lethargy.

At last my brother brought the horses close to the cabin and built fires to protect them and us. He was only twenty, but he showed himself a man during those early pioneer days. While he was picketing the horses and building us protecting fires my mother came to herself, but her face when she raised it was worse than her silence had been. She seemed to have died and to have returned to us from the grave, and I am sure she felt that she had done so. From that moment she took up again the burden of her life, a burden she did not lay down until she passed away; but her face never lost the deep lines those first hours of her pioneer life had cut upon it. . . .

We faced our situation with clear and unalarmed eyes the morning after our arrival. The problem of food, we knew, was at least temporarily solved. We had brought with us enough coffee, pork, and flour to last for several weeks; and the one necessity father had put inside the cabin walls was a great fireplace, made of mud and stones, in which our food could be cooked. The problem of our water-supply was less simple, but my brother James solved it for the time by showing us a creek a long distance from the house; and for months we carried from this creek, in pails, every drop of water we used, save that which we caught in troughs when the rain fell.

We held a family council after breakfast, and in this, though I was only twelve, I took an eager and determined part. I loved work—it has always been my favorite form of recreation—and my spirit rose to the opportunities of it which smiled on us from every side. . . .

During our first year there was no school within ten miles of us, but this lack failed to sadden Harry or me. We had brought with us from Lawrence a box of books, in which, in winter months, when our outdoor work was restricted, we found much comfort. They were the only books in that part of the country, and we read them until we knew them all by heart. Moreover, father sent us regularly the *New York Independent,* and with this admirable literature, after reading it, we papered our walls. Thus, on stormy days, we could lie on the settle or the floor and read the *Independent* over again with increased interest and pleasure.

Occasionally father sent us the *Ledger,* but here mother drew a definite line. She had a special dislike for that periodical, and her severest comment on any woman was that she was the type who would "keep a dog, make saleratus biscuit, and read the *New York Ledger* in the daytime." Our modest library also contained several histories of Greece and Rome, which must have been good ones, for years later, when I entered college, I passed my examination in ancient history with no other preparation than this reading. There were also a few arithmetics and algebras, a historical novel or two, and the inevitable copy of *Uncle Tom's Cabin,* whose pages I had freely moistened with my tears. . . .

Father joined us at the end of eighteen months, but though his presence gave us pleasure and moral support, he was not an addition to our executive staff. He brought with him a rocking-chair for mother and a new supply of books, on which I fell as a starving man falls upon food. Father read as eagerly as I, but much more steadily. His mind was always busy with problems, and if, while he was laboring in the field, a new problem presented itself to him, the imperishable curiosity that was in him made him scurry at once to the house to solve it. I have known him to spend a planting season in figuring on the production of a certain number of kernels of corn, instead of planting the corn and raising it. In the winter he was supposed to spend his time clearing land for orchards and the like, but instead he pored over his books and problems day after day and often half the night as well. It soon became known among our neighbors, who were rapidly increasing in number, that we had books and that father liked to read aloud, and men walked ten miles or more to spend the night with us and listen to his reading. Often, as his fame grew, ten or twelve men would arrive at our cabin on Saturday and remain over Sunday. When my mother once tried to check this influx of guests by mildly pointing out, among other things, the waste of candles represented by frequent all-night readings, every man humbly appeared again on the following Saturday with a candle in each hand. They were not sensitive; and, as they had brought their candles, it seemed fitting to them and to father that we girls should cook for them and supply them with food.

Father's tolerance of idleness in others, however, did not extend to tolerance of idleness in us, and this led to my first rebellion, which occurred when I was fourteen. For once, I had been in the woods all day, buried in my books; and when I returned at night, still in the dream world these books had opened to me, father was awaiting my coming with a brow dark with disapproval. As it happened, mother had felt that day some special need of me, and father reproached me bitterly for being beyond reach—an idler who wasted time while mother labored. He ended a long arraignment by predicting gloomily that with such tendencies I would make nothing of my life.

The injustice of the criticism cut deep; I knew I had done and was doing my share for the family, and already, too, I had begun to feel the call of my career. For some reason I wanted to preach—to talk to people, to tell them things. Just why, just what, I did not yet know—but I had begun to preach in the silent woods, to stand up on stumps and address the unresponsive trees, to feel the stir of aspiration within me.

When my father had finished all he wished to say, I looked at him and answered, quietly, "Father, some day I am going to college."

I can still see his slight, ironical smile. It drove me to a second prediction. I was young enough to measure success by material results, so I added, recklessly:

"And before I die I shall be worth ten thousand dollars!"

The amount staggered me even as it dropped from my lips. It was the largest fortune my imagination could conceive, and in my heart I believed that no woman ever had possessed or would possess so much. So far as I knew, too, no woman had gone to college. But now that I had put my secret hopes into words, I was desperately determined to make those hopes come true. After I became a wage-earner I lost my desire to make a fortune, but the college dream grew with the years; and though my college career seemed as remote as the most distant star, I hitched my little wagon to that star and never afterward wholly lost sight of its friendly gleam.

When I was fifteen years old I was offered a situation as school-teacher. By this time the community was growing around us with the rapidity characteristic of these Western settlements, and we had nearer neighbors whose children needed instruction. I passed an examination before a schoolboard consisting of three nervous and self-conscious men whose certificate I still hold, and I at once began my professional career on the modest salary of two dollars a week and my board. The school was four miles from my home, so I "boarded round" with the families of my pupils, staying two weeks in each place, and often walking from three to six miles a day to and from my little log school-house in every kind of weather. During the first year I had about fourteen pupils, of varying ages, sizes, and temperaments, and there was hardly a book in the school-room except those I owned. One little girl, I remember, read from an almanac, while a second used a hymn-book. . . .

[When the Civil War began, Shaw's father and two brothers volunteered for the Union Army. Shaw, her mother, and her sisters were left to support themselves. When the war ended, Shaw decided that she must pursue her dream of going to college. She moved to Grand Rapids, where she lived with her sister and entered high school.]

I took part in all our debates, recited yards of poetry to any audience we could attract, and even shone mildly in our amateur theatricals. It was probably owing to all this activity that I attracted the interest of the presiding elder of our district—Dr. Peck, a man of progressive ideas. There was at that time a movement on foot to license women to preach in the Methodist Church, and Dr. Peck was ambitious to be the first presiding elder to have a woman ordained for the Methodist ministry. . . .

[At Dr. Peck's request, Shaw preached her first sermon.]

There was no church in Ashton, so I preached my sermon in its one little school-house, which was filled with a curious crowd, eager to look at and hear the girl who was defying all conventions by getting out of the pew and into the pulpit. There was much whispering and suppressed excitement before I began, but when I gave out my text silence fell upon the room, and from that moment until I had finished my hearers listened quietly. A kerosene-lamp stood on a stand at my elbow, and as I preached I trembled so violently that the oil shook in its glass globe; but I finished without breaking down, and at the end Dr. Peck, who had his own reasons for nervousness, handsomely assured me that my first sermon was better than his maiden effort had been. It was evidently not a failure, for the next day he invited me to follow him around in his circuit, which included thirty-six appointments; he wished me to preach in each of the thirty-six places, as it was desirable to let the various ministers hear and know me before I applied for my license as a local preacher. . . .

[In fall 1873, at age 25, she entered Albion College in Albion, Michigan. She supported herself for two years by preaching and lecturing on temperance. Rather than continue her undergraduate education, however, she decided to enter the theological school of Boston University in 1876.]

I went through some grim months in Boston—months during which I learned what it was to go to bed cold and hungry, to wake up cold and hungry, and to have no knowledge of how long these conditions might continue. But not more than once or twice during the struggle there, and then only for an hour or two in the physical and mental depression attending malnutrition, did I regret coming. At that period in my life I believed that the Lord had my small personal affairs very much on His mind. If I starved and froze it was His test of my worthiness for the ministry, and if He had really chosen me for one of His servants, He would see me through. The faith that sustained me then has still a place in my life, and existence without it would be an infinitely more dreary affair than it is. But I admit that I now call upon the Lord less often and less imperatively than I did before the stern years taught me my unimportance in the great scheme of things.

My class at the theological school was composed of forty-two young men and my unworthy self, and before I had been a member of it an hour I realized that women theologians paid heavily for the privilege of being women. The young men of my class who were licensed preachers were given free accommodations in the dormitory, and their board, at a club formed for their assistance, cost each of them only one dollar and twenty-five cents a week. For me no such kindly provision was made. I was not allowed a place in the dormitory, but instead was given two dollars a week to pay the rent of a room outside. Neither was I admitted to the economical comforts of the club, but fed myself according to my income, a plan which worked admirably when there was an income, but left an obvious void when there was not.

With characteristic optimism, however, I hired a little attic room on Tremont Street and established myself therein. In lieu of a window the room offered a pale skylight to the February storms, and there was neither heat in it nor running water; but its possession gave me a pleasant sense of proprietorship, and the whole experience seemed a high adventure. I at once sought opportunities to preach and lecture, but these were even rarer than firelight and food. In Albion I had been practically the only licensed preacher available for substitute and special work. In Boston University's three theological classes there were a hundred men, each snatching eagerly at the slightest possibility of employment; and when, despite this competition, I received and responded to an invitation to preach, I never knew whether I was to be paid for my services in cash or in compliments. If, by a happy chance, the compensation came in cash, the amount was rarely more than five dollars, and never more than ten. There was no help in sight from my family, whose early opposition to my career as a minister had hotly flamed forth again when I started East. I lived, therefore, on milk and crackers, and for weeks at a time my hunger was never wholly satisfied. In my home in the wilderness I had often heard the wolves prowling around our door at night. Now, in Boston, I heard them even at high noon. . . .

[Financial support from an anonymous benefactor allowed her to finish her degree. After her graduation in 1878, she spent seven years as the pastor of two churches in East Dennis, Massachusetts. Refused ordination by the Methodist Episcopal Church, Shaw was ordained in 1880 by the Methodist Protestant Church. In 1882 she entered the medical school of Boston University and in 1885 received her medical degree.]

There is a theory that every seven years each human being undergoes a complete physical reconstruction, with corresponding changes in his mental and spiritual make-up. Possibly it was due to this reconstruction that, at the end of seven years on Cape Cod, my soul sent forth a sudden call to arms. I was, it reminded me, taking life too easily; I was in danger of settling into an agreeable routine. The work of my two churches made little drain on my superabundant vitality, and not even the winning of a medical degree and the increasing demands of my activities on the lecture platform wholly eased my conscience. I was happy, for I loved my people and they seemed to love me. It would have been pleasant to go on almost indefinitely, living the life of a country minister and telling myself that what I could give to my flock made such a life worth while.

But all the time, deep in my heart, I realized the needs of the outside world, and heard its prayer for workers. My theological and medical courses in Boston, with the experiences that accompanied them, had greatly widened my horizon. Moreover, at my invitation, many of the noble women of the day were coming to East Dennis to lecture, bringing with them the stirring atmosphere of the conflicts they were waging. One of the first of these was my friend Mary A. Livermore; and after her came Julia Ward Howe, Anna Garlin Spencer, Lucy Stone, Mary F. Eastman, and many others, each charged with inspiration for my people and with a special message for me, which she sent forth unknowingly and which I alone heard. They were fighting great battles, these women—for suffrage, for temperance, for social purity—and in every word they uttered I heard a rallying-cry. So it was that, in 1885, I suddenly pulled myself up to a radical decision and sent my resignation to the trustees of the two churches whose pastor I had been since 1878. . . .

We were entering upon a deeply significant period. For the first time women were going into industrial competition with men, and already men were intensely resenting their presence. Around me I saw women overworked and underpaid, doing men's work at half men's wages, not because their work was inferior, but because they were women. Again, too, I studied the obtrusive problems of the poor and of the women of the streets; and, looking at the whole social situation from every angle, I could find but one solution for women—the removal of the stigma of disfranchisement. As man's equal before the law, woman could demand her rights, asking favors from no one. With all my heart I joined in the crusade of the men and women who were fighting for her. My real work had begun. . . .

[She supported herself by lecturing on temperance and suffrage, experiencing the difficulties of life on the lecture circuit.]

To drive fifty or sixty miles in a day to meet a lecture engagement was a frequent experience. I have been driven across the prairies in June when they were like a mammoth flower-bed, and in January when they seemed one huge snow-covered grave—my grave, I thought, at times. Once during a thirty-mile drive, when the thermometer was twenty degrees below zero, I suddenly realized that my face was freezing. I opened my satchel, took out the tissue-paper that protected my best gown, and put the paper over my face as a veil, tucking it inside of my bonnet. When I reached my destination the tissue was a perfect mask, frozen stiff, and I had to be lifted from the sleigh. I was due on the lecture platform in half an hour, so I drank a huge bowl of boiling ginger tea and appeared on time. That night I went to bed expecting an attack of pneumonia as a result of the exposure, but I awoke next morning in superb condition. I possess what is called "an iron constitution," and in those days I needed it. . . .

[In 1890 the suffrage movement gained new strength from the establishment of the National American Woman's Suffrage Association by the merger of the American Woman's Suffrage Association and the more radical National Woman's Suffrage Association, which had been founded by Elizabeth Cady Stanton and Susan B. Anthony. Anthony became Shaw's mentor and beloved companion, and for several years they campaigned together for women's suffrage.]

The winning of the suffrage states, the work in the states not yet won, the conventions, gatherings, and international councils in which women of every nation have come together, have all combined to make this quarter of a century the most brilliant period for women in the history of the world. I have set forth the record baldly and without comment, because the bare facts are far more eloquent than words. It must not be forgotten, too, that these great achievements of the progressive women of to-day have been accomplished against the opposition of a large number of their own sex—who, while they are out in the world's arena fighting against progress for their sisters, still shatter the ear-drum with their incongruous war-cry, "Woman's place is in the home!"

Of our South Dakota campaign in 1890 there remains only one incident which should have a place here: We were attending the Republican state nominating convention at Mitchell—Miss Anthony, Mrs. [Carrie Chapman] Catt, other leaders, and myself—having been told that it would be at once the largest and the most interesting gathering ever held in the state—as it proved to be. All the leading politicians of the state were there, and in the wake of the white men had come tribes of Indians with their camp outfits, their wives and their children—the groups forming a picturesque circle of tents and tepees around the town. It was a great occasion for them, an Indian powwow, for by the law all Indians who had lands in severalty were to be permitted to vote the following year. They were present, therefore, to study the ways of the white man, and an edifying exhibition of these was promptly offered them.

The crowd was so great that it was only through the courtesy of Major Pickler, a member of Congress and a devoted believer in suffrage, that Miss Anthony, Mrs. Catt, and the rest of us were able to secure passes to the convention, and when we reached the hall we were escorted to the last row of seats on the crowded platform. As the space between us and the speakers was filled by rows upon rows of men, as well as by the band and their instruments, we could see very little that took place. Some of our friends pointed out this condition to the local committee and asked that we be given seats on the floor, but received the reply that there was "absolutely no room on the floor except for delegates and distinguished visitors." Our persistent friends then suggested that at least a front seat should be given to Miss Anthony, who certainly came under the head of a "distinguished visitor"; but this was not done—probably because a large number of the best seats were filled by Russian laborers wearing badges inscribed "Against Woman Suffrage and Susan B. Anthony." We remained, perforce, in our rear seats, finding such interest as we could in the back view of hundreds of heads.

Just before the convention was called to order it was announced that a delegation of influential Indians was waiting outside, and a motion to invite the red men into the hall was made and carried with great enthusiasm. A committee of leading citizens was appointed to act as escort, and these gentlemen filed out, returning a few moments later with a party of Indian warriors in full war regalia, even to their gay blankets, their feathered head-dresses, and their paint. When they appeared the band struck up a stirring march of welcome, and the entire audience cheered while the Indians, flanked by the admiring committee, stalked solemnly down the aisle and were given seats of honor directly in front of the platform.

All we could see of them were the brilliant feathers of their war-bonnets, but we got the full effect of their reception in the music and the cheers. I dared not look at Miss Anthony during this remarkable scene, and she, craning her venerable neck to get a glimpse of the incident from her obscure corner, made no comment to me; but I knew what she was thinking. The following year these Indians would have votes. Courtesy, therefore, must be shown them. But the women did not matter, the politicians reasoned, for even if they were enfranchised they would never support the element represented at that convention. It was not surprising that, notwithstanding our hard work, we did not win the state, though all the conditions had seemed most favorable; for the state was new, the men and women were working side by side in the fields, and there was discontent in the ranks of the political parties.

After the election, when we analyzed the vote county by county, we discovered that in every county whose residents were principally Americans the amendment was carried, whereas in all counties populated largely by foreigners it was lost. In certain counties—those inhabited by Russian Jews—the vote was almost solidly against us, and this notwithstanding the fact that the wives of these Russian voters were doing a man's work on their farms in addition to the usual women's work in their homes. The fact that our Cause could be defeated by ignorant laborers newly come to our country was a humiliating one to accept; and we realized more forcibly than ever before the difficulty of the task we had assumed—a

task far beyond any ever undertaken by a body of men in the history of democratic government throughout the world. We not only had to bring American men
back to a belief in the fundamental principles of republican government, but
we had also to educate ignorant immigrants, as well as our own Indians, whose
degree of civilization was indicated by their war-paint and the flaunting feathers of
their head-dresses. . . .

The interval between the winning of Idaho and Utah in 1896 and that of Washington in 1910 seemed very long to lovers of the Cause. We were working as hard
as ever—harder, indeed, for the opposition against us was growing stronger as
our opponents realized what triumphant woman suffrage would mean to the
underworld, the grafters, and the whited sepulchers in public office. But in
1910 we were cheered by our Washington victory, followed the next year by
the winning of California. Then, with our splendid banner year of 1912 came the
winning of three states—Arizona, Kansas, and Oregon—preceded by a campaign so full of vim and interest that it must have its brief chronicle here.

To begin, we conducted in 1912 the largest number of campaigns we had ever
undertaken, working in six states in which constitutional amendments were
pending—Ohio, Michigan, Wisconsin, Oregon, Arizona, and Kansas. Personally, I began my work in Ohio in August, with the modest aspiration of speaking
in each of the principal towns in every one of these states. In Michigan I had the
invaluable assistance of Mrs. Lawrence Lewis, of Philadelphia, and I visited at
this time the region of my old home, greatly changed since the days of my girl-
hood, and talked to the old friends and neighbors who had turned out in force to
welcome me. They showed their further interest in the most satisfactory way, by
carrying the amendment in their part of the state.

At least four and five speeches a day were expected, and as usual we traveled
in every sort of conveyance, from freight-cars to eighty horse-power French automobiles. In Eau Clair, Wisconsin, I spoke at the races immediately after the
passing of a procession of cattle. At the end of the procession rode a woman in an
ox-cart, to represent pioneer days. She wore a calico gown and a sunbonnet, and
drove her ox-team with genuine skill; and the last touch to the picture she made
was furnished by the presence of a beautiful biplane which whirred lightly in the
air above her. The obvious comparison was too good to ignore, so I told my
hearers that their women to-day were still riding in ox-teams while the men soared
in the air, and that women's work in the world's service could be properly done
only when they too were allowed to fly.

In Oregon we were joined by Miss Lucy Anthony. There, at Pendleton, I
spoke during the great "round up," holding the meeting at night on the street, in
which thousands of horsemen—cowboys, Indians, and ranchmen—were riding
up and down, blowing horns, shouting, and singing. It seemed impossible to
interest an audience under such conditions, but evidently the men liked variety,
for when we began to speak they quieted down and closed around us until we had
an audience that filled the streets in every direction and as far as our voices could
reach. Never have we had more courteous or enthusiastic listeners than those wild
and happy horsemen. Best of all, they not only cheered our sentiments, but they
followed up their cheers with their votes. I spoke from an automobile, and when
I had finished one of the cowboys rode close to me and asked for my New York
address. "You will hear from me later," he said, when he had made a note of it.
In time I received a great linen banner, on which he made a superb pen-and-ink
sketch of himself and his horse, and in every corner sketches of scenes in the

different states where women voted, together with drawings of all the details of cowboy equipment. Over these were drawn the words:

Woman Suffrage—We are all for it.

The banner hangs to-day in the National Headquarters. . . .

Under the gracious direction of Miss Kate Gordon and the Louisiana Woman Suffrage Association, we held an especially inspiring convention in New Orleans in 1903. In no previous convention were arrangements more perfect, and certainly nowhere else did the men of a community co-operate more generously with the women in entertaining us. A club of men paid the rent of our hall, chartered a steamboat and gave us a ride on the Mississippi, and in many other ways helped to make the occasion a success. Miss Gordon, who was chairman of the programme committee, introduced the innovation of putting me before the audience for twenty minutes every evening, at the close of the regular session, as a target for questions. Those present were privileged to ask any questions they pleased, and I answered them—if I could.

We were all conscious of the dangers attending a discussion of the negro question, and it was understood among the Northern women that we must take every precaution to avoid being led into such discussion. It had not been easy to persuade Miss Anthony of the wisdom of this course; her way was to face issues squarely and out in the open. But she agreed that we must respect the convictions of the Southern men and women who were entertaining us so hospitably.

On the opening night, as I took my place to answer questions, almost the first slip passed up bore these words:

> What is your purpose in bringing your convention to the South? Is it the desire of suffragists to force upon us the social equality of black and white women? Political equality lays the foundation for social equality. If you give the ballot to women, won't you make the black and white woman equal politically and therefore lay the foundation for a future claim of social equality?

I laid the paper on one side and did not answer the question. The second night it came to me again, put in the same words, and again I ignored it. The third night it came with this addition:

> Evidently you do not dare to answer this question. Therefore our conclusion is that this is your purpose.

When I had read this I went to the front of the platform.

"Here," I said, "is a question which has been asked me on three successive nights. I have not answered it because we Northern women had decided not to enter into any discussion of the race question. But now I am told by the writer of this note that we dare not answer it. I wish to say that we dare to answer it if you dare to have it answered—and I leave it to you to decide whether I shall answer it or not."

I read the question aloud. Then the audience called for the answer, and I gave it in these words, quoted as accurately as I can remember them:

"If political equality is the basis of social equality, and if by granting political equality you lay the foundation for a claim of social equality, I can only answer that you have already laid that claim. You did not wait for woman suffrage, but disfranchised both your black and your white women, thus making them politically equal. But you have done more than that. You have put the ballot into the hands of your black men, thus making them the political superiors of your white women. Never before in the history of the world have men made former slaves the political masters of their former mistresses!"

The point went home and it went deep. I drove it in a little further.

"The women of the South are not alone," I said, "in their humiliation. All the women of America share it with them. There is no other nation in the world in which women hold the position of political degradation our American women hold to-day. German women are governed by German men; French women are governed by French men. But in these United States American women are governed by every race of men under the light of the sun. There is not a color from white to black, from red to yellow, there is not a nation from pole to pole, that does not send its contingent to govern American women. If American men are willing to leave their women in a position as degrading as this they need not be surprised when American women resolve to lift themselves out of it."

For a full moment after I had finished there was absolute silence in the audience. We did not know what would happen. Then, suddenly, as the truth of the statement struck them, the men began to applaud—and the danger of that situation was over. . . .

[In 1904 Shaw was chosen president of the National American Woman's Suffrage Association.]

In looking back over the ten years of my administration as president of the National American Woman Suffrage Association, there can be no feeling but gratitude and elation over the growth of the work. Our membership has grown from 17,000 women to more than 200,000 and the number of auxiliary societies has increased in proportion.

Instead of the old-time experience of one campaign in ten years, we now have from five to ten campaigns each year. From an original yearly expenditure of $14,000 or $15,000 in our campaign work, we now expend from $40,000 to $50,000. In New York, in 1915, we have already received pledges of $150,000 for the New York State campaign alone, while Pennsylvania, Massachusetts, and New Jersey have made pledges in proportion.

In 1906 full suffrage prevailed in four states; we now have it in twelve. Our movement has advanced from its academic stage until it has become a vital political factor; no reform in the country is more heralded by the press or receives more attention from the public. It has become an issue which engages the attention of the entire nation—and toward this result every woman working for the Cause has contributed to an inspiring degree. Splendid team-work, and that alone, has made our present success possible and our eventual triumph in every state inevitable. Every officer in our organization, every leader in our campaigns, every speaker, every worker in the ranks, however humble, has done her share.

I do not claim anything so fantastic and Utopian as universal harmony among us. We have had our troubles and our differences. I have had mine. At every annual convention since the one at Washington in 1910 there has been an effort to depose me from the presidency. There have been some splendid fighters among my opponents—fine and high-minded women who sincerely believe that at sixty-eight I am getting too old for my big job. Possibly I am. Certainly I shall resign it with alacrity when the majority of women in the organization wish me to do so. At present a large majority proves annually that it still has faith in my leadership, and with this assurance I am content to work on.

Looking back over the period covered by these reminiscences, I realize that there is truth in the grave charge that I am no longer young; and this truth was once voiced by one of my little nieces in a way that brought it strongly home to me. She and her small sister of six had declared themselves suffragettes, and as the first result of their conversion to the Cause both had been laughed at by their schoolmates. The younger child came home after this tragic experience, weeping bitterly and declaring that she did not wish to be a suffragette any more—an exhibition of apostasy for which her wise sister of eight took her roundly to task.

"Aren't you ashamed of yourself," she demanded, "to stop just because you have been laughed at once? Look at Aunt Anna! *She* has been laughed at for hundreds of years!"

I sometimes feel that it has indeed been hundreds of years since my work began; and then again it seems so brief a time that, by listening for a moment, I fancy I can hear the echo of my childish voice preaching to the trees in the Michigan woods.

But long or short, the one sure thing is that, taking it all in all, the struggles, the discouragements, the failures, and the little victories, the fight has been, as Susan B. Anthony said in her last hours, "worth while." Nothing bigger can come to a human being than to love a great Cause more than life itself, and to have the privilege throughout life of working for that Cause.

As for life's other gifts, I have had some of them, too. I have made many friendships; I have looked upon the beauty of many lands; I have the assurance of the respect and affection of thousands of men and women I have never even met. Though I have given all I had, I have received a thousand times more than I have given. Neither the world nor my Cause is indebted to me—but from the depths of a full and very grateful heart I acknowledge my lasting indebtedness to them both.

WOODROW WILSON GUTHRIE
1912–1967

Woody Guthrie became a folk hero and gave voice to those down on their luck. He searched for life among the nation's common men and women in the hobo camps, skid rows, and Hoovervilles where people dispossessed by the Great Depression congregated to find work and gain strength from others who understood their plight.

Born in Okemah, Oklahoma, during the oil boom, Guthrie, after the oil bust of 1927, left home to find work. He ended up seeing the country. In the words of his most famous song, he went "from California to the New York Islands." He thumbed, hopped freight trains, and walked his way through backwater towns and glittering cities.

As the Great Depression entered its cruelest years in 1932 and 1933 with over 30 million people desperate for relief, Guthrie listened to the stories of the homeless and wrote over a thousand songs inspired by their courage and patriotism. Some of these populist ballads would be adapted as protest and hope songs during the civil rights movement of the 1960s. They are timeless renditions of faith in America even during the worst of times.

Bound for Glory, *Guthrie's story, serves, as does Black Elk's, to give voice to a people whose education and circumstances prevented them from gaining a louder hearing elsewhere. But unlike Black Elk, Guthrie could write in his optimistic collective autobiography that the people he knew as well as the country he loved were "bound for glory." John Steinbeck had ended his story about these same people,* The Grapes of Wrath, *with a further slip into poverty; Guthrie, with the knowledge that World War II was providing jobs for everyone, could reverse that judgment.*

He married twice and had five children, including folksinger Arlo Guthrie. In Los Angeles in 1941 he defended a group of Japanese-Americans from a racist mob angry about Pearl Harbor. In 1943, as part of the war effort, he joined the merchant marine. Afterward he sang with Pete Seeger, compiled a book called American Folksong, *and published a book of poetry,* Born to Win. *He died after thirteen years of hospitalization fighting a degenerative nerve disease.*

He was in a Brooklyn hospital when Vietnam veteran Ron Kovic was in nearby hospitals in Queens, then the Bronx. At the same time, Anne Moody was working for victims of historical racism in Mississippi. Their autobiographies call attention to the disparity between American dreams and the American reality.

Bound for Glory. *New York: E. P. Dutton & Co., Inc., 1943.*
(Reprinted with permission.)

Okemah was an Oklahoma farming town since the early days, and it had about an equal number of Indians, Negroes, and Whites doing their trading there. It had a railroad called the Fort Smith and Western—and there was no guarantee that you'd get any certain place any certain time by riding it. Our most famous railroad man was called "Boomer Swenson," and every time Boomer come to a spot along the rails where he'd run over somebody, he'd pull down on his whistle cord and blow the longest, moaningest, saddest whistle that ever blew on any man's railroad.

Ours was just another one of those little towns, I guess, about a thousand or so people, where everybody knows everybody else; and on your way to the post office, you'd nod and speak to so many friends that your neck would be rubbed raw when you went in to get your mail if there was any. It took you just about an hour to get up through town, say hello, talk over the late news, family gossip, sickness, weather, crops and lousy politics. Everybody had something to say about something, or somebody, and you usually knew almost word for word what it was going to be about before you heard them say it, as we had well-known and highly expert talkers on all subjects in and out of this world. . . .

I was what you'd call just a home-town kid and carved my initials on most everything that would stand still and let me. W. G. Okemah Boy. Born 1912. That was the year, I think, when Woodrow Wilson was named to be the president and my papa and mama got all worked up about good and bad politics and named me Woodrow Wilson too. I don't remember this any too clear.

I wasn't much more than two years old when we built our seven-room house over in the good part of Okemah. This was our new house, and Mama was awful glad and proud of it. I remember a bright yellow outside—a blurred haze of a dark inside—some vines looking in through windows.

Sometimes, I seem to remember trying to follow my big sister off to school. I'd gather up all of the loose books I could find around the house and start out through the gate and down the sidewalk, going to get myself a schoolhouse education, but Mama would run out and catch me and drag me back into the house kicking and bawling. When Mama would hide the books I'd walk back to the front porch, afraid to run away, but I'd use the porch for my stage, and the grass, flowers, and pickets along our fence would be my crowd of people; and I made up my first song right there:

> Listen to the music,
> Music, music;
> Listen to the music,
> Music band.

These days our family seemed to be getting along all right. People rode down our street in buggies and sarries, all dressed up, and they'd look over at our house and say, "Charlie and Nora Guthrie's place." "Right new."

Clara was somewhere between nine and ten, but she seemed like an awful big sister to me. She was always bending and whirling around, dancing away to school and singing her way back home; and she had long curls that swung in the wind and brushed in my face when she wrestled me across the floor.

WOODROW WILSON GUTHRIE

Roy was along in there between seven and eight. Quiet about everything. Walked so slow and thought so deep that I always wondered what was going on in his head. I watched him biff the tough kids on the noodle over the fence, and then he would just come on in home, and think and think about it. I wondered how he could fight so good and keep so quiet.

I guess I was going on three then.

Peace, pretty weather. Spring turning things green. Summer staining it all brown. Fall made everything redder, browner, and brittler. And winter was white and gray and the color of bare trees. Papa went to town and made real-estate deals with other people, and he brought their money home. Mama could sign a check for any amount, buy every little thing that her eyes liked the looks of. Roy and Clara could stop off in any store in Okemah and buy new clothes to fit the weather, new things to eat to make you healthy, and Papa was proud because we could all have anything we saw. Our house was packed full of things Mama liked, Roy liked, Clara liked, and that was what Papa liked. I remember his leather law books, Blackstone and others. He smoked a pipe and good tobacco and I wondered if this helped him to stretch out in his big easy-riding chair and try to think up some kind of a deal or swap to get some more money.

But those were fighting days in Oklahoma. If even the little newskids fought along the streets for corroded pennies, it's not hard to see that Papa had to outwit, outsmart, and outrun a pretty long string of people to have everything so nice. It kept Mama scared and nervous. She always had been a serious person with deep-running thoughts in her head; and the old songs and ballads that she sung over and over every day told me just about what she was thinking about. And they told Papa, but he didn't listen. She used to say to us kids, "We love your Papa, and if anything tries to hurt him and make him bad and mean, we'll fight it, won't we?" And Roy would jump up and pound his fist on his chest and say, "I'll fight!" Mama knew how dangerous the landtrading business was, and she wanted Papa to drop out of the fighting and the pushing, and settle down to some kind of a better life of growing things and helping other people to grow. But Papa was a man of brimstone and hot fire, in his mind and in his fists, and was known all over that section of the state as the champion of all the fist fighters. He used his fists on sharks and fakers, and all to give his family nice things. Mama was that kind of a woman who always looked at a pretty thing and wondered, "Who had to work to make it? Who owned it and loved it before?"

So our family was sort of divided up into two sides: Mama taught us kids to sing the old songs and told us long stories about each ballad; and in her own way she told us over and over to always try and see the world from the other fellow's side. Meanwhile Papa bought us all kinds of exercising rods and stretchers, and kept piles of kids boxing and wrestling out in the front yard; and taught us never and never to allow any earthly human to scare us, bully us, or run it over us. . . .

[After a fire destroyed their home, his family moved into a house none of them liked and his mother slowly slipped into depression and mental illness. After a cyclone wrecked this house and they relocated in Okemah, a town losing its small town atmosphere as it became an oil boom town, Woody's sister Clara died in a house fire.]

For a while it looked like trouble had made us closer friends with everybody, had drawn our whole family together and made us know each other better. But before long it was plainer than ever that it had been the breaking point for my mother.

She got worse, and lost control of the muscles in her body; and two or three times a day she would have bad spells of epileptics, first getting angry at things in the house, then arguing at every stick of furniture in every room until she would be talking so loud that all of the neighbors heard and wondered about it. I noticed that every day she would spend a minute or two staring at a lump of melted glass crystals, a door stop about as big as your two fists, and she told me, "Before our new six-room house burned down, this was a twenty-dollar cut-glass casserole. It was a present, and it was as pretty as I used to be. But now look how it looks, all crazy, all out of shape. It don't reflect pretty colors any more like it used to—it's all twisted, like everything pretty gets twisted, like my whole life is twisted. God, I want to die! I want to die! Now! Now! Now! Now!"

And she broke furniture and dishes to pieces.

She had always been one of the prettiest women in our part of the country: long black wavy hair that she combed and brushed for several minutes twice or three times a day, medium weight, round and healthy face and big dark eyes. She rode a one-hundred-dollar sidesaddle on a fast-stepping black horse; and Papa would ride along beside her on a light-foot pacing white mare. People said, "In them days your pa and ma made a mighty pretty picture," but there was a look in people's eyes like they was just talking about a pretty movie that come through town.

Mama had things on her mind. Troubles. She thought about them too much, or didn't fight back. Maybe she didn't know. Maybe she had faith in something that you can't see, something that would cause it all to come back, the house, the lands, the good furniture, the part-time maid, and the car to drive around the country. She concentrated on her worries until it got the best of her. The doctor said it would. He said for her to get up and run away, for us to take her to a place, a land somewhere where there wouldn't be any worries. She got to where she would shriek at the top of her voice and talk for hours on end about things that had went wrong. She didn't know where to put the blame. She turned on Papa. She thought he was to blame.

The whole town knew about her. She got careless with her appearance. She let herself run down. She walked around over the town, looking and thinking and crying. The doctor called it insanity and let it go at that. She lost control of the muscles of her face. Us kids would stand around in the house lost in silence, not saying a word for hours, and ashamed, somehow, to go out down the street and play with the kids, and wanting to stay there and see how long her spell would last, and if we could help her. She couldn't control her arms, nor her legs, nor the muscles in her body, and she would go into spasms and fall on the floor, and wallow around through the house, and ruin her clothes, and yell till people blocks up the street could hear her.

She would be all right for a while and treat us kids as good as any mother, and all at once it would start in—something bad and awful—something would start coming over her, and it come by slow degrees. Her face would twitch and her lips would snarl and her teeth would show. Spit would run out of her mouth and she would start out in a low grumbling voice and gradually get to talking as loud as her throat could stand it; and her arms would draw up at her sides, then behind her back, and swing in all kinds of curves. Her stomach would draw up into a hard ball, and she would double over into a terrible-looking hunch—and turn into another person, it looked like, standing right there before Roy and me.

I used to go to sleep at night and have dreams; it seemed like I dreamed the whole thing out. I dreamed that my mama was just like anybody else's. I saw her talking, smiling, and working just like other kids' mamas. But when I woke up it would still be all wrong, all twisted out of shape, helter-skelter, let go, the house not kept, the cooking skipped, the dishes not washed. Oh, Roy and me tried, I guess. We would take spells of working the house over, but I was only about nine years old, Roy about fifteen. Other things, things that kids of that age do, games they play, places they go, swimming holes, playing, running, laughing— we drifted into those things just to try to forget for a minute that a cyclone had hit our home, and how it was ripping and tearing away our family, and scattering it in the wind.

I hate a hundred times more to describe my own mother in any such words as these. You hate to read about a mother described in any such words as these. I know. I understand you. I hope you can understand me, for it must be broke down and said.

We had to move out of the house. Papa didn't have no money, so he couldn't pay the rent. He went down fighting, but he went right on down. He was a lost man in a lost world. Lost everything. Lost every cent. Owed ten times more than he could ever pay. Never could get caught up again, and get strung out down the road to success. He didn't know that. He still believed that he could start out on a peanut hull and fight his way back into the ten-thousand-dollar oil deals, the farms, and ranchlands, the royalties, and the leases, changing hands every day. I'll cut it short by saying that he fought back, but he didn't make the grade. He was down and out. No good to them. The big boys. They wouldn't back him. He went down and he stayed down.

We didn't want to send Mama away. It would be better some other place. We'd go off and start all over. So in 1923 we packed up and moved away to Oklahoma City. . . .

> [After a year of living hand to mouth with no job prospects, the Guthries moved back to Okemah. The oil wells were dry and bust had replaced boom. His father was badly burned in yet another house fire and went to Texas to recuperate. His mother was committed to an insane asylum. Woody lived on the streets for a few months with his brother Roy.]

I was thirteen when I went to live with a family of thirteen people in a two-room house. I was going on fifteen when I got me a job shining shoes, washing spittoons, meeting the night trains in a hotel up in town. I was a little past sixteen when I first hit the highway and took a trip down around the Gulf of Mexico, hoeing figs, watering strawberries, picking mustang grapes, helping carpenters and well drillers, cleaning yards, chopping weeds, and moving garbage cans. Then I got tired of being a stranger, so I stuck my thumb in the air again and landed back in the old home town, Okemah.

I found me a job at five dollars a week in a push-button service station. I got a letter twice a week as regular as a clock from Papa out on the Texas plains. I told him everything I thought and he told me everything he was hoping. Then, one day, he wrote that his burns had healed up enough for him to go to work, and he'd got him a job managing a whole block of property in Pampa, Texas.

In three days I was standing in the little office shaking his hand, talking old times, and all about my job with him as general handyman around the property. I was just past my seventeenth birthday. . . .

Lots of folks in the oil fields come in from the country. They heard about the high wages and the great number of jobs. The old farm has dried up and blowed away. The chickens are gone dry and the cows have quit laying. The wind has got high and the sky is black with dust. Blow flies are taking the place over, licking off the milk pails, falling into the cream, getting hung up in the molasses. Besides that, they ain't no more work to do on the farm; can't buy no seed for planting, nor feed for the horses and cows.

Hell, I can work. I like to work. Born working. Raised working. Married working. What kind of work do they want done in this oil boom town? If work is what they want done, plowing or digging or carrying something, I can do that. If they want a cellar dug or some dirt moved, I can do that. If they want some rock hauled and some cement shoveled, I can do that. If they want some boards sawed and some nails drove, hell's bells, I can do that. If they want a tank truck drove, I can do that, too, or if they want some steel towers bolted up, give me a day's practice, and I can do that. I could get pretty good at it. And I wouldn't quit. Even if I could, I wouldn't want to. . . .

I'll never feel as funny as the day I walked into the office and found Papa behind the flowery curtain, setting on the edge of the bed holding his face in his hands.

"Matter?" I asked him.

His finger pointed to the top of the dresser, and I found a check made out to me for a dollar and fifty cents.

At first I grinned and said, "Guess mebbe it's some o' my oil money a-rollin' in."

My blood turned to cold slush oil when my eyes saw on the corner of the check the name and address of the Insane Asylum in Norman, Oklahoma.

I set down by the side of Papa and put my arm around him.

The letter said that Nora B. Guthrie had died some days ago. Her death was a natural death. Because she only knew my address in Okemah, they were sending me the balance of her cash account.

Papa was wiping his eyes red with his knuckles, trying to quit crying. I patted him on the back and held the check down between my knees, reading it again.

I walked over across the tracks, uptown to the bank, not wanting to cash the check in our neighborhood. The man in the bank window could tell by my face that I was nervous and scared, and everybody standing in line was anxious for me to move on out of their way. I seen their hands full of checks, pink, tan, yellow and blue ones. My face turned a pale and sickly color, and my throat was just a wadding of dry cotton, and my eyes got hazy, and my whole life went through my head. It took every muscle in my body to pick up that dollar bill and fifty-cent piece. Somewhere on the outskirts of town, a high whining fire whistle seemed to be blowing.

I got a job selling root beer. It was just a big barrel with a coil running around inside of it, and it cost you a nickel for me to pull the handle, unless you was a personal friend of mine, in which case I'd draw you off a mug free.

Prohibition was on and folks seemed like they were dry. The first day that I was there, the boss come around and said, "Oh, here's your day's pay. We pay every day here, because we may have to close up any day. Business is rushing and good right now, but nobody can tell.

"Another thing I want to show you is about this little door right down here under the counter. You see this little door? Well, you push this trigger right here, just like that, and then you see the door comes open. Then you see inside. There's some little shelves. On these little shelves, as I suppose you see, are some little bottles. These little bottles are two ounces. They are fifty cents a bottle. They are a patented medicine, I think, and it's called Jamaica Ginger, or plain Jake—a mixture of ginger and alcohol. The alcohol is about ninety-nine percent. So now, in case anybody comes in with their thumbnail busted or ankle sprung, or is snake bit, or has got ancestors, or the hoof and mouth disease, or is otherwise sick and has got fifty cents cash money on him, get the fifty cents and then reach down here and give him one of these little bottles of Jake. Be sure to put the money in the register."

While I worked there only about a month, I saved up four dollars, and to boot I got an inside view of what the human race was drinking.

You couldn't tell any more about the rot gut called whiskey than you could about the Jake. It was just about as poison. Lots of people fell over dead and was found scattered here and yonder with different kinds of whiskey poisoning. I hated prohibition on that account. I hated it because it was killing people, paralyzing them, and causing them to die like flies. I've seen men set around and squeeze that old pink canned heat through an old dirty rag, get the alcohol drained out of it, and then drink it down. The papers carried tales about the men that drunk radiator alcohol and died from rust poisoning. Others came down with the beer head. That's where your head starts swelling up and it just don't quit. Usually you take the beer head from drinking home brew that ain't made right, or is fermented in old rusty cans, like garbage cans, oil drums, gasoline barrels, and slop buckets. It caused some of the people to die. They even had a kind of beer called Old Chock that was made by throwing everything under the sun into an old barrel, adding the yeast and sugar and water to it, and letting her go. Biscuit heels, corn-bread scraps, potato leavings, and all sorts of table scraps went into this beer. It is a whitish, milky, slicky-looking bunch of crap. But especially down in Oklahoma I've seen men drive fifteen miles out in the country just to get a hold of a few bottles of it. The name Chock come from the Choctaw Indians. I guess they just naturally wanted to celebrate some way or another, and thought a little drink would fire them up so's they'd break loose, forget their worries, and have a good time.

When I was behind the counter, men would come in and purchase bay rum, and I'd get a look into their puffy, red-speckled faces, and their bleary, batty eyes, that looked but didn't see, and that went shut, but never slept, that closed, but never rested, and dreamed but never arrived at a conclusion. I would see a man come in and buy a bottle of rubbing alcohol, and then buy a bottle of coke and go out and mix it half and half, hold his breath, wheeze for a few seconds, and then waddle on away.

One day my curiosity licked me. I said that I was going to taste a bottle of that Jake for myself. Man ought to be interested. I drawed up about a half a mug of root beer. It was cold and nice, and I popped the little stopper out of one of the Jake bottles, and poured the Jake into the root beer. When that Jake hit that beer, it commenced to cook it, and there was seven civil wars and two revolutions broke out inside of that mug. The beer was trying to tame the Jake down and the Jake was trying to eat the beer up. They sizzled and boiled and sounded about like bacon frying. The Jake was chasing the little bubbles and the little bubbles was chasing the Jake, and the beer spun like a whirlpool in a big swift river. It went around and around so fast that it made a little funnel right in the middle. I waited about twenty minutes for it to settle down. Finally it was about the color of a new tan saddle, and about as quiet as it would get. So I bent over it and stuck my ear down over the mug. It was spewing and crackling like a machine gun, but I thought I'd best to drink it before it turned into a waterspout or a dust storm. I took it up and took it down, and it was hot and dry and gingery and spicy, and cloudy, and smooth, and windy and cold, and threatening rain or snow. I took another big swallow and my shirt come unbuttoned and my insides burnt like I was pouring myself full of home-made soapy dishwater. I drank it all down, and when I woke up I was out of a job.

And then a couple of months wheeled past, and I found myself walking all around with my head down, still out of a job, and asking other folks why they had their heads down. But most people was tough, and they still kept their heads up.

I wanted to be my own boss. Have my own job of work whatever it was, and be on my own hook. I walked the streets in the drift of the dust and wondered where was I bound for, where was I going, what was I going to do? My whole life turned into one big question mark. And I was the only living person that could answer it. I went to the town library and scratched around in the books. I carried them home by the dozens and by the armloads, on any subject, I didn't care which. I wanted to look into everything a little bit, and pick out something, something that would turn me into a human being of some kind—free to work for my own self, and free to work for everybody.

My head was mixed up. I looked into every kind of an "ology," "osis," "itis," and "ism" there was. It seemed like it all turned to nothing. . . .

For the next few months I took a spell of spending all of the money I could rake and scrape for brushes, hunks of canvas, and all kinds of oil paints. Whole days would go by and I wouldn't know where they'd went. I put my whole mind and every single thought to the business of painting pictures, mostly people.

I made copies of Whistler's "Mother," "The Song of the Lark," "The Angelus," and lots of babies and boys and dogs, snow and green trees, birds singing on all kinds of limbs, and pictures of the dust across the oil fields and wheat country. I made a couple of dozen heads of Christ, and the cops that killed Him.

Things was starting to stack up in my head and I just felt like I was going out of my wits if I didn't find some way of saying what I was thinking. The world didn't mean any more than a smear to me if I couldn't find ways of putting it down on something. I painted cheap signs and pictures on store windows, warehouses, barns and hotels, hock shops, funeral parlors and blacksmith shops, and I spent the money I made for more tubes of oil colors. "I'll make 'em good an' tough," I said to myself, "so's they'll last a thousand years."

But canvas is too high priced, and so is paint and costly oils, and brushes that you've got to chase a camel or a seal or a Russian red sable forty miles to get.

An uncle of mine taught me to play the guitar and I got to going out a couple of nights a week to the cow ranches around to play for the square dances. I made up new words to old tunes and sung them everywhere I'd go. I had to give my pictures away to get anybody to hang them on their wall, but for singing a song, or a few songs at a country dance, they paid me as high as three dollars a night. A picture—you buy it once, and it bothers you for forty years; but with a song, you sing it out, and it soaks in people's ears and they all jump up and down and sing it with you, and then when you quit singing it, it's gone, and you get a job singing it again. On top of that, you can sing out what you think. You can tell tales of all kinds to put your idea across to the other fellow.

And there on the Texas plains right in the dead center of the dust bowl, with the oil boom over and the wheat blowed out and the hard-working people just stumbling about, bothered with mortgages, debts, bills, sickness, worries of every blowing kind, I seen there was plenty to make up songs about.

Some people liked me, hated me, walked with me, walked over me, jeered me, cheered me, rooted me and hooted me, and before long I was invited in and booted out of every public place of entertainment in that country. But I decided that songs was a music and a language of all tongues.

I never did make up many songs about the cow trails or the moon skipping through the sky, but at first it was funny songs of what all's wrong, and how it turned out good or bad. Then I got a little braver and made up songs telling what I thought was wrong and how to make it right, songs that said what everybody in that country was thinking.

And this has held me ever since.

My dad married a mail-order wife. She come to Pampa from Los Angeles, and after two or three wedding celebrations most of the relatives went on back to their farms, and Papa and his new wife, Betty Jane, settled down in a shack in a tourist court.

She put an ad in the paper and started telling fortunes. Her trade started out pretty slow at first, then it grew so fast that the customers overflowed her shack. . . .

[In 1936 the Pampa oil fields dried up, the Great Depression entered its seventh year, Hitler and Mussolini were beginning World War II, and Guthrie was twenty-four years old. He decided to leave the "dam dust" of Texas to live with his rich aunt in California. Penniless, he left Pampa hitching rides, hopping freights, and living by his wits.]

I had always played music, painted signs, and managed to do some kind of work to get a hold of a piece of money, with which I could walk in to town legal, and buy anything I wanted to eat or drink. I'd always felt that satisfied feeling of hearing a coin jingle across the counter, or at least, doing some kind of work to pay for my meals. I'd missed whole days without a meal. But I'd been pretty proud about bumming. I still hoped that I could find some kind of short job to earn me something to eat. This was the longest I had ever gone without anything to eat. More than two whole days and nights.

This was a strange town, with a funny feeling hanging over it, a feeling like there were lots of people in it—the Mexican workers, and the white workers, and the travelers of all skins and colors of eyes, caught hungry, hunting for some kind of work to do. I was too proud to go out like the other men and knock at the doors.

I kept getting weaker and emptier. I got so nervous that I commenced shaking, and couldn't hold myself still. I could smell a piece of bacon or corncake frying at a half a mile away. The very thought of fruit made me lick my hot lips. I kept shaking and looking blanker and blanker. My brain didn't work as good as usual. I couldn't think. Just got into a stupor of some kind, and sat there on the main line of the fast railroad, forgetting about even being there . . . and thinking of homes, with ice boxes, cook stoves, tables, hot meals, cold lunches, with hot coffee, ice-cold beer, homemade wine—and friends and relatives. And I swore to pay more attention to the hungry people that I would meet from there on down the line.

Pretty soon, a wiry-looking man came walking up across the low green patch, with a brown paper sack wadded up under his arm. He walked in my direction until he was about fifteen feet away, and I could see the brown stain of good-tasting grease soaking through his sack. I even sniffed, and stuck my nose up in the air, and swung my head in his direction as he got closer; and I could smell, by real instinct, the good homemade bread, onion, and salty pork that was in the sack. He sat down not more than fifty feet away, under the heavy squared timbers of the under-rigging of a water tank, and opened his sack and ate his meal, with me looking on.

He finished it slowly, taking his good easy time. He licked the ends of his fingers, and turned his head sideways to keep from spilling any of the drippings.

After he'd cleaned the sack out, he wadded it up properly and threw it over his shoulder. I wondered if there was any crumbs in it. When he left, I says to myself, I'll go and open it up and eat the crumbs. They'll put me on to the next town.

The man walked over to where I sat and said, "What the hell are you doing settin' here on the main line . . . ?"

"Waitin' fer a train," I said.

"You don't want one on top of you, do you?" he asked me.

"Nope," I says, "but I don't see none coming. . . ."

"How could you with your back to it?"

"Back?"

"Hell, yes, I seen guys end up like 'burger meat for just such carelessness as that. . . ."

"Pretty mornin'," I said to him.

"You hungry?" he asked me.

"Mister, I'm just as empty as one of them automobile cars there, headed back East to Detroit."

"How long you been this way?"

"More than two days."

"You're a dam fool. . . . Hit any houses for grub?"

"No—don't know which a way to strike out."

"Hell, you are a dam fool, for sure."

"I guess so."

"Guess, hell, I know so." He turned his eyes toward the better section of town. "Don't go up in the fine part of town to try to work for a meal. You'll starve to death, and they'll throw you in jail just for dying on the streets. But see them little shacks and houses over yonder? That's where the railroad workers live. You'll get a feed at the first house you go to, that is, if you're honest, willing to work for it, and ain't afraid to tell it just like it is."

I nodded my head up and down, but I was listening.

Before he quit talking, one of the last things that he said, was, "I been on the bum like this for a long time. I could have split my sack of eats with you right here, but you wouldn't have got any good out of it that way. Wouldn't learn you a dam thing. I had to learn it the hard way. I went to the rich part of town, and I learnt what it was like; and then I went to the working folks' end of town and seen what it was like. And now it's up to you to go out for yourself and get you some grub when your belly's empty.". . .

There was one more church that I had to make, the biggest one in town. A big mission, cathedral, or something. It was a great big, pretty building, with a tower, and lots of fancy rock carving on the high places. Heavy vines clumb around, holding onto the rough face of the rocks, and since it was a fairly new church, everything was just getting off to a good start. . . .

I knocked on the door, and in about three minutes the door swung open, and there was an old man with white hair, a keen shaved face, and a clean, stiff white collar that fit him right up around his neck. He was friendly and warm. He wore a black suit of clothes which was made out of good material. He said, "How do you do?"

I stuck out my hand to shake, grabbed his and squeezed as friendly as I knew how and said, "Mister Sanfrancisco, Frizsansco, Frisco, I'm glad to know you! Guthrie's my name. Texas. Panhandle country. Cattle. You know. Oil boom. That's what—fine day."

In a deep, quiet-sounding voice that somehow matched in with the halls of the church, he said that it was a fine day, and that he was very glad to meet me. I assured him again that I was glad to meet him, but would be somewhat gladder if I could also work for a meal. "Two days. No eats," I told him.

And then, soft and friendly as ever, his eyes shining out from the dark hall, his voice spoke up again and said, "Son, I have been in this service all my life. I have seen to it that thousands of men just like you got to work for a meal. But, right at this moment, there is no kind of work to do here, no kind of work at all; and therefore, it would be just a case of pure charity. Charity here is like charity everywhere; it helps for a moment, and then it helps no more. It is part of our policy to be charitable, for to give is better than to receive. You seem still to retain a good measure of your pride and dignity. You do not beg outright for food, but you offer to do hard labor in order to earn your meal. That is the best spirit in this world. To work for yourself is to help others, and to help others is to help yourself. But you have asked a certain question; and I must answer that question in your own words to satisfy your own thinking. You asked if there is work that you can do to earn a meal. My answer is this: There is no work around here that you can do, and therefore, you cannot earn a meal. And, as for charity, God knows, we live on charity ourselves."

The big, heavy door closed without making even a slight sound.

I walked a half a mile trembling past the yards, down to the shacks of the railroad workers, the Mexicanos, the Negroes, and the whites, and knocked on the first door. It was a little brown wooden house, costing, all together, less than one single rock in the church. A lady opened the door. She said that she didn't have anything for me to do; she acted crabby and fussy, chewing the rag, and talking sour to herself. She went back in the house again, still talking.

"Young men, old men, all kinds of men; walking, walking, all of the time walking, piling off of the freights, making a run across my tomato garden, and knocking on my door; men out gallivantin' around over the country; be better off if you'd of stayed at home; young boys taking all kinds of crazy chances, going hungry, thirsty, getting all dirty and ugly, ruining your clothes, maybe getting run over and killed by a truck or a train—who knows? Yes. Yes. Yes. Don't you dare run away, young nitwit. I'm a fixing you a plate of the best I got. Which is all I got. Blame fools." (Mumbling) "Ought to be at home with your family; that's where you'd ought to be. Here." (Opening the door again, coming out on the porch.) "Here, eat this. It'll at least stick to your ribs. You look like an old hungry hound dog. I'd be ashamed to ever let the world beat me down any such a way. Here. Eat every bite of this. I'll go and fix you a glass of good milk. Crazy world these days. Everybody's cutting loose and hitting the road."

Down the street, I stopped at another house. I walked up to the front door, and knocked. I could hear somebody moving around on the inside, but nobody come to the door. After a few more knocks, and five minutes of waiting, a little woman opened the door back a ways, took a peek out, but wouldn't open up all of the way.

She looked me over good. It was so dark in her house that I couldn't tell much about her. Just some messed-up hair, and her hand on the door. It was clean, and reddish, like she'd been in the dishwater, or putting out some clothes. Mexican or white, you couldn't tell which. She asked me in a whisper, "What, what do you want?"

"Lady, I'm headin' ta California lookin' for work. I just wondered if you had a job of work of some kind that a man could do to earn a lunch. Sack with somethin' in it ta carry along."

She gave me the feeling that she was afraid of something. "No, I haven't any kind of work. Sshhh. Don't talk so loud. And I haven't got anything in the house—that is—anything fit to pack for you to eat."

"I just got a meal off of th' lady down th' street here, an' just thought maybe—you know, thought maybe a little sack of somethin' might come in purty handy after a day or two out on the desert—any old thing. Not very hard ta please," I told her.

"My husband is sleeping. Don't talk so loud. I'm a little ashamed of what I've got left over here. Pretty poor when you need a good meal. But, if you're not too particular about it, you're welcome to take it with you. Wait here a minute."

I stood there looking back up across the tomato patch to the railroad yards. A switch engine was trotting loose cars up and down the track and I knew that our freight was making up.

She stuck her hand out through an old green screen door, and said, "Sshhh," and I tried to whisper "thank you," but she just kept motioning, nodding her head.

I was wearing a black slip-over sweater and I pulled the loose neck open, and pushed the sack down into the bosom. She'd put something good and warm from the warming-oven into the sack, because already I could feel the good hot feeling against my belly.

Trains were limbering up their big whistles, and there was a long string of cars made up and raring to step. A hundred and ten cars meant pretty certain that she was a hot one with the right-of-way to the next division. . . .

[As he rode the rails and lived in hobo camps, his biggest problem was food.]

Sign says: "Fruit, see, but don't pick it." Another one reads: "Fruit—beat it." Another one: "Trespassers prosecuted. Keep Out. Get away from Here."

Fruit is on the ground, and it looks like the trees have been just too glad to grow it, and give it to you. The tree likes to grow and you like to eat it; and there is a sign between you and the tree saying: "Beware The Mean Dog's Master."

Fruit is rotting on the ground all around me. Just what in the hell has gone wrong here, anyhow? I'm not a very smart man. Maybe it ought to be this way, with the crops laying all around over the ground. Maybe they couldn't get no pickers just when they wanted them, and they just let the fruit go to the bad.

There's enough here on the ground to feed every hungry kid from Maine to Florida, and from there to Seattle. . . .

I saw a sign tacked up in the Fresno yards that said: Free Meal & Nights Lodging. Rescue Mission.

Men looked at the sign and asked us, "Anybody here need ta be rescued?"

"From what?" somebody hollered.

"All ya got ta do is ta go down there an' kneel down an' say yer prayers, an' ya git a free meal an' a flop!" somebody explained.

"Yeah? Prayers? Which one o' youse boys knows any t'ing about any prayers?" an Eastern-sounding man yelled out.

"I'd do it, if I wuz just hungry 'nuff! I'd say 'em some prayers!"

"I don't hafta do no prayin' ta get fed!" a hard looker laughed out. He was poking a raw onion whole into his mouth, tears trickling down his jaws.

"Oh, I don't know," a quieter man answered him, "I sometimes believe in prayin'. Lots of folks believes in prayin' before they go out to work, an' others pray before they go out to fight. An' even if you don't believe in a God up on a cloud, still, prayin's a pretty good way to get your mind cleared up, or to get the nerve that it takes to do anything. People pray because it makes them think serious about things, and, God or no God, it's all that most of them know how to do." He was a friendly man with whitish hair, and his easy temper sounded in his voice. It was a thinking voice.

" 'Course," a big Swede told us, "we justa kid along. These monkeys dun't mean about halfa what they say. Now, like, you take me, Swede, I prayed long time ago. Usta believe in it strong. Then, whoof, an' a lot of other things happen that knock my prop out from under me, make me a railroad bum, an'—I just forget how to pray an' go church."

A guy that talked more and faster said, "I think it's dam crooks that cause folks like us to be down and out and hungry, worried about finding jobs, worried about our folks, and them a-worrying about us."

"Last two or three years, I been sorta thinkin' 'long them lines—an' it looks like I keep believin' in somethin'; I don't know exactly, but it's in me, an' in you, an' in ever' dam one of us." This talker was a young man with a smooth face, thick hair that was bushy, and a fairly honest look somewhere about him. "An' if we c'n jist find out how ta make good use of it, we'll find out who's causin' us alla th' trouble in the' world, like this Hitler rat, an' git ridda them, an' then not let anybody be outta work, or beat down an' wonderin' where their next meal's a comin' from, by God, with alla these crops an' orchards bubblin' up around here!"

"If God was ta do what's right," a heavy man said, "he'd give all of these here peaches an' cherries, an' oranges, an' grapes, an' stuff to eat, to th' folks that are hungry. An' for a hungry man to pray an' try to tell God how to run his business, looks sort of backwards, plumb silly to me. Hell, a man's got two hands an' a mind of his own, an' feet an' legs to take him where he wants to go; an' if he sees something wrong with the world, he'd ought to get a lot of people together, an' look up in th' air an' say, Hey, up there, God, I'm—I mean, we're goin' to fix this!"

Then I put my three cents worth in, saying, "I believe that when ya pray, you're tryin' ta get yer thinkin' straight, tryin' ta see what's wrong with th' world, an' who's ta blame fer it. Part of it is crooks, crooked laws, an' jist dam greedy people, people that's afraid of this an' afraid of that. Part of it's all of this, an' part of it's jist dam shore our own fault."

"Hell, from what you say, you think we're to blame for everybody here being on the freights?" This young traveler reared his head back and laughed to himself, chewing a mouthful of sticky bread.

"I dunno, fellers, just to be right real frank with you. But it's our own fault, all right, hell yes. It's our own personal fault if we don't talk up, 'er speak out, 'er somethin'—I ain't any too clear on it."

An old white-headed man spoke close to me and said, "Well, boys, I was on the bum, I suppose, before any of you was born into this world." Everybody looked around mostly because he was talking so quiet, interrupting his eating. "All of this talking about what's up in the sky, or down in hell, for that matter, isn't half as important as what's right here, right now, right in front of your eyes. Things are tough. Folks broke. Kids hungry. Sick. Everything. And people has just got to have more faith in one another, believe in each other. There's a spirit of some kind we've all got. That's got to draw us all together."

Heads nodded. Faces watched the old man. He didn't say any more. Toothless for years, he was a little bit slow finishing up his piece of old bread. . . .

[He got to his aunt's home in Sonora but did not even go inside. The affluence of her lifestyle made him feel "hemmed in" and shamed him to go back to the road life where he felt "alive again."]

In a bend of the Sacramento is the town of Redding, California. The word had scattered out that twenty-five hundred workers was needed to build the Kenneth Dam, and already eight thousand work hands had come to do the job. Redding was like a wild ant den. A mile to the north in a railroad bend had sprung up another camp, a thriving nest of two thousand people, which we just called by the name of the "jungle." In that summer of 1938, I learned a few little things about the folks in Redding, but a whole lot more, some way, down there by that big jungle where the people lived as close to nature, and as far from everything natural, as human beings can. . . .

I followed the trail out over the hill through the sun and the weeds. The camp was bigger than the town itself. People had dragged old car fenders up from the dumps, wired them from the limbs of oak trees a few feet off of the ground and this was a roof for some of them. Others had taken old canvas sacks or wagon sheets, stretched the canvas over little limbs cut so the forks braced each other, and that was a house for those folks. I heard two brothers standing back looking at their house saying, "I ain't lost my hand as a carpenter, yet." "My old eyes can still see to hit a nail." They'd carried buckets and tin cans out of the heap, flattened them on the ground, then nailed the tin onto crooked boards, and that was a mansion for them. Lots of people, families mostly, had some bedclothes with them, and I could see the old stinky, gummy quilts and blankets hung up like tents, and two or three kids of all ages playing around underneath. There was scatterings of cardboard shacks, where the people had lugged cartons, cases, packing boxes out from town and tacked them into a house. They was easy to build, but the first rain that hit them, they was goners.

Then about every few feet down the jungle hill you'd walk past a shack just sort of made out of everything in general—old strips of asphalt tar paper, double gunny sacks, an old dress, shirt, pair of overhalls, stretched up to cover half a side of a wall; bumpy corrugated iron, cement sacks, orange and apple crates took apart and nailed together with old rusty burnt nails from the cinder piles. Through a little square window on the side of a house, I'd hear bedsprings creaking and people talking. Men played cards, whittled, and women talked about work they'd struck and work they were hunting for. Dirt was on the floor of the house, and all kinds and colors of crawling and flying bugs come and went like they were getting paid for it. There were the big green blow-flies, the noisy little street flies, manure and lot flies, caterpillars and gnats from other dam jobs, bed bugs, fleas, and ticks sucking blood, while mosquitoes of all army and navy types, hummers, bombers, fighters, sung some good mosquito songs. In most cases, though, the families didn't even have a roof or shelter, but just got together once or twice every day and, squatting sort of Indian fashion around their fire, spaded a few bites of thickened flour gravy, old bread, or a thin watery stew. Gunny sacks, old clothes, hay and straw, fermenting bedclothes, are usually piled full of kids playing, or grown-ups resting and waiting for the word "work" to come.

The sun's shining through lots of places, other patches pretty shady, and right here at my elbow a couple of families are squatting down on an old slick piece of canvas; three or four quiet men, whittling, breaking grass stems, poking holes in leaves, digging into the hard ground; and the women rocking back and forth laughing out at something somebody'd said. A little baby sucks at a wind-burnt breast that nursed the four other kids that crawl about the fire. Cold rusty cans are their china cups and aluminum ware, and the hot still bucket of river water is as warm and clear as the air around. I watch a lot of little circles waving out from the middle of the water where a measuring worm has dropped from the limb of a tree and flips and flops for his very life. And I see a man with a forked stick reach the forks over into the bucket, smile, and go on talking about the work he's done; and in a moment, when the little worm clamps his feet around the forks of the stick, the man will lift him out, pull him up close to his face and look him over, then tap the stick over the rim of the bucket. When the little worm flips to the ground and goes humping away through the twigs and ashes, the whole bunch of people will smile and say, "Pretty close shave, mister worm. What do you think you are, a parshoot jumper?"

You've seen a million people like this already. Maybe you saw them down on the crowded side of your big city; the back side, that's jammed and packed, the hard section to drive through. Maybe you wondered where so many of them come from, how they eat, stay alive, what good they do, what makes them live like this? These people have had a house and a home just about like your own, settled down and had a job of work just about like you. Then something hit them and they lost all of that. They've been pushed out into the high lonesome highway, and they've gone down it, from coast to coast, from Canada to Mexico, looking for that home again. Now they're looking for a while, in your town. Ain't much difference between you and them. If you was to walk out into this big tangled jungle camp and stand there with the other two thousand, somebody would just walk up and shake hands with you and ask you, What kind of work do you do, pardner?

Then maybe, farther out on the ragged edge of your town you've seen these people after they've hit the road: the people that are called strangers, the people that follow the sun and the seasons to your country, follow the buds and the early leaves and come when the fruit and crops are ready to gather, and leave when the work is done. What kind of crops? Oil fields, power dams, pipe lines, canals, highways and hard-rock tunnels, skyscrapers, ships, are their crops. These are migrants now. They don't just set along in the sun—they go by the sun, and it lights up the country that they know is theirs.

If you'd go looking for social problems, you'd find just a good friendly bunch of people getting a lot of laughing and talking done, and some of it pretty good sense.

I listened to the talk in the tanglewood of the migratory jungle. "What'll be here to keep these people going," a man with baggy overhalls and a set of stickery whiskers is saying, "when this dam job is over? Nothing? No, mister, you're wrong as hell. What do you think we're putting in this dam for, anyhow? To catch water to irrigate new land, and water all of this desert-looking country here. And when a little drop of water hits the ground anywhere out across here—a crop, a bush, sometimes even a big tall tree comes jumping out of the dirt. Thousands and thousands of whole families are going to have all the good land they need, and I'm a-going to be on one of them little twenty acres!"

"Water, water," a young man about twenty or so, wearing a pair of handmade cowboy shoes, talks up. "You think water's gonna be th' best part? Well, you're just about half right, friend. Did you ever stop to think that th' most, th' best part of it all is th' electric power this dam's gonna turn out? I can just lay here on this old, rotten jungle hill with all of these half-starved people waiting to go to work, and you know, I don't so much see all of this filth and dirt. But I do see—just try to picture in my head, like—what's gonna be here. Th' big factories makin' all kinds of things from fertilizer to bombin' planes. Power lines, steel towers runnin' out acrost these old clumpy hills—most of all, people at work all of th' time on little farms, and whole bunches and bunches of people at work in th' big new factories."

"It's th' gifts of th' Lord, that's what 'tis." A little nervous man, about half Indian, is pulling up grass stems and talking. "Th' Lord gives you a mind to vision all of this, an' th' power to build it. He gives when He wants to. Then when He wants to, He takes it away—if we don't use it right."

"If we all get together, social like, and build something, say, like a big ship, any kind of a factory, railroad, big dam—that's social work, ain't it?" This is a young man with shell-rimmed glasses, a gray felt hat, blue work shirt with a fountain pen stuck with a notebook in his pocket, and his voice had the sound of books in it when he talked. "That's what 'social' means, me and you and you working on something together and owning it together. What the hell's wrong with this, anybody speak up! If Jesus Christ was sitting right here, right now, he'd say this very same dam thing. You just ask Jesus how the hell come a couple of thousand of us living out here in this jungle camp like a bunch of wild animals. You just ask Jesus how many million of other folks are living the same way? Sharecroppers down South, big city people that work in factories and live like rats in the slimy slums. You know what Jesus'll say back to you? He'll tell you we all just mortally got to work together, build things together, fix up old things together, clean out old filth together, put up new buildings, schools and churches, banks and factories together, and own everything together. Sure, they'll call it a bad ism. Jesus don't care if you call it socialism or communism, or just me and you."

When night come down, everything got a little stiller, and you could walk around from one bunch of people to the other one and talk about the weather. Although the weather wasn't such an ace-high subject to talk about, because around Redding for nine months and running the weather don't change (it's hot and dry, hot and dry, and tomorrow it's still going to be hot and dry), you can hear little bunches of folks getting acquainted with each other, saying, "Really hot, ain't it?" "Yeah, dry too." "Mighty dry."

I run onto a few young people of twelve to twenty-five, mostly kids with their families, who picked the banjo or guitar, and sung songs. Two of these people drew quite a bunch every evening along toward sundown and it always took place just about the same way. An old bed was under a tree in their yard, and a baby boy romped around on it when the shade got cool, because in the early parts of the day the flies and bugs nearly packed him off. So this was his ripping and romping time, and it was the job of his two sisters, one around twelve and the other one around fourteen, to watch him and keep him from falling off onto the ground. Their dad parked his self back on an old car cushion. He throwed his eyes out over the rims of some two-bit specks just about every line or two on his reading matter, and run his Adam's apple up and down; and his wife nearby was singing what all the Lord had done for her, while the right young baby stood up for his first time, and jumped up and down, bouncing toward the edge of the mattress. The old man puckered up his face and sprayed a tree with tobacco juice, and said, "Girls. You girls. Go in the house and get your music box, and set there on the bed and play with the baby, so's he won't fall off."

One of the sisters tuned a string or two, then chorded a little. People walked from all over the camp and gathered, and the kid, mama, and dad, and all of the visitors, kept as still as daylight while the girls sang:

> Takes a worried man to sing a worried song
> Takes a worried man to sing a worried song
> Takes a worried man to sing a worried song
> I'm worried nowwww
> But I won't be worried long. . . .

Everywhere I went I throwed my hat down in the floor and sung for my tips.

Sometimes I was lucky and found me a good job. I sung on the radio waves in Los Angeles, and I got a job from Uncle Samuel to come to the valley of the Columbia River and I made up and recorded twenty-six songs about the Grand Coulee Dam. I made two albums of records called "Dust Bowl Ballads," for the Victor people. I hit the road again and crossed the continent twice by way of highway and freights. Folks heard me on the nationwide radio programs CBS and NBC, and thought I was rich and famous, and I didn't have a nickel to my name, when I was hitting the hard way again. . . .

[He lived in skid rows as he traveled the country singing songs with the dispossessed. In 1942, he helped defend some Japanese-Americans from a mob in Los Angeles. His songs made him a folk hero and he was asked to audition at the Rockefeller Center for Performing Arts in New York City.]

"Next! Woody Guthrie!" a snazzy-looking gent was saying over the mike.

"Reckin that's me," I was mumbling under my chin, talking to myself, and looking out the window, thinking. I reached in my pocket and spun a thin dime out acrost the tablecloth and watched it whirl around and around, first heads, then tails, and said to myself, "Some difference 'tween that there apercot orchard las' June where th' folks wuz stuck down along th' river bottom, an' this here Rainbow Room on an August afternoon. Gosh, I come a long ways in th' last few months. Ain't made no money ta speak about, but I've stuck my head in a lot of plain an' fancy places. Some good, some just barely fair, an' some awful bad. I wrote up a lot of songs for union folks, sung 'em all over ever'where, wherever folks got together an' talked an' sung, from Madison Square Garden to a Cuban Cigar Makers' tavern in Spanish Harlem an hour later; from th' padded studios of CBS an' NBC to th' wild back country in th' raggedy Ghetto. In some places I was put on display as a freak, and others as a hero, an' in th' tough joints around th' Battery Park, I wuz jes' another shadow blund'rin' along with th' rest. It had been like this here little ol' dime spinnin', a whirl of heads an' tails. I'd liked mostly th' union workers, an' th' soldiers an' th' men in fightin' clothes, shootin' clothes, shippin' clothes, or farmin' clothes, 'cause singing with them made me friends with them, an' I felt like I was somehow in on their work. But this coin spinnin', that's my las' dime—an' this Rainbow Room job, well, rumors are it'll pay as much as seventy-five a week, an' seventy-five a week is dam shore seventy-five a week."

"Woody Guthrie!"

"Comin'!". . .

[Addicted to the traveling life, he turned down the job offer and took a train bound for the open road.]

MONICA SONE
1918–

Monica Sone's Nisei Daughter *dramatizes the ambiguities of the American immigrant experience. Born in the United States of Japanese parents, she came of age during the years of virulent anti-Japanese feeling that culminated in the internment of 112,000 persons of Japanese ancestry during World War II.*

Monica Sone's father, who had studied law in Tokyo, emigrated to the United States in 1904, hoping to continue his studies and practice law in this country. He never made enough money to achieve this dream but supported his family by managing a hotel for transients in Seattle. His wife emigrated with her family, headed by her father, a Congregational minister. Immigration law made Monica Sone's parents ineligible to become American citizens. They remained Isei; *their children, born in this country, were* Nisei.

Nisei Daughter, *in which the author takes the pseudonym Kazuko Itoi, emphasizes the duality of her experience: she had both Japanese and English names: "Kazuko" meaning "peace," and "Monica," after Saint Augustine's mother, Saint Monica. Her family's friends and business associates were Japanese or Japanese-American. Monica Sone and her three siblings spoke both Japanese and English and enjoyed Japanese and American food and customs. Nevertheless, there were cultural and generational disagreements as when her father refused to allow her to study ballet because, in Japan, dancing was associated with geisha girls. Monica Sone received her education at English-speaking schools although she briefly attended a Japanese school to learn Japanese etiquette. "Real Japanese," she thought in her childhood, lived in Japan.*

Living within this sheltered environment, Monica Sone experienced little racial prejudice beyond the family's inability to rent a beach house on the outskirts of Seattle. When Japan invaded China, hostility toward Japanese in the United States increased. Shortly after Japan bombed Pearl Harbor, she and her family were evacuated from Seattle. She and her siblings were soon released to find jobs in the Midwest, but her parents remained in the relocation camp for the duration of the war.

Nisei Daughter *has a theme found in much twentieth-century autobiography: the search for individual identity. The story of the author's search begins in the story's opening pages telling of her uncomfortable discovery that she was Japanese and ends with her celebration of being* Nisei—*both Japanese and American. The search is curiously painless. The inevitable tensions between clashing cultures and warring nations are muted. The only anger which Monica Sone allows herself to describe is what as a child she felt against her parents, never that of a young adult against the United States government that had torn her family from its home. Perhaps the persistent use of the pseudonym permitted the author to mask her real emotions. Anger would be inappropriate both for a Nisei, whose Japanese culture encouraged her acceptance of life's injustices, and for a daughter, whose gender encouraged her to be passive. The conservative politics of the early 1950s, in the full flush of McCarthyism, also made criticism of public policy unpopular.*

Nisei Daughter. *Boston: Little, Brown and Company, 1953. (Reprinted with permission.)*

The first five years of my life I lived in amoebic bliss, not knowing whether I was plant or animal, at the old Carrollton Hotel on the waterfront of Seattle. One day when I was a happy six-year-old, I made the shocking discovery that I had Japanese blood. I was a Japanese.

Mother announced this fact of life to us in a quiet, deliberate manner one Sunday afternoon as we gathered around for dinner in the small kitchen, converted from one of our hotel rooms. Our kitchen was cozily comfortable for all six of us as long as everyone remained in his place around the oblong table covered with an indestructible shiny black oilcloth; but if more than Mother stood up and fussed around, there was a serious traffic jam—soy sauce splattered on the floor and elbows jabbed into the pot of rice. So Father sat at the head of the table, Kenji, Henry, and I lined up on one side along the wall, while Mother and baby Sumiko occupied the other side, near the kitchen stove.

Now we watched as Mother lifted from a kettle of boiling water a straw basket of steaming slippery noodles. She directed her information at Henry and me, and I felt uneasy. Father paid strict attention to his noodles, dipping them into a bowl of fragrant pork broth and then sprinkling finely chopped raw green onion over them.

"Japanese blood—how is it I have that, Mama?" I asked, surreptitiously pouring hot tea over my bowl of rice. Mother said it was bad manners to wash rice down with tea, but rice was delicious with *obancha*.

"Your father and I have Japanese blood and so do you, too. And the same with Henry, Ken-chan, and Sumi-chan."

"Oh." I felt nothing unusual stirring inside me. I took a long cool sip of milk and then with my short red chopsticks I stabbed at a piece of pickled crisp white radish.

"So, Mama?" Henry looked up at her, trying to bring under control with his chopsticks the noodles swinging from his mouth like a pendulum.

"So, Papa and I have decided that you and Ka-chan will attend Japanese school after grammar school every day." She beamed at us.

I choked on my rice.

Terrible, terrible, terrible! So that's what it meant to be a Japanese—to lose my afternoon play hours! I fiercely resented this sudden intrusion of my blood into my affairs.

"But, Mama!" I shrieked. "I go to Bailey Gatzert School already. I don't want to go to another!"

Henry kicked the table leg and grumbled, "Aw gee, Mama, Dunks and Jiro don't have to—why do I!"

"They'll be going, too. Their mothers told me so."

My face grew hot with anger. I shouted, "I won't, I won't!"

Father and Mother painted glowing pictures for me. Just think you'll grow up to be a well-educated young lady, knowing two languages. One of these days you'll thank us for giving you this opportunity.

But they could not convince me. Until this shattering moment, I had thought life was sweet and reasonable. But not any more. Why did Father and Mother make such a fuss just because we had Japanese blood? Why did we have to go to Japanese school? I refused to eat and sat sobbing, letting great big tears splash down into my bowl of rice and tea.

Henry, who was smarter and adjusted more quickly to fate, continued his meal, looking gloomy, but with his appetite unimpaired.

Up to that moment, I had never thought of Father and Mother as Japanese. True, they had almond eyes and they spoke Japanese to us, but I never felt that it was strange. It was like one person's being red-haired and another black. . . .

And when I finally started grammar school, I found [an] enchanting world. Every morning I hurried to Adams Hotel, climbed its dark flight of stairs, and called for Matsuko. Together we made the long and fascinating journey—from First Avenue to Twelfth Avenue—to Bailey Gatzert School. We always walked over the bridge on Fourth Avenue where we hung over the iron rails, waiting until a train roared past under us, enveloping us completely in its hissing, billowing cloud of white, warm steam. We meandered through the international section of town, past the small Japanese shops and stores, already bustling in the early morning hour, past the cafés and barber shops filled with Filipino men, and through Chinatown. Then finally we went up a gentle sloping hill to the handsome low-slung, red-brick building with its velvet green lawn and huge play yard. I felt like a princess walking through its bright, sunny corridors on smooth, shiny floors. I was mystified by a few of the little boys and girls. There were some pale-looking children who spoke a strange dialect of English, rapidly like gunfire. Matsuko told me they were *"hagu-jins,"* white people. Then there were children who looked very much like me with their black hair and black eyes, but they spoke in high, musical singing voices. Matsuko whispered to me that they were Chinese.

And now Mother was telling us we were Japanese. I had always thought I was a Yankee, because after all I had been born on Occidental and Main Street. Montana, a wall-shaking mountain of a man who lived at our hotel, called me a Yankee. I didn't see how I could be a Yankee and Japanese at the same time. It was like being born with two heads. It sounded freakish and a lot of trouble. Above everything, I didn't want to go to Japanese school. . . .

Gradually I yielded to my double dose of schooling. Nihon Gakko was so different from grammar school I found myself switching my personality back and forth daily like a chameleon. At Bailey Gatzert School I was a jumping, screaming, roustabout Yankee, but at the stroke of three when the school bell rang and doors burst open everywhere, spewing out pupils like jelly beans from a broken bag, I suddenly became a modest, faltering, earnest little Japanese girl with a small, timid voice. I trudged down a steep hill and climbed up another steep hill to Nihon Gakko with other black-haired boys and girls. On the playground, we behaved cautiously. Whenever we spied a teacher within bowing distance, we hissed at each other to stop the game, put our feet neatly together, slid our hands down to our knees and bowed slowly and sanctimoniously. In just the proper, moderate tone, putting in every ounce of respect, we chanted, *"Konichi-wa, sensei.* Good day." . . .

[In her early adolescence Kazuko and her family visited her paternal grandfather in Japan, where she met "real Japanese."]

One of Father's brothers from Tokyo met us at the port. He was taller than Father, a handsome elderly man who held himself ceremoniously erect. A summer straw hat sat squarely on his freshly barbered head, and he wore a rustling black silk *hakama* and *haori* which men put on for special formal occasions. I waited for him and Father to fall upon each other's shoulders and greet each other noisily. After all, they had not seen each other for many years. But Uncle only bowed stiffly and began a short speech of welcome. Father and Mother looked a bit startled, but they too, not to be outdone, bowed their heads and plunged into an elaborate greeting.

We goggled at the scene around us. This was a strange land of bicycles. We had thought bicycles were only for boys and girls, but here, dignified men in Western-styled business suits pedaled by industriously. A delivery boy steered his bicycle with one hand while he balanced a towering pile of wooden boxes in his other hand. Mother was astonished to see a genteel-looking elderly woman wearing a *marumage* pompadour coiffure, cycling along with haughty composure.

"Mah, mah, how time has changed," Mother chuckled.

The Japanese women wore long kimonos and stiff wide sashes as I had expected, but their kimonos were almost drab in color and pattern. The men in their kimonos topped by a Homburg or a Panama hat looked odd to us.

We whooped with joy to see hundreds of two-wheeled carriages, jinrikishas, lined up near the dock. They were just as I had pictured them to be. It turned out that we were going to ride on them to our hotel. Mother held Sumiko in her lap and I sat beside her. The jinrikisha man, small, bronzed and muscular, smiled and ducked his head a great deal. A white towel was tied around his forehead and the hem of his short blue cotton kimono was tucked up into his sash, for the sake of speed. Father and Uncle rode up ahead; Henry and Kenji followed in another carriage. Our man ran along rhythmically and effortlessly, weaving in and out of the traffic of rickshaws, pedestrians, trams and automobiles. People stared at our foreign clothes and I felt self-conscious. . . .

We finally reached Takayama, the country village where Grandfather Itoi lived. It was another battling trip via jam-packed trains, hired automobiles, horse-drawn carts and jinrikishas. On country roads, farm folks seemed to know instinctively that foreigners were approaching. Wherever we went, a curious knot of people was gathered on the roadside. As we bounced by self-consciously on rickshaws, they nudged each other and whispered aloud, "Look, they must be from America. They certainly wear odd clothes."

Grandfather Itoi turned out to be a much beloved old patriarch. For forty years he had served as "soncho" or the head elder of four villages, and though he was retired now, people still consulted him about farm crops and personal matters. It was relaxing to sit on the cool porch while he chatted with Mother and Father about America. Sometimes we stretched our limbs and sprawled flat on our backs and listened to Grandfather tell us "Tanuki" stories, about the crafty badger who could turn into a teapot, a drum, or a rock to escape his enemies. . . .

By mid-August, we were on board ship again, sailing for home with bewildered, mixed feelings. . . . We longed to be back home among the familiar Seattle hills, but we did not want to leave Grandfather behind us. We tried to persuade him to come with us. Henry said, breathless with hope, "There's plenty of room for you, Ojih-chan, in our big hotel. You could share my room. I wish you'd live with me, Ojih-chan!"

Ojih-chan's face, parched and browned from the sun and wind, broke into a thousand wrinkles, and he smiled tenderly. "How I would love to see your fine home in Seattle, and to watch you grow. But when a man gets as old as I, he does not feel like moving from the place where he was born and where he had lived all his life. I long to go with you, but I'm too old now. You understand, don't you?"

We didn't understand, but we nodded our heads for he looked so sad and wistful even when he smiled. Many years later I learned why he could not come with us. In 1924 my country had passed an Immigration Law which kept all Orientals from migrating to America since that year. Those who had come in before that time could stay, but there would be no more new ones. That was why Father had taken us to Japan, so Grandfather could see us and say farewell to his son who had decided to make his home across the sea. The children who had been born in America belonged there and there he and Mother would stay.

On the last lap of our return trip, we passed the narrow straits of Juan de Fuca just at eventide. Every passenger was up on deck. The Pacific glimmered in the familiar golden orange glow of sunset. Suddenly as if a heavy weight had slipped from my chest, I realized we were home again, and my visit to Japan receded into the background like a sad, enchanted dream. We had explored the exotic island of the Japanese. I had felt the charm of its people. I had been impressed by its modern cities as well as by its historic beauty, but I had felt I was an alien among them.

This was home to me, this lovely Puget Sound Harbor stretched out before us. Tomorrow we would wake to the old familiar landmarks of Seattle—Magnolia Bluff, Smith Cove, the slender pinnacle of Smith Tower, and the stretch of Alki Beach. This America, where I was born, surrounded by people of different racial extractions, was still my home. . . .

[Kazuko first experienced anti-Japanese feeling when no one would rent her family a beach-side home.]

Gradually I learned in many other ways the terrible curse that went with having Japanese blood. As the nations went, so went their people. Japan and the United States were no longer seeing eye to eye, and we felt the repercussions in our daily lives.

International matters took a turn for the worse when Japan's army suddenly thrust into Shanghai. City officials, prominent men and women were interviewed and they all shouted for punishment and a boycott on Japanese goods. People stopped patronizing Japanese shops. The Chinese who were employed by Japanese resigned their jobs, one after another.

I dreaded going through Chinatown. The Chinese shopkeepers, gossiping and sunning themselves in front of their stores, invariably stopped their chatter to give me pointed, icicled glares.

The editorial sections of the newspapers and magazines were plastered with cartoons of hideous-looking Japanese. The Japanese was always caricatured with enormous, moon-shaped spectacles and beady, myopic eyes. A small mustache was perched arrogantly over massive, square buck teeth, and his bow-legged posture suggested a simian character. . . .

High school was a startling experience. For eight years at Nihon Gakko, Bailey Gatzert and Central Grammar, I had done only what I was told by my teachers. I opened my mouth only in reply to a question. I became a polished piece of inarticulateness. At high school, the teachers expected us to have opinions of our own and to express them. In classes like civics, history, current events and literature, the entire class hour was devoted to discussion and criticisms. Although I had opinions, I was so overcome with self-consciousness I could not bring myself to speak.

Some people would have explained this as an acute case of adolescence, but I knew it was also because I was Japanese. Almost all the students of Japanese blood sat like rocks during discussion period. Something compellingly Japanese made us feel it was better to seem stupid in a quiet way rather than to make boners out loud. I began to think of the Japanese as the Silent People, and I envied my fellow students who clamored to be heard. What they said was not always profound or even relevant, but they didn't seem worried about it. Only after a long, agonizing struggle was I able to deliver the simplest statement in class without flaming like a red tomato. . . .

[Her father insisted that she attend business school, and she finished the course in one year. She then planned to attend the University of Washington but instead spent nine months in a tuberculosis sanitarium, where she made many American friends.]

On a peaceful Sunday morning, December 7, 1941, Henry, Sumi and I were at choir rehearsal singing ourselves hoarse in preparation for the annual Christmas recital of Handel's "Messiah." Suddenly Chuck Mizuno, a young University of Washington student, burst into the chapel, gasping as if he had sprinted all the way up the stairs.

"Listen, everybody!" he shouted. "Japan just bombed Pearl Harbor . . . in Hawaii! It's war!"

The terrible words hit like a blockbuster, paralyzing us. Then we smiled feebly at each other, hoping this was one of Chuck's practical jokes. Miss Hara, our music director, rapped her baton impatiently on the music stand and chided him, "Now Chuck, fun's fun, but we have work to do. Please take your place. You're already half an hour late."

But Chuck strode vehemently back to the door, "I mean it, folks, honest! I just heard the news over my car radio. Reporters are talking a blue streak. Come on down and hear it for yourselves."

With that, Chuck swept out of the room, a swirl of young men following in his wake. Henry was one of them. The rest of us stayed, rooted to our places like a row of marionettes. I felt as if a fist had smashed my pleasant little existence, breaking it into jigsaw puzzle pieces. An old wound opened up again, and I found myself shrinking inwardly from my Japanese blood, the blood of an enemy. I knew instinctively that the fact that I was an American by birthright was not going to help me escape the consequences of this unhappy war.

One girl mumbled over and over again, "It can't be, God, it can't be!" Someone else was saying, "What a spot to be in! Do you think we'll be considered Japanese or Americans?"

A boy replied quietly, "We'll be Japs, same as always. But our parents are enemy aliens now, you know." . . .

Late that night Father got a shortwave broadcast from Japan. Static sputtered, then we caught a faint voice, speaking rapidly in Japanese. Father sat unmoving as a rock, his head cocked. The man was talking about the war between Japan and America. Father bit his lips and Mother whispered to him anxiously, "It's true then, isn't it, Papa? It's true?"

Father was muttering to himself, "So they really did it!" Now having heard the news in their native tongue, the war had become a reality to Father and Mother.

"I suppose from now on, we'll hear about nothing but the humiliating defeats of Japan in the papers here," Mother said, resignedly.

Henry and I glared indignantly at Mother, then Henry shrugged his shoulders and decided to say nothing. Discussion of politics, especially Japan versus America, had become taboo in our family for it sent tempers skyrocketing. Henry and I used to criticize Japan's aggressions in China and Manchuria while Father and Mother condemned Great Britain and America's superior attitude toward Asiatics and their interference with Japan's economic growth. During these arguments, we had eyed each other like strangers, parents against children. They left us with a hollow feeling at the pit of the stomach. . . .

In the afternoon President Roosevelt's formal declaration of war against Japan was broadcast throughout the nation. In grave, measured words, he described the attack on Pearl Harbor as shameful, infamous. I writhed involuntarily. I could no more have escaped the stab of self-consciousness than I could have changed my Oriental features. . . .

It made me positively hivey the way the FBI agents continued their raids into Japanese homes and business places and marched the Issei men away into the old red brick immigration building, systematically and efficiently, as if they were stocking a cellarful of choice bottles of wine. At first we noted that the men arrested were those who had been prominent in community affairs, like Mr. Kato, many times president of the Seattle Japanese Chamber of Commerce, and Mr. Ohashi, the principal of our Japanese language school, or individuals whose business was directly connected with firms in Japan; but as time went on, it became less and less apparent why the others were included in these raids.

We wondered when Father's time would come. We expected momentarily to hear strange footsteps on the porch and the sudden demanding ring of the front doorbell. Our ears became attuned like the sensitive antennas of moths, translating every soft swish of passing cars into the arrival of the FBI squad. . . .

We had a family conference to discuss the possibility of Father and Mother's internment. Henry was in graduate school and I was beginning my second year at the university. We agreed to drop out should they be taken and we would manage the hotel during our parents' absence. Every week end Henry and I accompanied Father to the hotel and learned how to keep the hotel books, how to open the office safe, and what kind of linen, paper towels, and soap to order.

Then a new menace appeared on the scene. Cries began to sound up and down the coast that everyone of Japanese ancestry should be taken into custody. For years the professional guardians of the Golden West had wanted to rid their land of the Yellow Peril, and the war provided an opportunity for them to push their program through. As the chain of Pacific islands fell to the Japanese, patriots shrieked for protection from us. A Californian sounded the alarm: "The Japanese are dangerous and they must leave. Remember the destruction and the sabotage perpetrated at Pearl Harbor. Notice how they have infiltrated into the harbor towns and taken our best land."

He and his kind refused to be comforted by Edgar Hoover's special report to the War Department stating that there had not been a single case of sabotage committed by a Japanese living in Hawaii or on the Mainland during the Pearl Harbor attack or after. I began to feel acutely uncomfortable for living on Beacon Hill. The Marine Hospital rose tall and handsome on our hill, and if I stood on the west shoulder of the Hill, I could not help but get an easily photographed view of the Puget Sound Harbor with its ships snuggled against the docks. And Boeing airfield, a few miles south of us, which had never bothered me before, suddenly seemed to have moved right up into my back yard, daring me to take just one spying glance at it.

In February, Executive Order No. 9066 came out, authorizing the War Department to remove the Japanese from such military areas as it saw fit, aliens and citizens alike. Even if a person had a fraction of Japanese blood in him, he must leave on demand.

A pall of gloom settled upon our home. We couldn't believe that the government meant that the Japanese-Americans must go, too. We had heard the clamoring of superpatriots who insisted loudly, "Throw the whole kaboodle out. A Jap's a Jap, no matter how you slice him. You can't make an American out of little Jap Junior just by handing him an American birth certificate." But we had dismissed these remarks as just hot blasts of air from an overheated patriot. We were quite sure that our rights as American citizens would not be violated, and we would not be marched out of our homes on the same basis as enemy aliens.

In anger, Henry and I read and reread the Executive Order. Henry crumpled the newspaper in his hand and threw it against the wall. "Doesn't my citizenship mean a single blessed thing to anyone? Why doesn't somebody make up my mind for me. First they want me in the army. Now they're going to slap an alien 4–C on me because of my ancestry. What the hell!"

Once more I felt like a despised, pathetic two-headed freak, a Japanese and an American, neither of which seemed to be doing me any good. The Nisei leaders in the community rose above their personal feelings and stated that they would cooperate and comply with the decision of the government as their sacrifice in keeping with the country's war effort, thus proving themselves loyal American citizens. I was too jealous of my recently acquired voting privilege to be gracious about giving in, and I felt most unco-operative. I noticed wryly that the feelings about the Japanese on the Hawaiian Islands were quite different from those on the West Coast. In Hawaii, a strategic military outpost, the Japanese were regarded as essential to the economy of the island and powerful economic forces fought against their removal. General Delos Emmons, in command of Hawaii at the time, lent his authoritative voice to calm the fears of the people on the island and to prevent chaos and upheaval. General Emmons established martial law, but he did not consider evacuation essential for the security of the island.

On the West Coast, General J. L. DeWitt of the Western Defense Command did not think martial law necessary, but he favored mass evacuation of the

Japanese and Nisei. We suspected the pressures from economic and political interests who would profit from such a wholesale evacuation influenced this decision.

Events moved rapidly. General DeWitt marked off Western Washington, Oregon, and all of California, and the southern half of Arizona as Military Area No. 1, hallowed ground from which we must remove ourselves as rapidly as possible. Unfortunately we could not simply vanish into thin air, and we had no place to go. We had no relatives in the east we could move in on. All our relatives were sitting with us in the forbidden area, themselves wondering where to go. The neighboring states in the line of exit for the Japanese protested violently at the prospect of any mass invasion. They said, very sensibly, that if the Coast didn't want the Japanese hanging around, they didn't either.

A few hardy families in the community liquidated their property, tied suitcases around their cars, and sallied eastward. They were greeted by signs in front of store windows, "Open season for Japs!" and "We kill rats and Japs here." On state lines, highway troopers swarmed around the objectionable migrants and turned them back under governor's orders.

General DeWitt must have finally realized that if he insisted on voluntary mass evacuation, hundreds and thousands of us would have wandered back and forth, clogging the highways and pitching tents along the roadside, eating and sleeping in colossal disorder. He suddenly called a halt to voluntary movement, although most of the Japanese were not budging an inch. He issued a new order, stating that no Japanese could leave the city, under penalty of arrest. The command had hatched another plan, a better one. The army would move us out as only the army could do it, and march us in neat, orderly fashion into assembly centers. We would stay in these centers only until permanent camps were set up inland to isolate us.

The orders were simple:

> Dispose of your homes and property. Wind up your business. Register the family. One seabag of bedding, two suitcases of clothing allowed per person. People in District #1 must report at 8th and Lane Street, 8 p.m. on April 28.

I wanted no part of this new order. I had read in the papers that the Japanese from the state of Washington would be taken to a camp in Puyallup, on the state fairgrounds. The article apologetically assured the public that the camp would be temporary and that the Japanese would be removed from the fairgrounds and parking lots in time for the opening of the annual State Fair. It neglected to say where we might be at the time when those fine breeds of Holstein cattle and York-shire hogs would be proudly wearing their blue satin ribbons. . . .

On the twenty-first of April, a Tuesday, the general gave us the shattering news. "All the Seattle Japanese will be moved to Puyallup by May 1. Everyone must be registered Saturday and Sunday between 8 a.m. and 5 p.m. They will leave next week in three groups, on Tuesday, Thursday and Friday."

Up to that moment, we had hoped against hope that something or someone would intervene for us. Now there was no time for moaning. A thousand and one details must be attended to in this one week of grace. Those seven days sputtered out like matches struck in the wind, as we rushed wildly about. Mother distributed sheets, pillowcases and blankets, which we stuffed into seabags. Into the two suitcases, we packed heavy winter overcoats, plenty of sweaters, woolen slacks and skirts, flannel pajamas and scarves. Personal toilet articles, one tin plate, tin cup and silverware completed our luggage. The one seabag and two suitcases apiece were going to be the backbone of our future home, and we planned it carefully.

Henry went to the Control Station to register the family. He came home with twenty tags, all numbered "10710," tags to be attached to each piece of baggage, and one to hang from our coat lapels. From then on, we were known as Family #10710. . . .

[The family was taken on a bus to the temporary camp site.]

Our bus idled a moment at the traffic signal and we noticed at the left of us an entire block filled with neat rows of low shacks, resembling chicken houses. Someone commented on it with awe, "Just look at those chicken houses. They sure go in for poultry in a big way here." Slowly the bus made a left turn, drove through a wire-fenced gate, and to our dismay, we were inside the oversized chicken farm. The bus driver opened the door, the guard stepped out and stationed himself at the door again. Jim, the young man who had shepherded us into the busses, popped his head inside and sang out, "Okay, folks, all off at Yokohama, Puyallup." . . .

Quickly we fell into the relentless camp routine in Puyallup. Every morning at six I was awakened by our sadistic cook beating mightily on an iron pot. He would thrust a heavy iron ladle inside the pot and hit all sides in a frightful, double-timed clamor, BONG! BONG! BONG! BONG! With my eyes glued together in sleep, I fumbled around for my washcloth and soap, and groped my way in the dark toward the community washroom.

At the mess hall I gnawed my way through canned stewed figs, thick French toast, and molten black coffee. With breakfast churning its way violently down to the pit of my stomach, I hurried each morning to the Area A gate. There I stood in line with other evacuees who had jobs in Area D. Area D was just across the street from A, but we required armed chaperones to make the crossing. After the guard carefully inspected our passes and counted noses, the iron gate yawned open for us, and we marched out in orderly formation, escorted fore and aft by military police. When we halted at the curb for the traffic signal to change, we were counted. We crossed the street and marched half a block to the Area D gate where we were counted again. I had a $16 a month job as stenographer at the administration office. A mere laborer who sweated it out by his brawn eight hours a day drew $12, while doctors, dentists, attorneys, and other professionals earned the lordly sum of $19 a month. For the most part, the camp was maintained by the evacuees who cooked, doctored, laid sewer pipes, repaired shoes, and provided their own entertainment. . . .

Sunday was the day we came to an abrupt halt, free from the busy round of activities in which we submerged our feelings. In the morning we went to church to listen to our Reverend Everett Thompson who visited us every Sunday. Our minister was a tall and lanky man whose open and friendly face quickly drew people to him. He had served as missionary in Japan at one time and he spoke fluent Japanese. He had worked with the young people in our church for many years, and it was a great comfort to see him and the many other ministers and church workers with whom we had been in contact back in Seattle. We felt that we were not entirely forgotten. . . .

[The family was soon transferred to a permanent internment camp.]

Camp Minidoka was located in the south central part of Idaho, north of Snake River. It was a semiarid region, reclaimed to some extent by an irrigation project with the Minidoka Dam. From where I was sitting, I could see nothing but flat prairies, clumps of greasewood, and the jack rabbits. And of course the hundreds and hundreds of barracks, to house ten thousand of us.

Our home was one room in a large army-type barracks, measuring about twenty by twenty-five feet. There were smaller rooms on both ends of the barracks reserved for couples, and larger rooms to accommodate a family of more than five. The only furnishings were an iron pot-belly stove and the cots.

On our first day in camp, we were given a rousing welcome by a dust storm. It caught up with us while we were still wandering about looking for our room. We felt as if we were standing in a gigantic sand-mixing machine as the sixty-mile gale lifted the loose earth up into the sky, obliterating everything. Sand filled our mouths and nostrils and stung our faces and hands like a thousand darting needles. Henry and Father pushed on ahead while Mother, Sumi and I followed, hanging onto their jackets, banging suitcases into each other. At last we staggered into our room, gasping and blinded. We sat on our suitcases to rest, peeling off our jackets and scarves. The window panes rattled madly, and the dust poured in through the cracks like smoke. Now and then when the wind subsided, I saw other evacuees, hanging on to their suitcases, heads bent against the stinging dust. The wind whipped their scarves and towels from their heads and zipped them out of sight. It seemed as if we had been sitting for hours in the stifling room before we were aroused by the familiar metallic clang of the dinner triangle.

The mess hall was a desolate sight with thick layers of dust covering the dining tables and benches, and filling teacups and bowls. The cooking in the kitchen filled the building with streaming vapor and the odor of fried fish. As we stood in the chow line, we stared out of the window, wondering when the storm would subside.

I saw a woman struggling toward the building. A miniature tornado enveloped her and she disappeared from sight. A few seconds later when it cleared, I saw that she had been pulling a child behind her, shielding it with her skirt. The little girl suddenly sat down on the ground and hid her face in her lap. The mother ripped off her jacket, threw it over her daughter's head and flung herself against the wind, carrying the child. Someone pulled the two inside the mess hall. For the next half hour we ate silently, accompanied by the child's persistent sobs.

Just as suddenly as the storm had broken out, it died. We walked out of the mess hall under a pure blue sky, startling in its serenity. It was as if there had been a quiet presence overhead, untouched and unaffected by the violence below, and the entire summer evening sky had lowered itself gently into a cradle of peace and silence.

The night sky of Idaho was beautiful and friendly. A translucent milk-glass moon hung low against its rich blue thickness, and diamond-cut stars were flung across it from horizon to horizon. This was a strange, gaunt country, fierce in the hot white light of day, but soft and gentle with a beauty all its own at night.

In the deepening blue shadows, people hurried to and fro, preparing for their first night in camp. The Issei men stomped along in their wooden *getas,* their loose suspenders swinging rhythmically with each step, while the Issei women in cool cotton print *yukatas,* Japanese house kimonos, slipped along noiselessly. They bowed to each other, murmuring *"Oyasumi nasai.* Rest well." . . .

By fall, Camp Minidoka had bloomed into a full-grown town. Children went to school in the barracks, taught by professional teachers among the evacuees and people hired from the outside. Except for the members of the administration staff, the evacuees themselves supplied the entire labor pool in the camp, in the mess halls, in the hospital, on the farm, on roadwork, and in internal policing. A small library was started with the donation of books from Seattle and the neighboring towns. All church activities, Protestant, Catholic and Buddhist, were in full session. The ministers, who had served among the Japanese people back home, moved to Twin Falls, a small town nearby, and continued their good work among us. Our own Mr. Thompson and his family were with us again. . . .

Then one day a group of army personnel marched into our dreaming camp on a special mission and our idyllic life of nothingness came to a violent end. They made a shocking announcement. "The United States War Department has decided to form a special combat unit for the Nisei. We have come to recruit volunteers."

We gasped and we spluttered. Dunks Oshima who had brought the news to us was on fire. Dunks had grown into a strapping young man with a brilliant record for high-school sports. He eyed us fiercely as he cried, "What do they take us for? Saps? First, they change my army status to 4–C because of my ancestry, run me out of town, and now they want me to volunteer for a suicide squad so I could get killed for this damn democracy. That's going some, for sheer brass!"

That was exactly the way most of us felt, but the recruiting officers were well prepared to cope with our emotional explosion. They called meetings and we flocked to them with an injured air.

An officer, a big, tall, dark-haired man with formidable poise spoke to us. "You're probably wondering why we are here, recruiting for volunteers from your group. I think that my explanation is best expressed in the statement recently issued by our President, regarding a citizen's right and privilege to serve his country. I want to read it to you:

> No loyal citizen of the United States should be denied the democratic right to exercise the responsibilities of his citizenship, regardless of his ancestry. The principle on which this country was founded and by which it has always been governed is that Americanism is a matter of the mind and the heart. Americanism is not, and never was, a matter of race or ancestry. Every loyal American citizen should be given the opportunity to serve this country wherever his skills will make the greatest contribution . . . whether it be in the ranks of our armed forces, war production, agriculture, Government service, or other work essential to the war effort."

It all sounded very well. It was the sort of declaration which rang true and clear in our hearts, but there were questions in our minds which needed answering. The speaker threw the meeting open for discussion. We said we didn't want a separate Nisei combat unit because it looked too much like segregation. We wanted to serve in the same way as other citizens, in a mixed group with the other Americans. The man replied, "But if the Nisei men were to be scattered throughout the army, you'd lose your significance as Nisei. Maybe you want it that way, because in the past you suffered with your Japanese faces. Well, why not accept your Japanese face? Why be ashamed of it? Why not capitalize on it for a change? This is no time for retiring into anonymity. There are powerful organizations who are now campaigning on the Coast to deport you all to Japan, citizens and residents alike. But there're also men and women who believe in you, who feel you should be given the chance to stand up and express yourselves. They thought that a Nisei combat unit would be just the thing so that whatever you accomplish, whatever you achieve, will be yours and yours alone." . . .

The birth of the Nisei combat team was the climax to our evacuee life, and the turning point. It was the road back to our rightful places. . . .

By 1943, scarcely a year after Evacuation Day, the War Relocation Authority was opening channels through which the Nisei could return to the main stream of life. It granted permanent leave to anyone cleared by the FBI who had proof of a job and a place to live. Students were also released if they had been accepted into colleges and universities.

The West Coast was still off-limits, but we had access to the rest of the continent where we could start all over again. The Midwest and East suddenly loomed before us, an exciting challenge. Up till then America for me had meant the lovely city of Seattle, a small Japanese community and a desperate struggle to be just myself. Now that I had shed my past, I hoped that I might come to know another aspect of America which would inject strength into my hyphenated Americanism instead of pulling it apart.

Matsuko, my childhood friend, was one of the first to leave camp. Through a church program, the Reverend Mr. and Mrs. W. Trumble of Chicago had become interested in helping individual evacuees. They had written Matsuko, telling her about a job as a stenographer in a large department store and inviting her to live with them. From Chicago, Matsuko deluged me with enthusiastic letters, telling me what wonderful folks the Trumbles were and how happy she was with her job. She said she no longer felt self-conscious about her Oriental face and that she was breathing free and easy for the first time in her life. Matsuko urged me to leave Minidoka and spoke to the Trumbles about me. One day I received a cordial letter from a Dr. and Mrs. John Richardson. Dr. Richardson was a pastor at a Presbyterian Church in a suburb of Chicago. He told me of a dentist, desperately in need of an assistant, who was willing to hire a Nisei. I was to live with the Richardsons.

I accepted Dr. Richardson's invitation posthaste, feeling as if it were a dream too good to be true. Father and Mother, although reluctant to see me go, accepted my decision to leave as part of the sadness which goes with bearing children who grow up and must be independent.

So when it was early in spring and the snow had thawed, I boarded a train in Shoshone, numbed with excitement and anxiety. For two days and two nights I remained wide-eyed and glued to my seat as we rushed headlong across the great continent. We finally hit Chicago, and I felt helpless in the giant, roaring metropolis, with its thundering vitality, perpetual wind and clouds of smoke. Hundreds of people and cars seemed to be rushing at each other at suicide speed. I was relieved to see that they were much too busy to notice the evacuees who had crept into town. I plunged and swam through this heaving mass of humanity until I found a taxi.

The Richardson residence was a large, two-story brown frame house in the suburbs. I pressed the doorbell with a nervous cold finger. A small woman with a beautiful halo of white hair and gentle gray eyes greeted me warmly. "Come in, Monica, I'm Mrs. Richardson. My husband and I've been expecting you. Here, let me help you with your suitcase." Her quiet, gracious manner disarmed me completely. . . .

[The Richardsons also arranged for Kazuko to attend college.]

I enrolled at Wendell College in southern Indiana. The cluster of ivy-covered red brick buildings stood gathered on the edge of a thick-wooded bluff which rose almost three hundred feet, overlooking the stately Ohio River. Wendell College was a Presbyterian-affiliated liberal arts school, and the atmosphere of its campus reflected a leisurely pace of life, simplicity and friendly charm. Young people from all walks of life were there . . . studying for the ministry, the teaching profession, the medical profession and other varied fields. There was also a distinct international air with foreign students from all parts of the world: South America, China, Java, India.

Mrs. Ashford, the widow with whom I lived on the edge of the campus, was an example of the college town's friendliness. She was a comfortable, motherly woman with silky, honey-colored hair done up in a bun, and merry blue eyes. Her husband had been a minister and college official. He had died several years before, and Mrs. Ashford had been living alone ever since. In the tall, two-storied gray frame house, my new friend had prepared a cozy room for me upstairs, where I could study quietly. Despite a stiff knee, Mrs. Ashford was up at dawn to fire up the furnace and prepare breakfast. I awakened to her cheerful call and the fragrant aroma of coffee wafting up to my room. In the evenings when I returned home from school, we sat in the two wooden rocking chairs in the sitting room, chatted about the days' events, listened to a favorite radio program or two, then I went upstairs to study. And always before bedtime, Mrs. Ashford called me down to the kitchen for a light snack because she firmly believed that mental work was just as exhausting as physical labor. Thus she provided me with the companionship I needed and a wealth of enchanting memories which I could conjure up at the thought of Wendell . . . the warm fragrance of freshly baked nutbread and homemade cookies filling the house on a cold winter night, the creaking porch swing where I could relax on warm spring evenings to watch the fireflies pinpoint the dark blue night, as I breathed in the thick sweet scent of lilacs surrounding the house.

There were three other Nisei girls enrolled at Wendell. Two were from southern California, and the third from my own home town. Faculty and students alike went out of their way to make us feel a real part of the campus life. We were swept into a round of teas and dinner parties, and invited to join the independent women's organization. The sororities included us in their rush parties, too, although because of a national ruling we could not be asked to join. I knew about this policy, and although I had ceased to feel personally hurt about it, one sorority apparently felt troubled by the restriction imposed on it. One day its officers, Alice Week, Lorraine Brown and the faculty advisor, Miss Knight, paid me a special visit. I remember how Alice looked at Miss Knight as if she were taking a deep breath before the plunge, and then spoke gently to me. "Monica, we've enjoyed meeting you, and we hope we'll get to know a lot more of each other from now on. But there are national restrictions placed on our membership.

Although many of us sincerely want to invite you into our group, we can't. I hope you understand." . . .

The first two school years at Wendell I worked for my tuition and board, waiting on tables in the women's dormitory. Being physically inept, I never learned to hoist the huge tray over my head with one hand as most students did within the first week. Instead I staggered and groaned under the weight of the tray until at last I was offered a job as secretary to Dr. Scott, and not a day too soon, I thought, for I had worn deep dents into my sides from carrying trays on my hips. During summer vacations, I went home to the Richardsons in Chicago where I worked as a stenographer in a law firm. Father's foresight in persuading me to go to business school was paying off at last.

My second year at Wendell, just before Christmas, I had a letter from Father and Mother, who were still in camp, urging me to spend the holiday with them. "It would be so nice to have at least one of you back." They enclosed a check for the railroad fare. So I packed a suitcase, kissed Mrs. Ashford "Good-by and Merry Christmas," and set off for Camp Minidoka.

At Shoshone, my last stop, I went into a crumbling old hotel and sat in its overheated lobby to wait for the bus to take me into camp. Bewhiskered, wrinkled old men lounged silently, reading every word in the newspaper, reaching around now and then to spit tobacco juice into the battered brass spittoon. I wondered if Father's hotel in Seattle was now filled with dried-up, dusty remnants of humanity like these.

At Camp Minidoka, I was startled to see an MP again, standing at the gate. I had forgotten about such things as MP's and barbed-wire fences. Mother rushed out of the gate shelter, her face beaming. "Ka-chan! It was so good of you to come. Have you been well and happy?" She looked closely into my face. I was relieved to see Mother looking well and still full of smiles, although I noticed a few gray streaks in her smooth jet-black head of hair as I hugged her.

"Where's Papa?" I asked.

"He had a bad cold, and he's resting at the hospital now. He'll be home in a day or two."

Although Mother tried to hide it, I learned that Father had had a close brush with pneumonia.

The camp was quiet and ghostly, drained of its young blood. All of the able-bodied Nisei men had been drafted into the army. The rest of the young people had relocated to the Midwest and East to jobs and schools. Some of the parents had followed them out. But the Issei who still wanted to go back West and had a home or a business to return to, remained in camp, hoping that the military restriction on the Coast would be lifted at the end of the war. . . .

The days passed by too quickly and it was time to leave Camp Minidoka. Father and Mother accompanied me to the camp gate. It was one of those crisp winter mornings when the pale sky and the snow were bathed in a taut cold pink.

"Ah, well, this parting is not a sad one for us, is it, Mama?" Father said. "It isn't as if she were a young son going off to war."

"This is what happens to all parents. Children grow, and they must fly away. But it is well . . . you all seem so happy in your letters, Henry and Minnie in St. Louis, and Sumi way out there in the East. When the war came and we were all evacuated, Papa and I were heartsick. We felt terribly bad about being your Japanese parents."

"No, don't say those things, Mama, please. If only you knew how much I have changed about being a Nisei. It wasn't such a tragedy. I don't resent my Japanese blood anymore. I'm proud of it, in fact, because of you and the Issei who've struggled so much for us. It's really nice to be born into two cultures, like getting a real bargain in life, two for the price of one. The hardest part, I guess, is the growing up, but after that, it can be interesting and stimulating. I used to feel like a two-headed monstrosity, but now I find that two heads are better than one."

Father beamed, "It makes us very happy to hear that."

"In spite of the war and the mental tortures we went through, I think the Nisei have attained a clearer understanding of America and its way of life, and we have learned to value her more. Her ideas and ideals of democracy are based essentially on religious principles and her very existence depends on the faith and moral responsibilities of each individual. I used to think of the government as a paternal organization. When it failed me, I felt bitter and sullen. Now I know I'm just as responsible as the men in Washington for its actions. Somehow it all makes me feel much more at home in America. All in all, I think the Issei's losses during this war are greater."

"If we consider material losses, maybe so, but our children's gain is our gain, too. Our deepest happiness we receive from our children," Father said.

"What are you and Mama going to do, the first thing after you return to Seattle?"

Father had a ready reply.

"Oh, first, we'll go and say 'Hello and thank you' to Joe, Sam and Peter for looking after the hotel. After that, we will take a walk along the waterfront and maybe dine on a crab or two. Then we will buy a little house and wait for visits from you all with your little children."

Mother smiled in assent. I gave a quick hug to Father and Mother and stepped inside the bus. As I looked out of the window, I saw them standing patiently, wrapped in heavy dark winter clothes, Father in his old navy pea jacket, Mother in black wool slacks and black coat. They looked like wistful immigrants. I wondered when they would be able to leave their no-man's land, pass through the legal barrier and become naturalized citizens. Then I thought, in America, many things are possible. When I caught Father and Mother's eyes, they smiled instantly.

I was returning to Wendell College with confidence and hope. I had discovered a deeper, stronger pulse in the American scene. I was going back into its main stream, still with my Oriental eyes, but with an entirely different outlook, for now I felt more like a whole person instead of a sadly split personality. The Japanese and the American parts of me were now blended into one.

ANNE MOODY
1940–

Anne Moody, who would come of age during a time historians call the Second Reconstruction, was born during the latter days of Jim Crow segregation in Mississippi. Called Essie Mae—a name she thought more appropriate "for a cow or hog"—Anne Moody had to grow up quickly. Her mother struggled for the family's survival after Anne's father deserted her and their three children. Anne was moved seven times and watched her mother give birth to two children and be pregnant with a third before the father agreed to marry her.

Anne was hardworking, athletic, attractive, and smart. From the age of nine she did odd jobs for the white women in town, bringing in necessary money for clothing, food, and school. She was a homecoming queen and athlete who applied herself to her schoolwork, finishing third academically in the Class of 1959 at all-black Johnson High School. Her grades and basketball skills earned her a scholarship to Natchez College before she studied her way into a full-tuition scholarship to "the best senior college in the state for Negroes"—Tougaloo, located in Jackson.

Moody came to maturity as the civil rights movement began to organize in the wake of Brown v. Board of Education *(1954), the Montgomery bus boycott of 1956, and the formation of the Student Nonviolent Coordinating Committee (SNCC) in 1960. At Tougaloo, she involved herself in the National Association for the Advancement of Colored People (NAACP) before working with SNCC and the Congress of Racial Equality (CORE), both organizations more insistent than the NAACP on swift and relentless action against white supremacy. She helped initiate the state's first sit-in of a Woolworth lunch counter, went to jail several times for attending demonstrations, and volunteered as a full-time field worker registering voters in the toughest areas of the state.*

Published when the author was twenty-eight, Moody's Coming of Age in Mississippi *recounts the poverty, terror, sexual exploitation, uncertainty, and family alienation of growing up black and female in the deep South during a time of hope and change. Her work asks and answers questions about the interplay of race, class, and gender. It is the skeptical and angry individual success story of a woman who fought against tremendous odds. But the autobiography should be read with a view to the social and political interactions that infiltrate every person's life. In that sense, it fits into the tradition of African-American writing that places the elevation of a race over the strivings of a single individual, family, or community.*

Coming of Age in Mississippi, *1968. Reprint, New York: Dell Publishing, 1976. (Reprinted with permission.)*

I'm still haunted by dreams of the time we lived on Mr. Carter's plantation. Lots of Negroes lived on his place. Like Mama and Daddy they were all farmers. We all lived in rotten wood two-room shacks. But ours stood out from the others because it was up on the hill with Mr. Carter's big white house, overlooking the farms and the other shacks below. It looked just like the Carters' barn with a chimney and a porch, but Mama and Daddy did what they could to make it livable. Since we had only one big room and a kitchen, we all slept in the same room. It was like three rooms in one. Mama slept in one corner and I had a little bed in another corner next to one of the big wooden windows. Around the fireplace a rocking chair and a couple of straight chairs formed a sitting area. This big room had a plain, dull-colored wallpaper tacked loosely to the walls with large thumbtacks. Under each tack was a piece of cardboard which had been taken from shoeboxes and cut into little squares to hold the paper and keep the tacks from tearing through. Because there were not enough tacks, the paper bulged in places. The kitchen didn't have any wallpaper and the only furniture in it was a wood stove, an old table and a safe.

Mama and Daddy had two girls. I was almost four and Adline was a crying baby about six or seven months. We rarely saw Mama and Daddy because they were in the field every day except Sunday. They would get up early in the morning and leave the house just before daylight. It was six o'clock in the evening when they returned, just before dark. . . .

[While her parents worked, her mother's eight-year-old brother babysat the Moody sisters. One day while he was playing with matches the house caught fire and burned down. He blamed Essie Mae and her father beat her.]

A week or so after the fire, every little thing began to get on Daddy's nerves. Now he was always yelling at me and snapping at Mama. The crop wasn't coming along as he had expected. Every evening when he came from the field he was terribly depressed. He was running around the house grumbling all the time.

"Shit, it was justa waste o' time. Didn't getta nuff rain for nuthin'. We ain't gonna even get two bales o' cotton this year. That corn ain't no good and them sweet potatoes jus' burning up in that hard-ass ground. Goddamn, ah'd a did better on a job than this. Ain't gonna have nuthin' left when Mr. Carter take out his share." We had to hear this sermon almost every night and he was always snapping at Mama like it was all her fault.

During the harvest, Daddy's best friend, Bush, was killed. Bush was driving his wagon when his horses went wild, turning the wagon over in the big ditch alongside the road. It landed on his neck and broke it. His death made Daddy even sadder.

The only times I saw him happy any more were when he was on the floor rolling dice. He used to practice shooting them at home before every big game and I would sit and watch him. He would even play with me then, and every time he won that money he would bring me lots of candy or some kind of present. He was good with a pair of dice and used to win the money all the time. He and most of the other men gambled every Saturday night through Sunday morning. One weekend he came home without a cent. He told Mama that he had lost every penny. He came home broke a few more times. Then one Sunday morning before he got home one of the women on the farm came by the house to tell Mama that he was spending his weekends with Florence, Bush's beautiful widow. I remember he and Mama had a real knockdown dragout session when he finally did come home. Mama fist-fought him like a man, but this didn't stop him from going by Florence's place. He even got bolder about it and soon went as often as he liked.

Florence was a mulatto, high yellow with straight black hair. She was the envy of all the women on the plantation. After Bush's death they got very particular about where their men were going. And they watched Florence like a bunch of hawks. She couldn't even go outdoors without some woman peeping at her and reporting that she was now coming out of the house.

Mama had never considered Florence or any of the other women a threat because she was so beautiful herself. She was slim, tall, and tawny-skinned, with high cheekbones and long dark hair. She was by and far the liveliest woman on the plantation and Daddy used to delight in her. When she played with me she was just like a child herself. Daddy used to call her an overgrown wildchild and tease her that she had too much Indian blood in her.

Meantime, Mama had begun to get very fat. Her belly kept getting bigger and bigger. Soon she acted as if she was fat and ugly. Every weekend, when she thought Daddy was with Florence she didn't do a thing but cry. Then one of those red-hot summer days, she sent me and Adline to one of the neighbors nearest to us. We were there all day. I didn't like the people so I was glad when we finally went home. When we returned I discovered why Mama had gotten so fat. She called me to the bed and said, "Look what Santa sent you." I was upset. Santa never brought live dolls before. It was a little baldheaded boy. He was some small and looked as soft as one of our little pigs when it was born.

"His name is Junior," Mama said. "He was named for your daddy."

My daddy's name was Fred so I didn't understand why she said the baby's name was Junior. Adline was a year old and walking good. She cried like crazy at the sight of the little baby.

While I stood by the bed looking at Mama, I realized her belly had gone down. I was glad of that. I had often wondered if Daddy was always gone because her belly had gotten so big. But that wasn't it, because after it went down, he was gone just as much as before, even more.

Next thing I knew, we were being thrown into a wagon with all our things. I really didn't know what was going on. But I knew something was wrong because Mama and Daddy barely spoke to each other and whenever they did exchange words, they snapped and cursed. Later in the night when we arrived at my Great-Aunt Cindy's place, all of our things were taken from the wagon and Daddy left.

"Where is Daddy goin'?" I cried to Mama.

"By his business," she answered.

Aunt Cindy and all the children stood around the porch looking at him drive the wagon away.

"That dog! That no-good dog!" I heard Mama mumble. I knew then that he was gone for good.

"Ain't he gonna stay with us?" I asked.

"No he ain't gonna stay with us! Shut up!" she yelled at me with her eyes full of water. She cried all that night. . . .

Shortly after we moved in I turned five years old and Mama started me at Mount Pleasant School. Now I had to walk four miles each day up and down that long rock road. Mount Pleasant was a big white stone church, the biggest Baptist church in the area.

The school was a little one-room rotten wood building located right next to it. There were about fifteen of us who went there. We sat on big wooden benches just like the ones in the church, pulled up close to the heater. But we were cold all day. That little rotten building had big cracks in it, and the heater was just too small.

Reverend Cason, the minister of the church, taught us in school. He was a tall yellow man with horn-rimmed glasses that sat on the edge of his big nose. He had the largest feet I had ever seen. He was so big, he towered over us in the little classroom like a giant. In church he preached loud and in school he talked loud. . . .

While Mama was working at the café in town, she began to get fat. She often told us how much she could eat while she was working. So I didn't think anything of her slowly growing "little pot." But one day after taking a good look, I noticed it wasn't a little pot any more. And I knew she was going to have a baby. She cried just about every night, then she would get up sick every morning. She didn't stop working until a week before the baby was born, and she was out of work only three weeks. She went right back to the café.

Mama called the baby James. His daddy was a soldier. One day the soldier and his mother came to get him. They were real yellow people. The only Negro near their color I had ever seen was Florence, the lady my daddy was now living with. The soldier's mother was a stout lady with long thin straight black hair and very thin lips. She looked like a slightly tanned white woman. Mama called her "Miss Pearl." All the time they were in our house, Mama acted as though she was scared of them. She smiled a couple of times when they made general comments about the baby. But I could tell she didn't mean it.

Just before the soldier and Miss Pearl left, Miss Pearl turned to Mama and said, "You can't work and feed them other children and keep this baby too." I guess Mama did want to keep the little boy. She looked so sad I thought she was going to cry, but she didn't say anything. Miss Pearl must have seen how Mama looked too. "You can stop in to see the baby when you are in town sometimes," she said. Then she and the soldier took him and drove away in their car. Mama cried all night. And she kept saying bad things about some Raymond. I figured that was the name of the soldier who gave her the baby.

At the end of that summer Mama found it necessary for us to move into town, in Centreville, where she worked. This time we moved into a two-room house that was twice the size of the other one. It was next to where a very poor white family lived in a large green frame house. It was also located on one of the main roads branching off Highway 24 running into Centreville. We were now a little less than a mile from the school that I was to attend, which was on the same road as our house. Here we had a sidewalk for the first time. It extended from town all the way to school where it ended. I was glad we lived on the sidewalk side of the road. Between the sidewalk and our house the top soil was sand about two feet deep. We were the only ones with clean white sand in our yard and it seemed beautiful and special. There was even more sand for us to play in in a large vacant lot on the other side of our house. The white people living next to us only had green grass in their yard just like everybody else.

A few weeks after we moved there, I was in school again. I was now six years old and in the second grade. At first, it was like being in heaven to have less than a mile to walk to school. And having a sidewalk from our house all the way there made things even better.

I was going to Willis High, the only Negro school in Centreville. It was named for Mr. C. H. Willis, its principal and founder, and had only been expanded into a high school the year before I started there. Before Mr. Willis came to town, the eighth grade had been the limit of schooling for Negro children in Centreville.

For the first month that I was in school a Negro family across the street kept Adline and Junior. But after that Mama had them stay at home alone and, every hour or so until I came home, the lady across the street would come down and look in on them. One day when I came home from school, Adline and Junior were naked playing in the sand in front of our house. All the children who lived in town used that sidewalk that passed our house. When they saw Adline and Junior sitting in the sand naked they started laughing and making fun of them. I was ashamed to go in the house or recognize Adline and Junior as my little sister and brother. I had never felt that way before. I got mad at Mama because she had to work and couldn't take care of Adline and Junior herself. Every day after that I hated the sand in front of the house.

Before school was out we moved again and I was glad. It seemed as though we were always moving. Every time it was to a house on some white man's place and every time it was a room and a kitchen. The new place was much smaller than the last one, but it was nicer. Here we had a larger pasture to play in that was dry, flat, and always closely cropped because of the cattle. Mama still worked at the café. But now she had someone to keep Adline and Junior until I came home from school. . . .

[After Anne's younger brother "Junior" burned down the house, the Moodys moved two more times.]

The Christmas after we moved there, I thought sure Mama would get us some skates. But she didn't. We didn't get anything but a couple of apples and oranges. I cried a week for those skates, I remember.

Every Saturday evening Mama would take us to the movies. The Negroes sat upstairs in the balcony and the whites sat downstairs. One Saturday we arrived at the movies at the same time as the white children. When we saw each other, we ran and met. Katie walked straight into the downstairs lobby and Adline, Junior, and I followed. Mama was talking to one of the white women and didn't notice that we had walked into the white lobby. I think she thought we were at the side entrance we had always used which led to the balcony. We were standing in the white lobby with our friends, when Mama came in and saw us. "C'mon! C'mon!" she yelled, pushing Adline face on into the door. "Essie Mae, um gonna try my best to kill you when I get you home. I told you 'bout running up in these stores and things like you own 'em!" she shouted, dragging me through the door. When we got outside, we stood there crying, and we could hear the white children crying inside the white lobby. After that, Mama didn't even let us stay at the movies. She carried us right home.

All the way back to our house, Mama kept telling us that we couldn't sit downstairs, we couldn't do this or that with white children. Up until that time I had never really thought about it. After all, we were playing together. I knew that we were going to separate schools and all, but I never knew why.

After the movie incident, the white children stopped playing in front of our house. For about two weeks we didn't see them at all. Then one day they were there again and we started playing. But things were not the same. I had never really thought of them as white before. Now all of a sudden they were white, and their whiteness made them better than me. I now realized that not only were they better than me because they were white, but everything they owned and everything connected with them was better than what was available to me. I hadn't realized before that downstairs in the movies was any better than upstairs. But now I saw that it was. Their whiteness provided them with a pass to downstairs in that nice section and my blackness sent me to the balcony.

Now that I was thinking about it, their schools, homes, and streets were better than mine. They had a large red brick school with nice sidewalks connecting the buildings. Their homes were large and beautiful with indoor toilets and every other convenience that I knew of at the time. Every house I had ever lived in was a one- or two-room shack with an outdoor toilet. It really bothered me that they had all these nice things and we had nothing. "There is a secret to it besides being white." I thought. Then my mind got all wrapped up in trying to uncover that secret.

One day when we were all playing in our playhouse in the ditch under the pecan tree, I got a crazy idea. I thought the secret was their "privates." I had seen everything they had but their privates and it wasn't any different than mine. So I made up a game called "The Doctor." I had never been to a doctor myself. However, Mama had told us that a doctor was the only person that could look at children's naked bodies besides their parents. Then I remembered the time my Grandma Winnie was sick. When I asked her what the doctor had done to her she said, "He examined me." Then I asked her about "examined" and she told me he looked at her teeth, in her ears, checked her heart, blood and privates. Now I was going to be the doctor. I had all of them, Katie, Bill, Sandra, and Paul plus Adline and Junior take off their clothes and stand in line as I sat on one of the apple crates and examined them. I looked in their mouths and ears, put my ear to their hearts to listen to their heartbeats. Then I had them lie down on the leaves and I looked at their privates. I examined each of them about three times, but I didn't see any differences. I still hadn't found that secret.

That night when I was taking my bath, soaping myself all over, I thought about it again. I remembered the day I had seen my two uncles Sam and Walter. They were just as white as Katie them. But Grandma Winnie was darker than Mama, so how could Sam and Walter be white? I must have been thinking about it for a long time because Mama finally called out, "Essie Mae! Stop using up all that soap! And hurry up so Adline and Junior can bathe 'fore that water gits cold."

"Mama," I said, "why ain't Sam and Walter white?"

" 'Cause they mama ain't white," she answered.

"But you say a long time ago they daddy is white."

"If the daddy is white and the mama is colored, then that don't make the children white."

"But they got the same hair and color like Bill and Katie them got," I said.

"That still don't make them white! Now git out of that tub!" she snapped.

Every time I tried to talk to Mama about white people she got mad. Now I was more confused than before. If it wasn't the straight hair and the white skin that made you white, then what was it? . . .

[Raymond got out of the army and moved her mother and the children into a house with him. Essie learned to play basketball, chopped cotton on Raymond's farm, went to a revival at the Baptist church and was baptized in a muddy pond that had "big piles of cow manure floating around." She sold pecans to buy school clothes. Her mother had another baby—her sixth—and then "forced" Raymond to marry her. Essie worked as a maid for Linda Jean Jenkins.]

I worked for Linda Jean throughout my seventh grade year. But that spring and summer Raymond tried farming again, and I was only able to help her on weekends. When I entered eighth grade the following fall we were poorer than ever. Raymond had worse luck with the farm than the year before, so we weren't able to buy any new school clothes. I had added so much meat to my bones that I could squeeze into only two of my old school dresses. They were so tight I was embarrassed to put them on. I had gotten new jeans for the field that summer, so I started wearing them to school two and three days a week. But I continued to fill out so fast that even my jeans got too tight. I got so many wolf whistles from the boys in the class that the faster girls started wearing jeans that were even tighter than mine. When the high school boys started talking about how fine those eighth grade girls were, the high school girls started wearing tight jeans too. I had started a blue jeans fad.

One Friday in early October before school let out, Mrs. Willis announced that first thing Monday morning the class would choose its queen for the Homecoming competition. I couldn't think of any girl in the class I liked enough to nominate. I figured that the boys would get together and pick one of the fast girls, so I didn't worry myself about it.

Homecoming Day was in November. Each grade from fifth to twelfth was represented by a queen in the parade before the football game; the queen whose class raised the most money became Miss Willis High and was crowned Homecoming Queen during half time. Every girl in my class knew that our queen would certainly be the winner because Mrs. Willis' class always raised the most money. Mrs. Willis knew more about raising money than any other teacher on campus.

On Monday morning, after roll call, Mrs. Willis passed out little slips of paper and asked us to write the names of our nominees. Just for the hell of it I nominated myself. I knew that the outcome of the election depended on how the boys voted because all the girls except Darlene and me, who stood alone, were split into two groups, the fast and the quiet. Even so it would be close since there were nearly as many girls as there were boys. All that day I could see the three groups in their separate huddles, speculating. When we finally got back to Mrs. Willis' class in the last period, everybody got quiet.

"Class, durin' my break I counted the votes," Mrs. Willis said, "and I'm mighty glad I did because we've elected ourselves *three* queens!"

Everybody gasped and oohed and ahed. All the girls were looking at each other wondering who was the third queen, the one the *boys* had undoubtedly picked.

"Will the queens come forward as I call your names, please," Mrs. Willis said. "Queen Amanda!"

Amanda, the prettiest girl in the quiet group, went shyly up to the front of the room and stood by the side of Mrs. Willis' desk, looking down at the floor.

"Queen Dorothy!" Mrs. Willis called.

Some of the girls in the fast group clapped their hands as Dorothy switched up front in a real tight pair of jeans and with an overconfident look on her face. As she stood next to Amanda, she put her hands on her hips and stuck out her ass. A couple of the boys gave a low "boo" and all of a sudden she didn't seem so confident. I was surprised at the boos because I also thought Dorothy was the boys' favorite since she was the fastest girl in the eighth grade.

Mrs. Willis cleared her throat. I could tell she was enjoying the surprises.

"Queen Essie," she said. The girls in both groups nearly fainted and the boys started whistling and cheering. I began to look around for Queen Essie. Suddenly it struck me that *I* was Queen Essie. "The boys picked *me*?" I thought, with my mouth wide open.

"Queen Essie, we're waitin'," Mrs. Willis said, smiling.

"You mean me?" I said, poking myself in the chest.

"You're Essie, ain't you?" Mrs. Willis said.

As I started to get up and the boys began to whistle even louder, I realized I had on those tight jeans. So I sat right back down in my seat. One of the fast girls who didn't like me whispered from behind me, " 'Shamed to show that ass now, Moody?" I felt like spitting in her face, but instead I got up and purposely swayed my ass all the way up to Mrs. Willis' desk. The boys were going crazy, whistling all over the place. Mrs. Willis was laughing like she got a big kick out of the whole thing. . . .

[In a runoff, Essie became the homecoming queen. The name on her Eighth Grade diploma read "Annie Mae Moody." Because it would cost a fee to change the diploma—and because she preferred the mistake over her real name—Essie Mae adopted it as her given name. Her mother had another baby.]

Not only did I enter high school with a new name, but also with a completely new insight into the life of Negroes in Mississippi. I was now working for one of the meanest white women in town, and a week before school started Emmett Till was killed.

Up until his death, I had heard of Negroes found floating in a river or dead somewhere with their bodies riddled with bullets. But I didn't know the mystery behind these killings then. I remember once when I was only seven I heard Mama and one of my aunts talking about some Negro who had been beaten to death. "Just like them low-down skunks killed him they will do the same to us," Mama had said. When I asked her who killed the man and why, she said, "An Evil Spirit killed him. You gotta be a good girl or it will kill you too." So since I was seven, I had lived in fear of that "Evil Spirit." It took me eight years to learn what that spirit was.

I was coming from school the evening I heard about Emmett Till's death. There was a whole group of us, girls and boys, walking down the road headed home. A group of about six high school boys were walking a few paces ahead of me and several other girls. We were laughing and talking about something that had happened in school that day. However, the six boys in front of us weren't talking very loud. Usually they kept up so much noise. But today they were just walking and talking among themselves. All of a sudden they began to shout at each other.

"Man, what in the hell do you mean?"

"What I mean is these goddamned white folks is gonna start some shit here you just watch!"

"That boy wasn't but fourteen years old and they killed him. Now what kin a fourteen-year-old boy do with a white woman? What if he did whistle at her, he might have thought the whore was pretty."

"Look at all these white men here that's fucking over our women. Everybody knows it too and what's done about that? Look how many white babies we got walking around in our neighborhoods. Their mama's ain't white either. That boy was from Chicago, shit, everybody fuck everybody up there. He probably didn't even think of the bitch as white."

What they were saying shocked me. I knew all of those boys and I had never heard them talk like that. We walked on behind them for a while listening. Questions about who was killed, where, and why started running through my mind. I walked up to one of the boys.

"Eddie, what boy was killed?"

"Moody, where've you been?" he asked me. "Everybody talking about that fourteen-year-old boy who was killed in Greenwood by some white men. You don't know nothing that's going on besides what's in them books of yours, huh?"

Standing there before the rest of the girls, I felt so stupid. It was then that I realized I really didn't know what was going on all around me. It wasn't that I was dumb. It was just that ever since I was nine, I'd had to work after school and do my lessons on lunch hour. I never had time to learn anything, to hang around with people my own age. And you never were told anything by adults. . . .

I was fifteen years old when I began to hate people. I hated the white men who murdered Emmett Till and I hated all the other whites who were responsible for the countless murders Mrs. Rice told me about and those I vaguely remembered from childhood. But I also hated Negroes. I hated them for not standing up and doing something about the murders. In fact, I think I had a stronger resentment toward Negroes for letting the whites kill them than toward the whites. Anyway, it was at this stage in my life that I began to look upon Negro men as cowards. I could not respect them for smiling in a white man's face, addressing him as Mr. So-and-So, saying yessuh and nossuh when after they were home behind closed doors that same white man was a son of a bitch, a bastard, or any other name more suitable than mister.

Emmett Till's murder provoked a lot of anger and excitement among whites in Centreville. Now just about every evening when I got to work, Mrs. Burke had to attend a guild meeting. She had more women coming over now than ever. She and her friends had organized canvassing teams and a telephone campaign, to solicit for new members. Within a couple of months most of the whites in Centreville were taking part in the Guild. The meetings were initially held in the various houses. There were lawn parties and church gatherings. Then when it began to get cold, they were held in the high school auditorium.

After the Guild had organized about two-thirds of the whites in Centreville, all kinds of happenings were unveiled. The talk was on. White housewives began firing their maids and scolding their husbands and the Negro communities were full of whispered gossip.

The most talked-about subject was a love affair Mr. Fox, the deputy sheriff, and one of my classmates were carrying on. Bess was one of the oldest girls in my class. She was a shapely, high brown girl of about seventeen. She did general housekeeping and nursing for Fox and his wife.

It was general policy that most young white couples in Centreville hired only older Negro women as helpers. However, when there were two or more children in the family, it was more advantageous to hire a young Negro girl. That way, they always had someone to baby-sit when there was a need for a baby-sitter. My job with Linda Jean had been this kind. I kept Donna and Johnny on Sundays and baby-sat at night when they needed me.

Even though the teen-age Negro girls were more desirable for such jobs, very few if any were trusted in the homes of the young couples. The young white housewife didn't dare leave one alone in the house with her loyal and obedient husband. She was afraid that the Negro girl would seduce him, never the contrary.

There had been whispering in the Negro communities about Bess and Fox for some time. Just about every young white man in Centreville had a Negro lover. Therefore Fox, even though he was the deputy sheriff, wasn't doing anything worse than the rest of the men. At least that's the way the Negroes looked at the situation. Fox wasn't anyone special to them. But the whites didn't see it that way. The sheriff and all of his deputies were, in the eyes of their white compatriots, honorable men. And these honorable men were not put into office because they loved Negroes. So when the white community caught on about Fox and Bess, naturally they were out to expose the affair. Such exposure would discourage other officers from similar misbehavior.

Mrs. Fox was completely devoted to her husband. She too thought he was an honest man and she was willing to do anything that would prove him innocent. Soon a scheme was under way. Mrs. Fox was to leave home every so often. It had been reported that every time she was out and Bess was left there alone, Fox found his way home for one reason or another. Mrs. Fox left home purposely a couple of times while the neighbors kept watch. They confirmed the report that Fox would always return home. So one day Mrs. Fox decided to take the children and visit her mother—but she only went as far as the house next door. Bess was to come and give the house a thorough cleaning on the same day.

Mrs. Fox waited almost an hour at her neighbors' and nothing happened. It was said she was ready to go home and apologize to Bess and call her husband and do likewise. But just as she was about to do so, Fox drove up and went inside. She waited about thirty minutes more, then went home.

When she walked into her bedroom there they were, her husband and Bess, lying in her bed all curled up together. Poor Bess was so frightened that she ran out of the house clothed only in her slip with her panties in her hands. She never set foot in Mrs. Fox's house again. Neither did she return to school afterward. She took a job in the quarters where we lived, in a Negro café. It was said that she didn't need the job, though. Because after her embarrassing episode with Fox, her reputation was beyond repair, and he felt obligated to take care of her. Last I heard of Bess, she was still in Centreville, wearing fine clothes and carrying on as usual. Fox is no longer deputy, I understand, but he and his wife are still together.

It appeared after a while that the much talked about maids raids were only a means of diverting attention from what was really taking place in those guild meetings. In the midst of all the talk about what white man was screwing which Negro woman, new gossip emerged—about what Negro man was screwing which white woman. This gossip created so much tension, every Negro man in Centreville became afraid to walk the streets. They knew too well that they would not get off as easily as the white man who was caught screwing a Negro woman. They had only to look at a white woman and be hanged for it. Emmett Till's murder had proved it was a crime, punishable by death, for a Negro man to even whistle at a white woman in Mississippi.

I had never heard of a single affair in Centreville between a Negro man and a white woman. It was almost impossible for such an affair to take place. Negro men did not have access to white women. Whereas almost every white man in town had a Negro woman in his kitchen or nursing his babies. . . .

[In the wake of Emmett Till's murder, racial tensions grew worse, threats and beatings were frequent, and a family of nine was burned alive by an arsonist. Anne went to Baton Rouge to stay with her uncle and for a summer job before she returned to Centreville. She excelled at school and in basketball while she worked in the household of Mrs. Burke. Anne tutored Wayne Burke in algebra and brought on Mrs. Burke's wrath for getting too familiar with the white boy.]

The dining room in Mrs. Burke's house had come to mean many things to me. It symbolized hatred, love, and fear in many variations. The hatred and the love caused me much anxiety and fear. But courage was growing in me too. Little by little it was getting harder and harder for me not to speak out. Then one Wednesday night it happened.

Mrs. Burke seemed to discuss her most intimate concerns with me whenever I was ironing. This time she came in, sat down, and asked me, "Essie, what do you think of all this talk about integrating the schools in the South?"

At first I looked at her stunned with my mouth wide open. Then Mama's words ran through my head: "Just do your work like you don't know nothin'." I changed my expression to one of stupidity.

"Haven't you heard about the Supreme Court decision, and all this talk about integrating the schools?" she asked.

I shook my head no. But I lied.

"Well, we have a lot of talk about it here and people seemingly just don't know what to do. But I am not in favor of integrating schools. We'll move to Liberty first. I am sure that they won't stand for it there. You see, Essie, I wouldn't mind Wayne going to school with *you*. But all Negroes aren't like you and your family. You wouldn't like to go to school with Wayne, would you?" She said all this with so much honesty and concern, I felt compelled to be truthful.

"I don't know, Mrs. Burke. I think we could learn a lot from each other. I like Wayne and his friends. I don't see the difference in me helping Wayne and his friends at home and setting in a classroom with them. I've learned a lot from Judy them. Just like all Negroes ain't like me, all white children I know ain't like Wayne and Judy them. I was going to the post office the other day and a group of white girls tried to force me off the sidewalk. And I have seen Judy with one of them. But I know Judy ain't like that. She wouldn't push me or any other Negro off the street."

"What I asked you, Essie, is if you wanted to go to school with Wayne," Mrs. Burke said stiffly. "I am not interested in what Judy's friends did to you. So you are telling me you want to go to school with Wayne!" She stormed out of the dining room, her face burning with anger.

After she left I stood at the ironing board waiting—waiting for her to return with my money and tell me she didn't need me any more. But she didn't. She didn't confront me at all before I left that evening. And I went home shaking with fear. . . .

[She spent the summer working in a chicken factory in New Orleans and staying with her grandmother. She breezed through the academics of high school, learned to play piano, and became the best player on her basketball team. After her stepfather began to make sexual advances toward her, Anne moved in with her father and changed schools. She graduated in 1959 with a basketball scholarship to Natchez Junior College. In 1961 she entered Tougaloo College on a full academic scholarship.]

By the time mid-semester exams rolled in, I had gotten off to a very good start. It looked as though I could make the honor roll if I continued at this pace. I began to relax. I started taking time with my clothes, watching my weight, and wanting to look good. Keemp had not written in about a month. I started to worry because I knew that most of my girlfriends at Natchez College wanted him. I thought I'd better find me someone at Tougaloo to pass the time with. I knew I'd have to do some looking since there were three girls on campus to every boy. Three or four guys showed lots of interest in me, but they were already dating girls I knew. Finally, in December, I started dating one of them—a guy named Dave Jones.

As it turned out, when the semester ended, I didn't make that damn honor roll. I came out with three points less than I needed. I rationalized by blaming my downfall on my adjustment to the white teachers. However, the real cause was that damn Dave. All he could think of after we had gone together for a month was going to bed. I didn't even like him that much—not enough to go to bed with him anyway. When we had a so-called "adult discussion" about sex, as he called it, I told him that I was a virgin and I was afraid to be screwing around on campus. He kept telling me that he would take care of me, that he wouldn't hurt me, and all that shit. To get him off my back, I told him that I would only when I felt that I was ready. After another month or so when I still wasn't ready, he got mad, and one night in the park, he tried to take me. We were walking back from the "Greasy Spoon," a little student hangout right outside the campus gate. He had drunk quite a bit of beer and now he suggested that we sit on a bench and talk for a while. I agreed only to discover that he wanted to start petting and going on.

"Dave, let's go. O.K.?" I said.

"Why are you in such a hurry? It's Saturday night. You could sleep late tomorrow."

"I just want to go," I said, trembling.

"O.K.," he said, "give me one sweet kiss and we can leave."

When I kissed him, I could taste the beer and cigarettes he'd had at the Greasy Spoon. I didn't like this at all, so I drew away. He got mad and jerked me to him, kissing me hard. He started caressing my breasts and breathing on my neck and everything.

"Let go of me, Dave!" I started crying. Then we saw another couple coming through the gate. Dave didn't want to act as if something was going on, so he let me go, but held on to my sweater. I jumped up to leave and tore every button off it. I ran back to the dormitory, vowing I would never see Dave again.

On Monday I got a letter from him begging me to forgive him. He promised to buy me a new sweater and everything. I didn't want to go through that shit again, so I just acted as if I hadn't got the letter. He had asked me to call him, but I wouldn't. I was through and that was that.

One night, shortly after Dave and I had broken up, I asked Trotter what kind of meetings she was always going to. She said, "I thought you knew. I'm secretary of the NAACP chapter here on campus."

"I didn't even know they had a chapter here," I said.

"Why don't you become a member? We're starting a voter registration drive in Hinds County and we need canvassers. Besides, it would give you something to do in your spare time, now that you don't see Dave any more."

I promised her that I would go to the next meeting. All that night I didn't sleep. Everything started coming back to me. I thought of Samuel O'Quinn. I thought of how he had been shot in the back with a shotgun because they suspected him of being a member. I thought of Reverend Dupree and his family who had been run out of Woodville when I was a senior in high school, and all he had done was to get up and mention NAACP in a sermon. The more I remembered the killings, beatings, and intimidations, the more I worried what might possibly happen to me or my family if I joined the NAACP. But I knew I was going to join, anyway. I had wanted to for a long time.

A few weeks after I got involved with the Tougaloo chapter of the NAACP, they organized a demonstration at the state fair in Jackson. Just before it was to come off, Medgar Evers came to campus and gave a big hearty speech about how "Jackson was gonna move." Tougaloo sent four picketers to the fair, and one of them was Dave Jones. Because he was chosen to be the spokesman for the group, he was the first to be interviewed on TV. That evening when the demonstration was televised on all the news programs, it seemed as though every girl in the dorm was down in the lounge in front of the set. They were all shooting off about how they would take part in the next demonstration. The girl Dave was now seeing was running all around talking about how good he looked.

Dave and the other demonstrators had been arrested and were to be bailed out around eight that night. By eight-thirty a lot of us were sitting outside on the dormitory steps awaiting their arrival, and they still hadn't shown up. One of the girls had just gone inside to call the NAACP headquarters in Jackson, when suddenly two police cars came speeding through the campus. Students came running from every building. Within minutes the police cars were completely surrounded, blocked in from every direction. There were two cops in the front seat of each car. They looked frightened to death of us. When the students got out of the cars, they were hugged, kissed, and congratulated for well over an hour. All during this time the cops remained in their seats behind locked doors. Finally someone started singing "We Shall Overcome," and everyone joined in. When we finished singing, someone suggested we go to the football field and have a big rally. In minutes every student was on the football field singing all kinds of freedom songs, giving testimonies as to what we were going to do, and praying and carrying on something terrible. The rally ended at twelve-thirty and by this time, all the students were ready to tear Jackson to pieces.

The following evening Medgar Evers again came to campus to, as he put it, "get some of Tougaloo's spirit and try and spread it around all over Jackson." He gave us a good pep talk and said we would be called upon from time to time to demonstrate.

That spring term I had really wanted to do well in all my subjects, but I had become so wrapped up in the Movement that by the time mid-semester grades came out, I had barely a one-point average. Other students who had gotten involved with the NAACP were actually flunking. I started concentrating more on my work—with little success. It seemed as though everything was going wrong. . . .

During the summer a white student moved into the room across the hall from me. Her name was Joan Trumpauer, and she told me she worked for SNCC as a secretary. In a short time we got to know each other very well, and soon I was going into Jackson with Joan and hanging out at her office. SNCC was starting a voter registration drive in the Delta (Greenwood and Greenville) and was recruiting students at Tougaloo. When they asked me if I wanted to canvass every other weekend, I agreed to go.

The first time I went to the Delta, I was with three other girls. A local family put us up and we slept two to a room. The second time I was there I stayed at the Freedom House—a huge white frame house that SNCC was renting from a widow for sixty dollars a month. This time I was with Bettye Poole, who had been canvassing for SNCC for a couple of months, and Carolyn Quinn, a new recruit like me. We arrived at the Freedom House on a Friday night about twelve-thirty and found fifteen boys all sleeping in one large room on triple-decker beds. They were all sleeping in their clothes. Some of the boys got up and we played cards for a while. A couple of them were from McComb, Mississippi, which was only twenty miles from Centreville. We cracked jokes about how bad the whites were in Wilkinson County. Around 2 a.m. I started to get sleepy and asked where the girls were going to stay. I was told we were going to stay right in the same room with all those boys. I was some shocked. Now I understood why Bettye Poole was wearing jeans; just then she was climbing into one of the empty bunks and settling down for the night. Here I was with only a transparent nylon pajama set to sleep in. Carolyn Quinn wasn't prepared either. The two of us just sat up in chairs until some extra pairs of pants were found for us. The boys explained that they slept in their clothes because they had had bomb threats, and had to be ready to run anytime. They all slept here in this one big room because it was sheltered by another house. . . .

I really got to like all of the SNCC workers. I had never known people so willing and determined to help others. I thought Bob Moses, the director of SNCC in Mississippi, was Jesus Christ in the flesh. A lot of other people thought of him as J.C., too. . . .

Things didn't seem to be coming along too well in the Delta. On Saturdays we would spend all day canvassing and often at night we would have mass rallies. But these were usually poorly attended. Many Negroes were afraid to come. In the beginning some were even afraid to talk to us. Most of these old plantation Negroes had been brainwashed so by the whites, they really thought that only whites were supposed to vote. There were even a few who had never heard of voting. The only thing most of them knew was how to handle a hoe. For years they had demonstrated how well they could do that. Some of them had calluses on their hands so thick they would hide them if they noticed you looking at them.

On Sundays we usually went to Negro churches to speak. We were split into groups according to our religious affiliation. We were supposed to know how to reach those with the same faith as ourselves. In church we hoped to be able to reach many more Negroes. We knew that even those that slammed doors in our faces or said, "I don't want no part of voting" would be there. There would also be the schoolteachers and the middle-class professional Negroes who dared not participate. They knew that once they did, they would lose that $250 a month job. But the people started getting wise to us. Most of them stopped coming to church. They knew if they came, they would have to face us. Then the ministers started asking us not to come because we scared their congregations away. SNCC had to come up with a new strategy.

As the work continued that summer, people began to come around. I guess they saw that our intentions were good. But some began getting fired from their jobs, thrown off plantations and left homeless. They could often find somewhere else to stay, but food and clothing became a problem. SNCC started to send representatives to Northern college campuses. They went begging for food, clothing and money for the people in Mississippi, and the food, clothing and money started coming in. The Delta Negroes still didn't understand the voting, but they knew they had found friends, friends they could trust.

That summer I could feel myself beginning to change. For the first time I began to think something would be done about whites killing, beating, and misusing Negroes. I knew I was going to be a part of whatever happened. . . .

In mid-September I was back on campus. But didn't very much happen until February when the NAACP held its annual convention in Jackson. They were having a whole lot of interesting speakers: Jackie Robinson, Floyd Patterson, Curt Flood, Margaretta Belafonte, and many others. I wouldn't have missed it for anything. I was so excited that I sent one of the leaflets home to Mama and asked her to come.

Three days later I got a letter from Mama with dried-up tears on it, forbidding me to go to the convention. It went on for more than six pages. She said if I didn't stop that shit she would come to Tougaloo and kill me herself. She told me about the time I last visited her, on Thanksgiving, and she had picked me up at the bus station. She said she picked me up because she was scared some white in my hometown would try to do something to me. She said the sheriff had been by, telling her I was messing around with that NAACP group. She said he told her if I didn't stop it, I could not come back there any more. He said that they didn't need any of the NAACP people messing around in Centreville. She ended the letter by saying that she had burned the leaflet I sent her. "Please don't send any more of that stuff here. I don't want nothing to happen to us here," she said. "If you keep that up, you will never be able to come home again."

I was so damn mad after her letter, I felt like taking the NAACP convention to Centreville. I think I would have, if it had been in my power to do so. The remainder of the week I thought of nothing except going to the convention. I didn't know exactly what to do about it. I didn't want Mama or anyone at home to get hurt because of me. . . .

[In May 1963, Anne was one of three students to sit-in at the segregated Woolworth lunch counter in Jackson.]

At noon, students from a nearby white high school started pouring in to Woolworth's. When they first saw us they were sort of surprised. They didn't know how to react. A few started to heckle and the newsmen became interested again. Then the white students started chanting all kinds of anti-Negro slogans. We were called a little bit of everything. The rest of the seats except the three we were occupying had been roped off to prevent others from sitting down. A couple of the boys took one end of the rope and made it into a hangman's noose. Several attempts were made to put it around our necks. The crowds grew as more students and adults came in for lunch.

We kept our eyes straight forward and did not look at the crowd except for occasional glances to see what was going on. All of a sudden I saw a face I remembered—the drunkard from the bus station sit-in. My eyes lingered on him just long enough for us to recognize each other. Today he was drunk too, so I don't think he remembered where he had seen me before. He took out a knife, opened it, put it in his pocket, and then began to pace the floor. At this point, I told Memphis and Pearlena what was going on. Memphis suggested that we pray. We bowed our heads, and all hell broke loose. A man rushed forward, threw Memphis from his seat, and slapped my face. Then another man who worked in the store threw me against an adjoining counter.

Down on my knees on the floor, I saw Memphis lying near the lunch counter with blood running out of the corner of his mouth. As he tried to protect his face, the man who'd thrown him down kept kicking him against the head. If he had worn hard-soled shoes instead of sneakers, the first kick probably would have killed Memphis. Finally, a man dressed in plain clothes identified himself as a police officer and arrested Memphis and his attacker.

Pearlena had been thrown to the floor. She and I got back on our stools after Memphis was arrested. There were some white Tougaloo teachers in the crowd. They asked Pearlena and me if we wanted to leave. They said that things were getting too rough. We didn't know what to do. While we were trying to make up our minds, we were joined by Joan Trumpauer. Now there were three of us and we were integrated. The crowd began to chant, "Communists, Communists, Communists." Some old man in the crowd ordered the students to take us off the stools.

"Which one should I get first?" a big husky boy said.

"That white nigger," the old man said.

The boy lifted Joan from the counter by her waist and carried her out of the store. Simultaneously, I was snatched from my stool by two high school students. I was dragged about thirty feet toward the door by my hair when someone made them turn me loose. As I was getting up off the floor, I saw Joan coming back inside. We started back to the center of the counter to join Pearlena. Lois Chaffee, a white Tougaloo faculty member, was now sitting next to her. So Joan and I just climbed across the rope at the front end of the counter and sat down. There were now four of us, two whites and two Negroes, all women. The mob started smearing us with ketchup, mustard, sugar, pies, and everything on the counter. Soon Joan and I were joined by John Salter, but the moment he sat down he was hit on the jaw with what appeared to be brass knuckles. Blood gushed from his face and someone threw salt into the open wound. Ed King, Tougaloo's chaplain, rushed to him.

At the other end of the counter, Lois and Pearlena were joined by George Raymond, a CORE field worker and a student from Jackson State College. Then a Negro high school boy sat down next to me. The mob took spray paint from the counter and sprayed it on the new demonstrators. The high school student had on a white shirt; the word "nigger" was written on his back with red spray paint.

We sat there for three hours taking a beating when the manager decided to close the store because the mob had begun to go wild with stuff from other counters. He begged and begged everyone to leave. But even after fifteen minutes of begging, no one budged. They would not leave until we did. Then Dr. Beittel, the president of Tougaloo College, came running in. He said he had just heard what was happening.

About ninety policemen were standing outside the store; they had been watching the whole thing through the windows, but had not come in to stop the mob or do anything. President Beittel went outside and asked Captain Ray to come and escort us out. The captain refused, stating the manager had to invite him in before he could enter the premises, so Dr. Beittel himself brought us out. He had told the police that they had better protect us after we were outside the store. When we got outside, the policemen formed a single line that blocked the mob from us. . . .

There was a mass rally that night at the Pearl Street Church in Jackson, and the place was packed. People were standing two abreast in the aisles. Before the speakers began, all the sit-inners walked out on the stage and were introduced by Medgar Evers. People stood and applauded for what seemed like thirty minutes or more. Medgar told the audience that this was just the beginning of such demonstrations. He asked them to pledge themselves to unite in a massive offensive against segregation in Jackson, and throughout the state. The rally ended with "We Shall Overcome" and sent home hundreds of determined people. It seemed as though Mississippi Negroes were about to get together at last.

Before I demonstrated, I had written Mama. She wrote me back a letter, begging me not to take part in the sit-in. She even sent ten dollars for bus fare to New Orleans. I didn't have one penny, so I kept the money. Mama's letter made me mad. I had to live my life as I saw fit. I had made that decision when I left home. But it hurt to have my family prove to me how scared they were. It hurt me more than anything else—I knew the whites had already started the threats and intimidations. I was the first Negro from my hometown who had openly demonstrated, worked with the NAACP, or anything. . . .

[The demonstrations gained strength in Jackson and many arrests were made as national television focused on events. Tougaloo students and faculty were in the forefront of the movement and Anne spent time in jail. After a sniper killed NAACP field secretary Medgar Evers, Anne was arrested again with hundreds of others protesting his murder. Authorities released them in time to attend the funeral.]

When they reached the funeral home, the body was taken inside, and most of the procession dispersed. But one hard core of angry Negroes decided they didn't want to go home. With some encouragement from SNCC workers who were singing freedom songs outside the funeral home, these people began walking back toward Capitol Street.

Policemen had been placed along the route of the march, and they were still there. They allowed the crowd of Negroes to march seven blocks, but they formed a solid blockade just short of Capitol Street. This was where they made everyone stop. They had everything—shotguns, fire trucks, gas masks, dogs, fire hoses, and billy clubs. Along the sidewalks and on the fringes of the crowd, the cops knocked heads, set dogs on some marchers, and made about thirty arrests, but the main body of people in the middle of the street was just stopped.

They sang and shouted things like "Shoot, shoot" to the police, and then the police started to push them back slowly. After being pushed back about a block, they stopped. They wouldn't go any farther. So the cops brought the fire trucks up closer and got ready to use the fire hoses on the crowd. That really broke up the demonstration. People moved back faster and started to go home. But it also made them angrier. Bystanders began throwing stones and bottles at the cops and then the crowd started too; other Negroes were pitching stuff from second- and third-story windows. The crowd drew back another block, leaving the space between them and the fire trucks littered with rocks and broken glass. John Doar came out from behind the police barricade and walked toward the crowd of Negroes, with bottles flying all around him. He talked to some of the people at the front, telling them he was from the Justice Department and that this wasn't "the way." After he talked for a few minutes, things calmed down considerably, and Dave Dennis and a few others began taking bottles away from people and telling them they should go home. After that it was just a clean-up operation. One of the ministers borrowed Captain Ray's bull horn and ran up and down the street telling people to disperse, but by that time there were just a few stragglers.

After Medgar's death there was a period of confusion. Each Negro leader and organization in Jackson received threats. They were all told they were "next on the list." Things began to fall apart. The ministers, in particular, didn't want to be "next"; a number of them took that long-promised vacation to Africa or else-where. Meanwhile SNCC and CORE became more militant and began to press for more demonstrations. A lot of the young Negroes wanted to let the whites of Jackson know that even by killing off Medgar they hadn't touched the real core of the Movement. For the NAACP and the older, more conservative groups, however, voter registration had now become number one on the agenda. After the NAACP exerted its influence at a number of strategy meetings, the militants lost. . . .

In July, CORE opened up an office in Canton, Mississippi, to start a voter registration campaign in Madison County. By this time, I was so fed up with the fighting and bickering among the organizations in Jackson, I was ready to go almost anywhere, even Madison County, where Negroes frequently turned up dead. Shortly before Christmas a man's headless corpse had been found on the road between Canton and Tougaloo with the genitals cut off and with K's cut into the flesh all over his body. Around the time the body was found, Tougaloo College had received a lot of threats, so an inventory was made of all the males on campus to see if any were missing.

When Reverend King discovered that I had agreed to work with CORE in the area, he was very much concerned. He discussed Canton with me, telling me he thought the place was too rough for girls. Some of my girlfriends also begged me not to go. But I just had to. I don't know why I felt that way, but I did.

Because I had come from Wilkinson County, I just didn't think Madison could be any worse. Things might even be a little better, I thought, since in Madison there were three Negroes to every white. I remembered that in Jackson there had been one point when I could see the white folks actually tremble with fear. At times when we were having mass demonstrations we had them so confused they didn't know what to do. Whenever I could detect the least amount of fear in any white Mississippian, I felt good. I also felt there was a chance of winning the battle regardless of how costly it turned out to be.

Disregarding all acts of violence, Madison County was considered a place with a possible future for Negroes. In addition to the fact that our records showed that there was a population of twenty-nine thousand Negroes as against nine thousand whites, Negroes owned over 40 percent of the land in the county. However, there were only about one hundred and fifty to two hundred registered to vote, and these had registered as a result of a campaign conducted by a few local citizens a couple of years earlier. Of this number, less than half were actually voting. . . .

> [Anne was frustrated trying to get people to register to vote because most of them feared for their jobs and lives if they bucked the system. A few tried to register and were turned away by the white registrar who determined that they could not pass the literacy requirements for registration. Whites increased violent attacks and made threats to kill the CORE workers. Anne hid all night in a field of tall grass to escape a raid on her building.]

After this incident, Robert and a group of men all in their middle or late twenties formed a group to protect us. Three or four of them had already lost their jobs because they tried to register. They couldn't find other jobs so they followed us around everywhere we went, walking with us as if they were bulletproof. They also spread rumors that the Freedom House was protected by armed men. We were all still a little up tight and afraid to sleep at night, but after a while, when the whites didn't come back, we figured the rumors worked. The threats didn't bother me as much now. I began to feel almost safe with those men around all the time. Their interest, courage, and concern gave all of us that extra lift we needed.

Now every Negro church in the county was opened for workshops. The nine of us split into groups of three. Almost every night we had workshops in different churches, sometimes sixteen to thirty miles out of town.

One or two of our protective guys had cars. They were usually sent along with the girls out in the country. It was dark and dangerous driving down those long country rock roads, but now that we always had two or three of the guys riding with us, it wasn't so bad. In fact, once we got to the churches, everything was fine. Listening to those old Negroes sing freedom songs was like listening to music from heaven. They sang them as though they were singing away the chains of slavery. Sometimes I just looked at the expressions on their faces as they sang and cold chills would run down my back. Whenever God was mentioned in a song, I could tell by the way they said the word that most of them had given up here on earth. They seemed to be waiting just for God to call them home and end all the suffering.

The nightly church workshops were beginning to be the big thing going for us at this point in the campaign. However, the white folks found out about this and tried to put a stop to it. One night out in the country three carloads of whites chased George and a group of the guys all the way to Canton. George said they were shooting at them like crazy. Since George thought the whites could have killed them if they had wanted to, we took it as a warning. We were extra careful after that. . . .

[Anne went to the August 1963 March on Washington. In Canton, she distributed clothes to the poor. On her 23rd birthday, September 15, 1963, she heard horrible news from Birmingham.]

We were all eating and listening to the radio when the music stopped abruptly in the middle of a record. "A special news bulletin just in from Birmingham," the DJ was saying. "A church was just bombed in Birmingham, Alabama. It is believed that several Sunday school students were killed." We all sat glued to our seats, avoiding each other's eyes. No one was eating now. Everyone was waiting for the next report on the bombing. The second report confirmed that four girls had been killed. I looked at George; he sat with his face buried in the palms of his hands. Dave sat motionless with tears in his eyes. Mattie looked at Dave as if she had been grounded by an electric shock. I put my hand up to my face. Tears were pouring out of my eyes, and I hadn't even known I was crying.

"Why! Why! Why! Oh, God, why? Why us? Why us?" I found myself asking. "I gotta find myself some woods, trees, or water—anything. I gotta talk to you, God, and you gotta answer. Please don't play Rip Van Winkle with me today."

I rushed out of the house and started walking aimlessly. I ran up a hill where there were trees. I found myself in a graveyard I didn't even know was there. I sat there looking up through the trees, trying to communicate with God: "Now talk to me, God. Come on down and talk to me.

"You know, I used to go to Sunday school when I was a little girl. I went to Sunday school, church, and B.T.U. every Sunday. We were taught how merciful and forgiving you are. Mama used to tell us that you would forgive me seventy-seven times a day, and I believed in you. I bet you those girls in Sunday school were being taught the same as I was when I was their age. Is that teaching wrong? Are you going to forgive their killers? You not gonna answer me, God, hmm? Well, if you don't want to talk, then listen to me.

"As long as I live, I'll never be beaten by a white man again. Not like in Woolworth's. Not any more. That's out. You know something else, God? Nonviolence is out. I have a good idea Martin Luther King is talking to you, too. If he is, tell him that nonviolence has served its purpose. Tell him that for me, God, and for a lot of other Negroes who must be thinking it today. If you don't believe that, then I know you must be white, too. And if I ever find out you are white, then I'm through with you. And if I find out you are black, I'll try my best to kill you when I get to heaven.

"I'm through with you. Yes, I am going to put you down. From now on, I am my own God. I am going to live by the rules I set for myself. I'll discard everything I was once taught about you. Then I'll be you. I will be my own God, living my life as I see fit. Not as Mr. Charlie says I should live it, or Mama, or anybody else. I shall do as I want to in this society that apparently wasn't meant for me and my kind. If you are getting angry because I'm talking to you like this, then just kill me, leave me here in this graveyard dead. Maybe that's where all of us belong, anyway. Maybe then we wouldn't have to suffer so much. At the rate we are being killed now, we'll all soon be dead anyway."

When I got back to the Freedom House, Dave and Mattie were gone. I found George stretched out on his bed.

"What happened to Mattie and Dave?" I asked.

"Dave was called for a meeting in Jackson, and they had to leave. Where have you been all this time?"

"Walking," I said. "Was there any more news about the bombing?"

"No," he said, "except that the four girls were killed, and the city is getting pretty tense, the closer it gets to dark. They'll probably tear Birmingham to bits tonight. I pray that they don't have any violence."

"Pray! Pray, George! Why in the hell should we be praying all the time? Those white men who hurled that bomb into the church today weren't on their knees, were they? If those girls weren't at Sunday school today, maybe they would be alive. How do you know they weren't on their knees? That's what's wrong now. We've been praying too long. Yes, as a race all we've got is a lot of religion. And the white man's got everything else, including all the dynamite."

"Hold it—is that Miss Woolworth, the Nonviolent Miss Woolworth talking like that?" he asked.

"Let's face it, George. Nonviolence is through and you know it. Don't you think we've had enough of it? First of all we were only using it as a tactic to show, or rather dramatize, to the world how bad the situation is in the South. Well, I think we've had enough examples. I think we are overdoing it. After this bombing, if there are any more nonviolent demonstrations for the mere sake of proving what all the rest of them have, then I think we are overdramatizing the issue."

"You feel like talking about anything else?" he asked.

"Yeah, let's talk about that beautiful march on Washington," I said, almost yelling. "It was just two weeks ago, believe it or not. And 250,000 people were there yelling, 'We want freedom.' Well, I guess this bombing is Birmingham's answer to the march. But what's gonna be our answer to the bombing? We're gonna send more of our children right back to Sunday school to be killed. Then the President will probably issue a statement saying, 'We are doing Everything in our Power to apprehend the killers. And we are in close touch with the situation.' After which we will still run out in the streets and bow our heads and pray to be spat upon in the process. I call that real religion, real, honest-to-goodness nigger religion. If Martin Luther King thinks nonviolence is really going to work for the South as it did for India, then he is out of his mind." . . .

We opened up two or three workshops in the county again, and that made things worse. We no longer had our protective guys riding around with us. Most of them had gone north or to California trying to find jobs. Now either George went with us, or we went alone. Doris and I were coming from a workshop twenty-six miles out in the country one night, when we were chased by a group of drunken whites. Doris panicked. She began driving like a crazy woman, making every curve on two wheels, sending rocks sailing everywhere. I just knew we would turn over in a ditch and be killed. I wondered whether it would be better to force Doris to stop, or to jump out of the car into a ditch, as Doris turned a curve, hoping the other car would pass without seeing me. If I forced Doris to stop the car, I thought, maybe we would just be beaten or raped by the drunks and not killed. Finally, I just closed my eyes and hoped that whatever would happen wouldn't take too long or be too painful. I must have blacked out, because when I opened my eyes we were at the Freedom House.

The next night George went with us but the fear was still there. All the jokes we were able to come up with couldn't erase the experience we had encountered on those long, dark, country roads. . . .

[She worked to get out a "Freedom Vote" to show that black Mississippians would vote if given the chance. 80,000 of 400,000 possible voters cast ballots. Anne quit the movement for a while and went to New Orleans. Her mother, with a new baby, visited her there.]

While sitting there I could see Mama in the mirror behind the bar. She was looking at me with her eyes full of water. I sat there talking to Jennie Ann for about an hour and all that time Mama never took her eyes off me. I could see that a thousand questions were going on in her mind. I looked at her and wondered how she had brought me into this world and did not understand me or it. Maybe she understood Adline better. I looked at Adline. She was running all around the place tonight acting as content as anyone. Sometimes I hated her because she was so content with nothing. I hated her now as I looked at her. We were sisters, but there was no likeness between us. Junior walked in and I directed my thoughts to him. We looked a little alike. And sometimes when I was with him, I could feel that he was just as rebellious and discontent as I was. But his discontent would come and go. I had never been able to do away with mine like that. It was always there. Sometimes I used to try to suppress it and it didn't show. Now it showed all the time.

I got tired of everyone staring at me so I decided to leave the party. I told Mama that I had a terrible headache, and that I had left a present on the bed for her. I wished her a happy birthday and left. On my way back to the apartment, I was almost blinded by tears running down my cheeks. I couldn't understand why I seemed so strange to everyone. At the party I felt like I had committed a crime and everyone was punishing me by not talking to me. All of a sudden, I found myself wishing I was in Canton again working in the Movement with people who understood me. Here among my own people, I seemed crazy because I was grieved over problems they didn't even think about.

I walked around most of the next week wondering what to do about the Movement. At one point, I made up my mind to go back to Canton. But then I couldn't think up any reasons for going. I had the feeling that I should be back in the Movement, but involved in some different way that I could not yet define. I decided to give up thinking about it for a while.

On Friday, November 22, 1963, I was headed for the pantry during the rush hour at the restaurant with a tray of dishes when Julian, the new cashier, a white Tulane Law student, walked up behind me and said, "President Kennedy was just shot!" Everything around me went black. When things were light again, I found myself sitting dazed in a chair with Julian holding my tray. Just that morning, I remembered, James had made a crack about President Kennedy coming to the South—I hadn't even given it much thought. Julian went out front to see if there was any further news. A short while later, he came back and said that President Kennedy was dead. For a while I just sat there staring at everyone and not seeing a thing. "So much killing," I thought, "so, so much killing. And when will it end? When? . . . ."

[She waited tables and registered voters for CORE in New Orleans. After her uncle was murdered for not staying in his "place," Anne returned to Canton to register voters again. She attended her graduation at Tougaloo before visiting New Orleans.]

I didn't stay long in New Orleans—just a couple of days—because I realized I had no way of making any money during the next two weeks. I was a little sorry I had quit my job at the restaurant so soon. The evening after I got back, Tim and Carol, a white married couple from California working with New Orleans CORE, stopped by the apartment and asked if I wanted a ride into Mississippi with them the following morning. They were going to visit a friend of theirs who had been arrested in the Canton Freedom Day march. I just couldn't resist that free ride to Mississippi.

The following morning I was back in Canton, ready to start work on the Summer Project. As soon as I had left my suitcase at the Freedom House, I went to see Mrs. Chinn. I found her looking terribly depressed.

"Anne," she said, "if I were you and didn't have no ties to Canton, I wouldn't waste no time here. Looka here, alla that work we put into that march and McKinley almost beaten to death and things are even worse than they were before. These niggers done went into hiding again, scared to stick their heads outta the door. C.O.'s in jail, them goddamn cops coming by my house every night, just about to drive me crazy. This ain't the way, Anne. This just ain't the way. We ain't big enough to do it by ourselves."

I had never seen Mrs. Chinn that depressed. What she said got me to thinking real hard. I walked around Canton for hours looking at the familiar streets. There were hardly any Negroes to be seen. The whole place looked dead. Walking past the jail, I saw C. O. Chinn coming in with the chain gang. They had been digging ditches all day and he was filthy from head to toe. When he saw me, he waved trying to look happy. I couldn't hardly bring myself to wave back. I walked away as quickly as I could. I couldn't get that picture of C.O. out of my mind. A year ago when I first came to Canton, C.O. was a big man in town, one of Canton's wealthiest Negroes. He had opened up Canton for the Movement. He had sacrificed and lost all he had trying to get the Negroes moving. Now he was trying to look happy on a chain gang!

I felt worse about everything than I had ever felt before. Mrs. Chinn's words kept pounding through my head: "We ain't big enough to do it by ourselves." My head began to ache. I found myself running. I was trying to get away. I felt like the walls of Mississippi were closing in on me and Mrs. Chinn and C.O. and all the other Negroes in the state, crushing us. I had to get out and let the world know what was happening to us. I ran faster, and faster. I soon got back to the Freedom House out of breath, just in time to stumble into Dave Dennis' car and head for Jackson. About twenty minutes later, Dave was parking in front of the COFO headquarters on Lynch Street. Parked right in front of us was a Greyhound bus. The motor was running and smoke was shooting out of its exhaust pipe. It looked and sounded like it was about to pull off. Getting out of the car, I saw Bob Moses holding the door open waving goodbye to the people inside. I ran up to him and asked:

"Hey Bob, where's this bus going?"

"Oh! Moody, I'm glad you came. Can you go? We need you to testify," he said.

"Testify? What do you . . . ?"

"Hey Moody! C'mon get on, we're going to Washington!" It was little twelve-year-old Gene Young, leaning his head out of the window. As the bus began to pull out, Bob grabbed the door and held it for me. I just managed to squeeze in. The bus was packed. To avoid the staring, smiling faces I knew, I just bopped down between Gene and his friend. As soon as the bus was really moving, everybody began singing, "We Shall Overcome." I closed my eyes and leaned back in the seat listening to them.

> We shall overcome, We shall overcome
> We shall overcome some day.
> Oh, deep in my heart I do believe
> We shall overcome some day.

"C'mon, Annie Moody, wake up! Get the Spirit on!" little Gene yelled right in my ear. I opened my eyes and looked at him.

"We're gonna go up there to Washington and we're gonna *tell* 'em somethin' at those COFO hearings. We're gonna tell 'em what Mississippi is all *about*," Gene said excitedly, joining in the singing. His eyes were gleaming with life and he clapped his hands in time with the song. Watching him, I felt very old.

> The truth will make us free,
>   The truth will make us free,
> The truth will make us free some day.
> Oh, deep in my heart I do believe
> The truth will make us free some day.

Suddenly he looked at me again and saw that I still wasn't singing.

"Moody, what's wrong? What's the matter with you? You cracking up or something?" he asked, looking worried for the first time. When I didn't answer, he gave me a puzzled look and joined the singing again, but this time he was not so lively.

I sat there listening to "We Shall Overcome," looking out of the window at the passing Mississippi landscape. Images of all that had happened kept crossing my mind: the Taplin burning, the Birmingham church bombing, Medgar Evers' murder, the blood gushing out of McKinley's head, and all the other murders. I saw the face of Mrs. Chinn as she said, "We ain't big enough to do it by ourselves," C.O.'s face when he gave me that pitiful wave from the chain gang. I could feel the tears welling up in my eyes.

"Moody . . ." it was little Gene again interrupting his singing. "Moody, we're gonna git things straight in Washington, huh?"

I didn't answer him. I knew I didn't have to. He looked as if he knew exactly what I was thinking.

"I wonder. I wonder."

> We shall overcome, We shall overcome
> We shall overcome some day.

I WONDER. I really WONDER.

RON KOVIC
1946–

Nothing about the early life of Ron Kovic is atypical. Many baby boomers raised in conventional ways in the years following World War II lived months of unconventional lives in a small country ten thousand miles from "the World"—as Vietnam veterans called the United States. Kovic had the special middle-American distinction of being born on the most patriotic, or nationalistic, day of the year.

Born on the Fourth of July *opens with the most important experience of Kovic's life, the firefight that paralyzed him in Nam. From there his story is often interrupted with flashbacks and nightmares about the Vietnamese children his unit unwittingly killed and an American soldier he mistakenly shot to death. At times, Kovic refers to himself as "he" as if to distance himself from actions he cannot quite own up to or understand. These literary techniques very vividly demonstrate the war's effects on many of the men and women who sacrificed their youth or life to that war. While nearly 58,000 Americans died, thousands of others have committed suicide since it ended in 1975. For veterans and their families, the war is an "endless storm."*

Kovic's autobiography, written as therapy for himself and for his generation, recalls that time of innocence for white middle-class kids raised in the 1950s. He had grown up when Mickey Mantle batted cleanup for the Yankees, Elvis Presley gyrated on the Ed Sullivan Show, John Wayne led the Marines across the sands of Iwo Jimo, and Catholic priests warned that kissing and petting led to sin. In high school he lettered in wrestling, watched American Bandstand, and stayed on the lookout for communist infiltration of his hometown. In summary, he believed.

Vietnam changed that. Kovic concludes that what ruined his life was not the bullet in Nam, but the community and nation that had taught him to believe in things that never were. His autobiography presents a spiritual coming of age, depressing and reminiscent of Black Elk's closing comment, "I, to whom so great a vision was given in my youth ... have done nothing, for the nation's hoop is broken and scattered. There is no center any longer, and the sacred tree is dead."

In 1989 Kovic's autobiography was made into a film by the same name starring Tom Cruise and directed by Oliver Stone. The movie garnered seven Academy Award nominations, including Best Picture.

Born on the Fourth of July, *1976. Reprint, N.Y.: Simon & Schuster, 1977. (Reprinted with permission.)*

The blood is still rolling off my flak jacket from the hole in my shoulder and there are bullets cracking into the sand all around me. I keep trying to move my legs but I cannot feel them. I try to breathe but it is difficult. I have to get out of this place, make it out of here somehow.

Someone shouts from my left now, screaming for me to get up. Again and again he screams, but I am trapped in the sand.

Oh get me out of here, get me out of here, please someone help me! Oh help me, please help me. Oh God oh Jesus! "Is there a corpsman?" I cry. "Can you get a corpsman?"

There is a loud crack and I hear the guy begin to sob. "They've shot my fucking finger off! Let's go, sarge! Let's get outta here!"

"I can't move," I gasp. "I can't move my legs! I can't feel anything!"

I watch him go running back to the tree line.

"Sarge, are you all right?" Someone else is calling to me now and I try to turn around. Again there is the sudden crack of a bullet and a boy's voice crying. "Oh Jesus! Oh Jesus Christ!" I hear his body fall in back of me.

I think he must be dead but I feel nothing for him, I just want to live. I feel nothing.

And now I hear another man coming up from behind, trying to save me. "Get outta here!" I scream. "Get the fuck outta here!"

A tall black man with long skinny arms and enormous hands picks me up and throws me over his shoulder as bullets begin cracking over our heads like strings of firecrackers. Again and again they crack as the sky swirls around us like a cyclone. "Motherfuckers motherfuckers!" he screams. And the rounds keep cracking and the sky and the sun on my face and my body all gone, all twisted up dangling like a puppet's, diving again and again into the sand, up and down, rolling and cursing, gasping for breath. "Goddamn goddamn motherfuckers!"

And finally I am dragged into a hole in the sand with the bottom of my body that can no longer feel, twisted and bent underneath me. The black man runs from the hole without ever saying a thing. I never see his face. I will never know who he is. He is gone. And others now are in the hole helping me. They are bandaging my wounds. There is fear in their faces.

"It's all right," I say to them. "Everything is fine."

Someone has just saved my life. My rifle is gone and I don't feel like finding it or picking it up ever again. The only thing I can think of, the only thing that crosses my mind, is living. . . .

[Along with the other wounded and dead, he was taken from the field and flown to a military hospital where a priest administered last rites and doctors tried to save lives.]

I awake to the screams of other men around me. I have made it. I think that maybe the wound is my punishment for killing the corporal and the children. That now everything is okay and the score is evened up. And now I am packed in this place with the others who have been wounded like myself, strapped onto a strange circular bed. I feel tubes going into my nose and hear the clanking, pumping sound of a machine. I still cannot feel any of my body but I know I am alive. I feel a terrible pain in my chest. My body is so cold. It has never been this weak. It feels so tired and out of touch, so lost and in pain. I can still barely breathe. I look around me, at people moving in shadows of numbness. There is the man who had been in the ambulance with me, screaming louder than ever, kicking his bloody stumps in the air, crying for his mother, crying for his morphine. . . .

I am in this place for seven days and seven nights. I write notes on scraps of paper telling myself over and over that I will make it out of here, that I am going to live. I am squeezing rubber balls with my hands to try to get strong again. I write letters home to Mom and Dad. I dictate them to a woman named Lucy who is with the USO. I am telling Mom and Dad that I am hurt pretty bad but I have done it for America and that it is worth it. I tell them not to worry. I will be home soon.

The day I am supposed to leave has come. I am strapped in a long frame and taken from the place of the wounded. I am moved from hangar to hangar, then finally put on a plane, and I leave Vietnam forever. . . .

[He convalesced in St. Albans Naval Hospital in Queens, New York, before being transferred to an under-staffed, under-equipped Veterans' Administration hospital nearby.]

The aide pushes me into the line-up in the hallway. There are frames all over the place now, lined up in front of the blue room for their enemas. It is the Six o'Clock Special. There are maybe twenty guys waiting by now. It looks like a long train, a long assembly line of broken, twisted bodies waiting for deliverance. It is very depressing, all these bodies, half of them asleep, tied down to their frames with their rear ends sticking out. All these bodies bloated, waiting to be released. Every third day I go for my enema and wait with the long line of men shoved against the green hospital wall. I watch the dead bodies being pushed into the enema room, then finally myself.

It is a small blue room and they cram us into it like sardines. Tommy runs back and forth placing the bedpans under our rear ends, laughing and joking, a cigarette dangling from the corner of his mouth. "Okay, okay, let's go!" he shouts. There is a big can of soapy water above each man's head and a tube that comes down from it. Tommy is jumping all around and whistling like a little kid, running to each body, sticking the rubber tubes up into them. He is jangling the pans, undoing little clips on the rubber tubes and filling the bellies up with soapy water. Everyone is trying to sleep, refusing to admit that this whole thing is happening to them. A couple of the bodies in the frames have small radios close to their ears. Tommy keeps running from one frame to the other, changing the rubber gloves on his hands and squirting the tube of lubricant onto his fingers, ramming his hands up into the rear ends, checking each of the bodies out, undoing the little clips. The aide keeps grabbing the bedpans and emptying all the shit into the garbage cans, occasionally missing and splattering the stuff on the floor. She places the empty pans in a machine and closes it up. There is a steam sound and the machine opens with all the bedpans as clean as new.

Oh God, what is happening to me? What is going on here? I want to get out of this place! All these broken men are very depressing, all these bodies so emaciated and twisted in these bedsheets. This is a nightmare. This isn't like the poster down by the post office where the guy stood with the shiny shoes; this is a concentration camp. It is like the pictures of all the Jews that I have seen. This is as horrible as that. I want to scream. I want to yell and tell them that I want out of this. All of this, all these people, this place, these sounds, I want out of this forever. I am only twenty-one and there is still so much ahead of me, there is so much ahead of me.

I am wiped clean and pushed past the garbage cans. The stench is terrible. I try to breathe through my mouth but I can't. I'm trapped. I have to watch, I have to smell. I think the war has made me a little mad—the dead corporal from Georgia, the old man that was shot in the village with his brains hanging out. But it is the living deaths I am breathing and smelling now, the living deaths, the bodies broken in the same war that I have come from. . . .

At first I felt that the wound was very interesting. I saw it almost as an adventure. But now it is not an adventure any longer. I see it more and more as a terrible thing that I will have to live with for the rest of my life. Nobody wants to know that I can't fuck anymore. I will never go up to them and tell them I have this big yellow rubber thing sticking in my penis, attached to the rubber bag on the side of my leg. I am afraid of letting them know how lonely and scared I have become thinking about this wound. It is like some kind of numb twilight zone to me. I am angry and want to kill everyone—all the volunteers and the priests and the pretty girls with the tight short skirts. I am twenty-one and the whole thing is shot, done forever. There is no real healing left anymore, everything that is going to heal has healed already and now I am left with the corpse, the living dead man, the man with the numb legs, the man in the wheelchair, the Easter Seal boy, the cripple, the sexless man, the sexlessman, the man with the numb dick, the man who can't make children, the man who can't stand, the man who can't walk, the angry lonely man, the bitter man with the nightmares, the murder man, the man who cries in the shower.

In one big bang they have taken it all from me, in one clean sweep, and now I am in this place around all the others like me, and though I keep trying not to feel sorry for myself, I want to cry. There is no shortcut around this thing. It is too soon to die even for a man who has died once already. . . .

For me it began in 1946 when I was born on the Fourth of July. The whole sky lit up in a tremendous fireworks display and my mother told me the doctor said I was a real firecracker. Every birthday after that was something the whole country celebrated. It was a proud day to be born on.

I hit a home run my first time at bat in the Massapequa Little League, and I can still remember my Mom and Dad and all the rest of the kids going crazy as I rounded the bases on seven errors and slid into home a hero. We lost the game to the Midgets that night, 22 to 7, and I cried all the way home. It was a long time ago, but sometimes I can still hear them shouting out in front of Pete's house on Hamilton Avenue. There was Bobby Zimmer, the tall kid from down the street, Kenny and Pete, little Tommy Law, and my best friend Richie Castiglia, who lived across from us on Lee Place.

Baseball was good to me and I played it all I could. I got this baseball mitt when I was seven. I had to save up my allowance for it and cash in some soda bottles. It was a cheap piece of shit, but it seemed pretty nice, I mean it seemed beautiful to me before Bobby and some of the other guys tore the hell out of it.

I remember that I loved baseball more than anything else in the world and my favorite team was the New York Yankees. Every chance I got I watched the games on the TV in my house with Castiglia, waiting for Mickey Mantle to come to the plate. We'd turn up the sound of the television as the crowd went wild roaring like thunder. I'd run over to Richie's house screaming to his mother to tell Richie that Mantle was at bat. . . .

I remember Elvis Presley on the Ed Sullivan Show and my sister Sue going crazy in the living room jumping up and down. He kept twanging this big guitar and wiggling his hips, but for some reason they were mostly showing just the top of him. My mother was sitting on the couch with her hands folded in her lap like she was praying, and my dad was in the other room talking about how the Church had advised us all that Sunday that watching Elvis Presley could lead to sin.

I loved God more than anything else in the world back then and I prayed to Him and the Virgin Mary and Jesus and all the saints to be a good boy and a good American. Every night before I went to sleep I knelt down in front of my bed, making the sign of the cross and cupping my hands over my face, sometimes praying so hard I would cry. I asked every night to be good enough to make the major leagues someday. With God anything was possible. I made my first Holy Communion with a cowboy hat on my head and two six-shooters in my hands. . . .

[He lived the normal childhood and high school years of working-class America. He played touch football, hooked up a "telegraph" to his friend's house, sledded in the snow, made heroes of Mickey Mantle and John Wayne, shot plastic Mattel machine guns while he played war, joined the cub scouts, and worried about Sputnik, communists, pimples, and girls.]

President Kennedy got killed that last year and we played football in the huge snowdrifts that had settled on the Long Island streets that afternoon. We played in silence, I guess because you're supposed to be silent when someone dies. I truly felt I had lost a dear friend. I was deeply hurt for a long time afterward. We went to the movies that Sunday. I can't remember what was playing, but how ashamed I was that I was even there, that people could sit through a movie or have the nerve to want to go to football games when our president had been killed in Dallas. The pain stuck with me for a long time after he died. I still remember Oswald being shot and screaming to my mother to come into the living room. It all seemed wild and crazy like some Texas shootout, but it was real for all of us back then, it was very real. I remember Johnson being sworn in on the plane and the fear in the eyes of the woman judge from Texas. And then the funeral and the casket. I guess all of us, the whole country, watched it like a big football game. Down the street the black horses came and his little boy saluting the way he did, the perfect way he did. Soon after he died there was a memorial picture of him that went up in the candy store down the block. At the bottom of it it said he had been born in 1917 and had died in 1963. It stayed up in the candy store on the wall for a long time after we all went to the war.

That spring before I graduated, my father took me down to the shopping center in Levittown and made me get my first job. It was in a supermarket not far from the marine recruiting station. I worked stacking shelves and numbing my fingers and hands unloading cases of frozen food from the trucks. Working with Kenny each day after school, all I could think of, day after day, was joining the marines. My legs and my back ached, but I knew that soon I would be signing the papers and leaving home.

I didn't want to be like my Dad, coming home from the A&P every night. He was a strong man, a good man, but it made him so tired, it took all the energy out of him. I didn't want to be like that, working in that stinking A&P, six days a week, twelve hours a day. I wanted to be somebody. I wanted to make something out of my life.

I was getting older now, I was seventeen, and I looked at myself in the mirror that hung from the back of the door in my room and saw how tall and strong I had suddenly become. I took a deep breath, flexing my muscles, and stared straight into the mirror, turning to the side and looking at myself for a long time.

In the last month of school, the marine recruiters came and spoke to my senior class. They marched, both in perfect step, into the auditorium with their dress blue uniforms and their magnificently shined shoes. It was like all the movies and all the books and all the dreams of becoming a hero come true. I watched them and listened as they stood in front of all the young boys, looking almost like statues and not like real men at all. They spoke in loud voices and one of them was tall and the other was short and very strong looking.

"Good afternoon men," the tall marine said, "We have come today because they told us that some of you want to become marines." He told us that the marines took nothing but the best, that if any of us did not think we were good enough, we should not even think of joining. The tall marine spoke in a very beautiful way about the exciting history of the marines and how they had never lost and America had never been defeated.

"The marines have been the first in everything, first to fight and first to uphold the honor of our country. We have served on distant shores and at home, and we have always come when our country has called. There is nothing finer, nothing prouder, than a United States Marine."

When they were finished, they efficiently picked up their papers and marched together down the steps of the stage to where a small crowd of boys began to gather. I couldn't wait to run down after them, meet with them and shake their hands. And as I shook their hands and stared up into their eyes, I couldn't help but feel I was shaking hands with John Wayne and Audie Murphy. They told us that day that the Marine Corps built men—body, mind, and spirit. And that we could serve our country like the young president had asked us to do.

We were all going in different directions and we had our whole lives ahead of us, and a million different dreams. I can still remember the last stickball game. I stood at home plate with the sun in my face and looked out at Richie, Pete, and the rest. It was our last summer together and the last stickball game we ever played on Hamilton Avenue.

One day that summer I quit my job at the food store and went to the little red, white, and blue shack in Levittown. My father and I went down together. It was September by the time all the paperwork was completed, September 1964. I was going to leave on a train one morning and become a marine.

I stayed up most of the night before I left, watching the late movie. Then "The Star-Spangled Banner" played. I remember standing up and feeling very patriotic, chills running up and down my spine. I put my hand over my heart and stood rigid at attention until the screen went blank.

"Awright, ladies!" shouted the sergeant again. "My name is Staff Sergeant Joseph. This—" he said, pointing to the short sergeant at the end of the formation, "this is Sergeant Mullins. I am your senior drill instructor. You will obey both of us. You will listen to everything we say. You will do everything we tell you to do. Your souls today may belong to God, but your asses belong to the United

States Marine Corps!" The sergeant swaggered sharply back and forth in front of the formation, almost bouncing up and down on his heels, his long thin hands sliding up and down against his hips. "I want you swinging dicks to stand straight at attention, do you hear me? I don't want you people to look left or right, I want you people to stand straight ahead."....

[At Parris Island, S.C., the U.S. Marine Corps boot camp, Kovic was turned into a soldier.]

"It's late!" screamed the short sergeant. "And I know how tired you ladies are tonight. Are you tired ladies?" screamed the sergeant.

"Yessir!" shouted the men.

"I can't hear you!" screamed the sergeant. "Louder!"

"Yessir!" the young men screamed again.

"That's more like it."

The sergeant repeated a long list of names including the president and vice president of the United States and everyone else right on down to the senior drill instructor himself, and after completing the list, he shouted to the men that every night from here on out they would repeat those names. And then he shouted, "Ready—Mount!" And they shouted back "Ready—Mount! Aye aye, sir!" And all eighty jumped into bed, still standing at attention, lying in their racks.

"Awright! I want you to stand at attention all night! I think it's good practice for you."

And as they lay in their racks at attention, one of the sergeants had a young black boy from Georgia sing the Lord's Prayer: "Our Father, Who art in heaven, hallo-o-wed be Thy name," he sang. "Thy kingdom come, Thy will be done, on earth as it is in hea-ven." And when he was finished the lights went out and they slowly closed their eyes.

And the first day had ended.

(Lights flash, flash, flash standing by my rack now) sir! the private requests to make an emergency sitting head call WHAT DO YOU WANT KOVIC? sir! o god of jesus yessir aye aye sir one two aye aye sir If I die in a combat zone pack me up and ship me home COUNTDOWN—READY—SEATS! GET IN THE PASSAGEWAY SWEETPEA AND GIVE ME FIVE HUNDRED BENDS AND THRUSTS—DO IT! BY THE LEFT FLANK—one two three four I love the Marine Corps THIS IS YOUR RIFLE LADIES I WANT YOU TO KNOW IT ALL OF IT EVERY PART OF IT! CAN'T YOU READ SWEETPEA? this is my rifle this is my gun this is for fighting this is for fun, Ask not what your country (the formation now) remember i can talk no i can't talk no i can't bring back by the river—with the rifle—America. America. God shed His grace on thee, Eenie meenie mynie moe catch a nigger by the toe EYES RIGHT! I WANT YOU TO BELIEVE THIS AFTERNOON THAT THIS THING OUT THERE IS A COMMIE SONOFABITCH and wops and spics and chinks and japs and GET IN FRONT OF YOUR RACKS!! THAT'S NOT QUICK ENOUGH! (never quick enough, eighteen i'm eighteen now) UP! DOWN! GET IT! OUT! GET IT! o mom o please o someone someone help now somebody BY THE RIGHT FLANK! GET DOWN! GET UP! (hot deck parades faces mirror face still pimples now boots and socks) o lights flashes GET THE FUCK UP! We will bear any burden by your leave sir excuse me sir pardon me sir suffer any hardships i'm sorry

sir o yessir no sir aye aye sir, sir! (push-ups, push-ups clanking sounds steel)
READY—SEATS! (plates forks and) EAT AND HURRY UP AND RUN AND
HURRY UP AND EAT AND HURRY UP AND RUN AND HURRY UP
HURRY UP! There is something I believe—we'll be home by Christmas Eve *sir*
my service number is two-oh-three-oh-two-six-one sir the president of the united
states is the honorable lyndon baines johnson sir the vice president is Our Father,
Who art in heaven *PREPARE TO MOUNT aye aye sir* hallowed be Thy name
MOUNT! Thy kingdom come, if I die on the Russian front bury me with a
Russian cunt *DO IT! DO IT! DO IT! DO IT!* Thy will be done *DO IT! DO IT!*
DO IT IN YOUR SLEEP ON THE FLOOR ON YOUR HEAD DO IT NOW
WANT TO BECOME MEN WANT TO BECOME MEN WANT TO BECOME
MEN. . . .

**[As a wounded veteran, Kovic was "displayed" at parades and
ceremonies while American legion members made speeches about
winning wars so that the sacrifice of Kovic and others would not be
in vain.]**

He watched the island disappear as the plane took off from Kennedy Airport. For
the first time since he had come home from the war, he was getting away, going
off somewhere by himself. His chair was safely packed in the belly of the plane,
and he was just one of the other passengers, sitting there just like everybody else.
Sometimes when he was out in his car, driving around, cruising up and down the
block and into the town with his hand controls, he would get the same kind of
feeling. It was a really free feeling that he couldn't get unless he was out of the
chair.

He had been thinking about going to Mexico for a long time. In the hospital
there had been a brochure that said there was this place down there where people
like himself were cared for. It was a place called the Village of the Sun. He'd even
met one guy who'd been there and talked about a whorehouse he'd gone to where
the whores were very understanding, where even paralyzed men could get fucked.
He thought about the Village of the Sun all the time after that. He just knew
inside he could make love again, even though all the parts had been destroyed by
the war.

It was night by the time he arrived in Guadalajara. A man named Rahilio met
him at the airport and put him in his Ford pickup. It had been a long trip and now
it was going to be a long ride to Las Fuentes and the Village, but he was happy
to be in Mexico. Rahilio's small son lay on the seat next to him singing a song
he couldn't understand. He opened up his window and looked out into the dark
Mexican countryside. . . .

Finally one afternoon he went up to the guy who worked behind the desk at
the Hilton and asked him where the biggest whorehouse in town was. The guy
behind the desk wrote down the address for him and he wheeled out to the street
and caught a cab.

The girl was very beautiful and the jukebox was playing as she pushed his chair
into the small room. There was an old mattress on the floor and he got himself
onto it and began to take his shirt off, watching the girl as she took off all her
clothing. She lay down in the bed next to him and asked him why he wasn't taking
off his pants.

"I can't." He hesitated. It was very hard for him to talk about. "I can't take them off," he said. He pointed to his legs. "They were paralyzed in the war."

She looked at him and seemed very confused.

"The war," he said. "Vietnam. Have you ever heard of Vietnam?"

"Vietnam, yes."

"I can't move it," he said, showing her his penis. "You see this?" he said, pointing at the yellow catheter tube. "It doesn't move anymore and I have to use this tube. You see this tube," he said, pointing to it again. "It's okay," he said. "Don't worry about it, *senorita* is *muy bonita*," he said, staring at her dark eyes. "We can still love," he said.

The tears began to roll down her face. She was sitting in the bed next to him crying.

"You see?" he said, pointing to the scar on his chest. "This is where they stuck a chest tube. . . ."

She was getting up now and putting her clothes back on. She was still crying. She was so very beautiful and he wanted so much to lie with her body warm and soft against the top of him, where he could still feel. But now she was walking out the door, leaving for good. She didn't even ask for his money, she didn't even want that.

He lay there for a long time until the madam came in and said it was time for him to leave. It was getting very late, she said. He put on his shirt and dragged his body across the bed, back into the wheelchair. The madam helped him out into the street.

It was early in the morning and the sun was about to come up and he sat crying outside the whorehouse. A cab came by. The driver stopped and asked him if he needed anything. "Do you need a woman?" he said. "Hey, want to go to a great whorehouse? There's a woman in there that will knock you out, really knows how to fuck."

There wasn't anything left to lose, he thought.

The driver got out of his cab and pushed him down the street to a place that was still open. "Wait a minute out here. I'll be right back," he told him. He came back with a big smile on his face. "Maria will be right out," he said, and pushed him into the bar.

A very young girl came into the room, walking past all the tables and then up to his. She had long brown hair down to her waist. "Do you want to sleep with me?" she said. He looked at her and said, "Yes." She seemed very excited, her brown eyes as bright as a little child's. He thanked the cabdriver and gave him some money and followed the girl into one of the tiny cubicles.

She was so much more relaxed than the other woman. He didn't have to explain anything to her. She lay down and touched his face gently. She kissed him and pushed her breasts next to his chest. She felt warm and good. She didn't seem to notice his pants were still on, or the catheter, the rubber urine bag, or any of that. She loved him, they loved each other on the bed in the little room, for what seemed a very long time. She didn't care about the war or any of the other things. They laughed and rolled on top of each other, hiding under the blankets, and talked about a lot of things. She told him she had a kid, a little girl, and they lived in the city. It was very lonely she told him and she really didn't want to do what she was doing, but it was the only way she could make money for herself and her baby. He held her in his arms as if she were his sister as well as his lover.

There was a loud knock on the door and the cabdriver yelled in a taunting voice that it was time for him to get out. But she laughed and said something in Spanish and they stayed in bed almost an extra ten minutes over the limit. When she was getting dressed she asked him if he wanted to get married. She told him she loved him very much and wrote down her address on a small piece of paper. "Here. You take this," she said. She helped him put on his shirt and buttoned each one of the buttons for him. "Come see me tomorrow at four," she said. "You can live with me. *Dinero*," she said, and he gave her fifteen dollars and she helped him into the chair.

All the way back to the village he thought about her and how they would live together and learn each other's language. He saw them sitting naked in bed together studying their books, the child playing at their feet. But then he began to think she hadn't really meant it and he didn't go back the next day at four. He went to a different place and lay with a different girl.

He went out almost every night after that, coming in every morning just after the sun came up and sleeping until four in the afternoon. Then he would get up and get ready to go into the city. Rahilio would call a cab for him and he would wait for it outside the gate of the Village of the Sun.

He would go from whorehouse to whorehouse, wheeling the chair in past the pretty painted Mexican women. He would find a table and wait for one to come up and talk to him. Usually they were kind and did not pity him. They would smile back, very interested, very curious, and he would smell their perfume and look at their breasts. He would sleep with a different one every night. He wanted to sleep with as many as he could, trying one after the other. . . .

[He flew back to New York and entered a university.]

I was in Vietnam when I first heard about the thousands of people protesting the war in the streets of America. I didn't want to believe it at first—people protesting against *us* when we were putting our lives on the line for our country. The men in my outfit used to talk about it a lot. How could they do this to us? Many of us would not be coming back and many others would be wounded or maimed. We swore they would pay, the hippies and draftcard burners. They would pay if we ever ran into them.

But the hospital had changed all that. It was the end of whatever belief I'd still had in what I'd done in Vietnam. Now I wanted to know what I had lost my legs for, why I and the others had gone at all. But it was still very hard for me to think of speaking out against the war, to think of joining those I'd once called traitors.

I settled into my apartment again and went back to classes at the university. It was the spring of 1970. I still wore a tie and sweater every day to school and had a short haircut. I was very sensitive to people looking at me in the wheelchair. I buried myself in my books, cutting myself off from the other students. It was as if they threatened me—particularly the activists, the radicals.

I was sitting alone in my apartment listening to the radio when I first heard the news about Kent State. Four students had just been shot in a demonstration against the invasion of Cambodia. For a moment there was a shock through my body. I felt like crying. The last time I had felt that way was the day Kennedy was killed. I remember saying to myself, The whole thing is coming down now. I wheeled out to my car. I didn't know where I was going but I had to find other people who felt the way I did. I drove down the street to the university. Students were congregating in small groups all over the place. The campus looked as if it were going to explode. Banners were going up and monitors with red armbands were walking up and down handing out leaflets. There was going to be a march and demonstration. I thought carefully for a moment or two, then decided to participate, driving my car past the hundreds of students marching down to the big parking lot where the rally was to be held. I honked my horn in support but I was still feeling a little hesitant. I stayed in my car all during the rally, listening intently to each speaker and cheering and shouting with the crowd. I was still acting like an observer. The last speaker was a woman who said there would be a huge rally in Washington that Saturday and that it was hoped that everyone would make it down. I decided I would go. . . .

We listened as the speakers one after another denounced the invasion of Cambodia and the slaying of the students at Kent State. The sun was getting very hot and Skip and I decided to move around. We wanted to get to the White House where Nixon was holed up, probably watching television. We were in a great sea of people, thousands and thousands all around us. We finally made it to Lafayette Park. On the other side of the avenue the government had lined up thirty or forty buses, making a huge wall between the people and the White House. I remember wondering back then why they had to put all those buses in front of the president. Was the government so afraid of its own people that it needed such a gigantic barricade? I'll always remember those buses lined up that day and not being able to see the White House from my wheelchair. . . .

When we got to the memorial, I remember looking at Lincoln's face and reading the words carved on the walls in back of him. I felt certain that if he were alive he would be there with us.

I told Skip that I was never going to be the same. The demonstration had stirred something in my mind that would be there from now on. It was so very different from boot camp and fighting in the war. There was a togetherness, just as there had been in Vietnam, but it was a togetherness of a different kind of people and for a much different reason. In the war we were killing and maiming people. In Washington on that Saturday afternoon in May we were trying to heal them and set them free.

It will be my turn to speak soon. They have put me up on the platform of this auditorium in this high school that is so much like the one I went to, in this town that is like the one I grew up in. I am looking at all the young faces. Kids. They were laughing, horsing around when they came in, just the way we used to. Now they are silent, looking at me and Bobby Muller, my friend from the V.A. hospital who is speaking to them from his wheelchair.

It is like the day the marine recruiters came. I remember it like it was yesterday—their shiny shoes and their uniforms, their firm handshakes, all the dreams, the medals, the hills taken with Castiglia by my side his army-navy store canteen rattling, the movies the books the plastic guns, everything in 3-D and the explosive spiraling colors of a rainbow. Except this time, this time it is Bobby and me. What if I had seen someone like me that day, a guy in a wheelchair, just sitting there in front of the senior class not saying a word? Maybe things would have been different. Maybe that's all it would have taken.

Bobby is telling his story and I will tell mine. I am glad he has brought me here and that all of them are looking at us, seeing the war firsthand—the dead while still living, the living reminders, two young men who had the shit shot out of them.

I have never spoken before but it is time now, I am thinking about what I can tell them. I wheel myself to the center of the platform. I begin by telling them about the hospital. . . .

[He dropped out of the university and moved to California.]

I had been in California for about a month when one day there was a big photo on the front page of the *L.A. Times*—a group of vets had gone to Washington and thrown away their medals. It was one of the most moving antiwar demonstrations there had been. I would have given anything to have been there with them. I read about it sitting by the pool of the Santa Monica Bay Club, wearing a ridiculous Mickey Mouse shirt. Suddenly I knew my easy life could never be enough for me. The war had not ended. It was time for me to join forces with other vets.

I went home and called a couple of people I knew. One of them told me there was going to be a meeting of Vietnam Veterans Against the War that night in an apartment in L.A. I was still a bit unsure of myself but I couldn't wait to get into my car and drive over.

I remember how kind they were to me from the moment I arrived. When I got there, a bunch of vets were in front of the house waiting to carry me up the stairs in my chair. "Hi brother," they said to me warmly. "Can we help you brother? Is there anything we can do?"

All of a sudden everything seemed to change—the loneliness seemed to vanish. I was surrounded by friends. They were the new veterans, the new soldiers with floppy bush hats and jungle uniforms right here on the streets of America. I began to feel closer to them than I ever had to the people at the university and at the hospital and all the people who had welcomed me back to Massapequa. It had a lot to do with what we had all been through. We could talk and laugh once again. We could be honest about the war and ourselves. Before each meeting there was the thumb-and-fist handshake—it meant you cared about your brother.

We were men who had gone to war. Each of us had his story to tell, his own nightmare. Each of us had been made cold by this thing. We wore ribbons and uniforms. We talked of death and atrocity to each other with unaccustomed gentleness. . . .

I went totally into speaking out against the war after that. I went into it the same way I'd gone into everything else I've wanted to do in my life—the way I'd gone into pole vaulting or baseball or the marines. But this was something that meant much more than being an athlete or a marine. I could see that this thing— this body I had trained so hard to be strong and quick, this body I now dragged around with me like an empty corpse—was to mean much more than I had ever realized. Much more than I'd known the night I cried into my pillow in Massapequa because my youth had been desecrated, my physical humanity defiled. I think I honestly believed that if only I could speak out to enough people I could stop the war myself. I honestly believed people would listen to me because of who I was, a wounded American veteran. They would have to listen. Every chance I had to get my broken body on the tube or in front of an audience I went hog wild. Yes, let them get a look at me. Let them be reminded of what they'd done when they'd sent my generation off to war. One look would be enough—worth more than a thousand speeches. But if they wanted speeches I could give them speeches too. There was no end to what I had to tell them.

"I'm the example of the war," I would say. "Look at me. Do you want your sons to look like this? Do you want to put on the uniform and come home like me?" Some people could not believe the conditions I told them about in the hospitals. Others could not believe anything at all. After one of the TV shows a cameraman called me a commie traitor to my face. He was pushing me down the studio steps in my chair and I wondered if he was going to drop me. I kept receiving letters from people calling me names and telling me what they would do if I didn't stop aiding the enemy. . . .

[He increasingly demonstrated with the group called Vietnam Veterans Against the War. He was arrested, beat up and condemned by the public and the police for his protests. He joined the massive veterans' protest of the 1972 Republican National Convention in Miami, where Richard Nixon was nominated for "four more years."]

A couple of newsmen, including Roger Mudd from CBS, had worked their way through the security barricades and begun to ask me questions.

"Why are you here tonight?" Roger Mudd asked me. "But don't start talking until I get the camera here," he shouted.

It was too good to be true. In a few seconds Roger Mudd and I would be going on live all over the country. I would be doing what I had come here for, showing the whole nation what the war was all about. The camera began to roll, and I began to explain why I and the others had come, that the war was wrong and it had to stop immediately. "I'm a Vietnam veteran," I said. "I gave America my all and the leaders of this government threw me and the others away to rot in their V.A. hospitals. What's happening in Vietnam is a crime against humanity, and I just want the American people to know that we have come all the way across this country, sleeping on the ground and in the rain, to let the American people see for themselves the men who fought their war and have come to oppose it. If you can't believe the veteran who fought the war and was wounded in the war, who can you believe?"

"Thank you," said Roger Mudd, visibly moved by what I had said. "This is Roger Mudd," he said, "down on the convention floor with Ron Kovic, a disabled veteran protesting President Nixon's policy in Vietnam.". . .

President Nixon began to speak and all three of us took a deep breath and shouted at the top of our lungs, "Stop the bombing, stop the war, stop the bombing, stop the war," as loud and as hard as we could, looking directly at Nixon. The security agents immediately threw up their arms, trying to hide us from the cameras and the president. "Stop the bombing, stop the bombing," I screamed. For an instant Cronkite looked down, then turned his head away. They're not going to show it, I thought. They're going to try and hide us like they did in the hospitals. Hundreds of people around us began to clap and shout "Four more years," trying to drown out our protest. They all seemed very angry and shouted at us to stop. We continued shouting, interrupting Nixon again and again until Secret Service agents grabbed our chairs from behind and began pulling us backward as fast as they could out of the convention hall. "Take it easy," Bobby said to me. "Don't fight back."

I wanted to take a swing and fight right there in the middle of the convention hall in front of the president and the whole country. "So this is how they treat their wounded veterans!" I screamed.

A short guy with a big Four More Years button ran up to me and spat in my face. "Traitor!" he screamed, as he was yanked back by police. Pandemonium was breaking out all around us and the Secret Service men kept pulling us out backward.

"I served two tours of duty in Vietnam!" I screamed to one newsman. "I gave three-quarters of my body for America. And what do I get? Spit in the face!" I kept screaming until we hit the side entrance where the agents pushed us outside and shut the doors, locking them with chains and padlocks so reporters wouldn't be able to follow us out for interviews.

All three of us sat holding on to each other shaking. We had done it. It had been the biggest moment of our lives, we had shouted down the president of the United States and disrupted his acceptance speech. What more was there left to do but go home?

I sat in my chair still shaking and began to cry. . . .

[He relived the accident in Nam when he killed an American corporal by mistake. He confessed his crime to a superior.]

"There were a bunch of shots," he said carefully. "Everybody was shooting, it was a bad firefight." He paused. "It was pretty bad and then corporal was shot. He was shot and he fell down in front of us and a couple of the men ran out to get him. They pulled him back in. I think the others were still firing. The corpsman tried to help . . . the corporal was shot in the neck . . . The corpsman tried to help. . . ."

It was becoming very difficult for him to talk now. "Major," he said, "I think I might have . . . I think I might have killed the corporal."

"I don't think so," said the major quickly.

"It was very confusing. It was hard to tell what was happening."

"Yes I know," said the major. "Sometimes it gets very hard out there. I was out a couple of weeks ago and sometimes it's very hard to tell what's happening."

He stared down at the floor of the bunker until he could make himself say it again. He wasn't quite sure the major had heard him the first time.

"But I just want you to know, major, I think I was the one who killed him. I think it might have been me."

There, he had said it. And now he was walking away.

For some reason he was feeling a lot better. He had told the major everything and the major hadn't believed it. It was like going to confession when he was a kid and the priest saying everything was okay. He walked by the men outside the radio shack. They turned their faces away as he passed. Let them talk, he thought. He was only human, he had made a mistake. The corporal was dead now and no one could bring him back.

The chaplain held a memorial service that afternoon for the man he had killed and he sat in the tent with the rest of the men. There was a wife and a kid, someone said. He tried to listen to the words the chaplain was saying, the name he kept repeating over and over again. Who was this man he'd just killed? Who had he been? He wanted to scream right there in the church tent, right there during the ceremony. He kept hearing the name too many times, the name of the dead man, the man with the friends, the man with the wife, the one he didn't know or care to know, the kid from Georgia who was now being carefully wrapped up in some plastic bag and sent back in a cheap wooden box to be buried in the earth at nineteen.

He had panicked with the rest of them that night and murdered his first man, but it wasn't the enemy, it wasn't the one they had all been taught and trained to kill, it wasn't the silhouette at the rifle range he had pumped holes in from five hundred yards, or the German soldiers with plastic machine guns in Sally's Woods. He'd never figured it would ever happen this way. It never did in the movies. There were always the good guys and the bad guys, the cowboys and the Indians. There was always the enemy and the good guys and each of them killed the other.

He went back to his tent after the ceremony was over and sat down. There was some mail but he couldn't get interested in it. Someone had sent him a Sergeant Rock comicbook. But it wasn't funny anymore. The good guys weren't supposed to kill the good guys. . . .

He went out on patrol with the others the night of the ambush at exactly eight o'clock, loading a round into the chamber of his weapon before he walked outside the tent and into the dark and rain. As usual he had made all the men put on camouflage from head to toe, made sure they had all blackened their faces, and attached twigs and branches to their arms and legs with rubber bands.

One by one the scouts moved slowly past the thick barbed wire and began to walk along the bank of the river, heading toward the graveyard where the ambush would be set up. They were moving north exactly as planned, a line of shadows tightly bunched in the rain. Sometimes it would stop raining and they would spread out somewhat more, but mostly they continued to bunch up together, as if they were afraid of losing their way.

There was a rice paddy on the edge of the graveyard. No one said a word as they walked through it and he thought he could hear voices from the village. He could smell the familiar smoke from the fires in the huts and he knew that the people who went out fishing each day must have come home. They were the people he watched every morning moving quietly in their small boats down toward the mouth of the river, heading out to the sea. Some of the older men reminded him of his father, going to work each morning and coming back home every night to sit by their fires with their children cooking their fish. They must talk about us sometimes, he thought. He wondered a lot what it was they thought about him and the men.

He remembered how difficult it had been when he had first come to the war to tell the villagers from the enemy and sometimes it had seemed easier to hate all of them, but he had always tried very hard not to. He wished he could be sure they understood that he and the men were there because they were trying to help all of them save their country from the Communists. . . .

Suddenly someone was firing from the end with his rifle, and now the whole line opened up, roaring their weapons like thunder, pulling their triggers again and again without even thinking, emptying everything they had into the hut in a tremendous stream of bright orange tracers that crisscrossed each other in the night.

The flare arched its last sputtering bits into the village and it became dark, and all he could see were the bright orange embers from the fire that had gone out.

And he could hear them.

There were voices screaming.

"What happened? Goddamn it, what happened?" yelled the lieutenant.

The voices were screaming from inside the hut.

"Who gave the order to fire? I wanna know who gave the order to fire."

The lieutenant was standing up now, looking up and down the line of men still lying in the rain.

He found that he was shaking. It had all happened so quickly.

"We better get a killer team out there," he heard Molina say.

"All right, all right. Sergeant," the lieutenant said to him, "get out there with Molina and tell me how many we got."

He got to his feet and quickly got five of the men together, leading them over the dike and through the water to the hut from where the screams were still coming. It was much closer than he had first thought. Now he could see very clearly the smoldering embers of the fire that had been blown out by the terrific blast of their rifles.

Molina turned the beam of his flashlight into the hut. "Oh God," he said. "Oh Jesus Christ." He started to cry. "We just shot up a bunch of kids!"

The floor of the small hut was covered with them, screaming and thrashing their arms back and forth, lying in pools of blood, crying wildly, screaming again and again. They were shot in the face, in the chest, in the legs, moaning and crying.

"Oh Jesus!" he cried.

He could hear the lieutenant shouting at them, wanting to know how many they had killed.

There was an old man in the corner with his head blown off from his eyes up, his brains hanging out of his head like jelly. He kept looking at the strange sight, he had never seen anything like it before. A small boy next to the old man was still alive, although he had been shot many times. He was crying softly, lying in a large pool of blood. His small foot had been shot almost completely off and seemed to be hanging by a thread.

"What's happening? What's going on up there?" The lieutenant was getting very impatient now.

Molina shouted for the lieutenant to come quickly. "You better get up here. There's a lot of wounded people up here."

He heard a small girl moaning now. She was shot through the stomach and bleeding out of the rear end. All he could see now was blood everywhere and he heard their screams with his heart racing like it had never raced before. He felt crazy and weak as he stood there staring at them with the rest of the men, staring down onto the floor like it was a nightmare, like it was some kind of dream and it really wasn't happening.

And then he could no longer stand watching. They were people, he thought, children and old men, people, people like himself, and he had to do something, he had to move, he had to help, do something. He jerked the green medical bag off his back, ripping it open and grabbing for bandages, yelling at Molina to please come and help him. He knelt down in the middle of the screaming bodies and began bandaging them, trying to cover the holes where the blood was still spurting out. "It's gonna be okay. It's gonna be okay," he tried to say, but he was crying now, crying and still trying to bandage them all up. He moved from body to body searching in the dark with his fingers for the holes the bullets had made, bandaging each one as quickly as he could, his shaking hands wet with the blood. It was raining into the hut and a cold wind swept his face as he moved in the dark.

The lieutenant had just come up with the others.

"Help me!" he screamed. "Somebody help!"

"Well, goddamn it sergeant! What's the matter? How many did we kill?"

"They're children!" he screamed at the lieutenant.

"Children and old men!" cried Molina.

"Where are their rifles?" the lieutenant asked.

"There aren't any rifles," he said. . . .

[His unit suffered through an artillery attack where they could only hide in the ground and pray for life. Many died.]

Another crowd had gathered around a trench. It was hard to tell what had happened there, how many bodies there were. Maybe three all mangled together in a heap, a bunch of arms and legs. There was a smell of gunpowder and blood mixed with burning flesh. One of the heads was completely severed, chopped off, with the exception of a strand of muscle—that was the only thing that continued to connect the head to the stinking corpse. There was nothing any of us could do but pick up the pieces. They seemed very cold and gray and someone in back of me was taking pictures. I fished around for identification in one corpse's dead back pocket and found a wallet. It was Sergeant Bo, one of my friends. He was the supply sergeant and had a wife somewhere. He was sort of the Sergeant Bilko of the battalion. He never went on patrol and had the most comfortable quarters of anyone, with a rug and a desk and a picture of his pretty wife. He had a very young face and now he was in that hole, mangled in that hole, stinking with the others.

The lieutenant came by and ordered the men to put the pieces on a stretcher. Sergeant Bo was my friend and now he was dead. They were going to put him in a plastic bag. They were going to do that with the pieces just like they were going to do with MacCarthy and like they'd done with the corporal from Georgia whom I'd killed the month before. Out by the command bunker they had all the dead lined up in a neat long line. They were all stripped of their clothes and staring up at the sky. Bo and Mac were there with a lot of others I hadn't seen before. About eleven men had been killed in the attack.

There were scores of wounded. Sergeant Peters had been hit in the eye and Corporal Swanson was lying in the command tent with a large piece of metal still stuck in his head. I went up to him and held his hand, telling him everything was going to be all right. He told me to send a letter right away to his wife in California and tell her what had happened. I promised him I'd do it that night but I never did and I never heard from him again.

The men were beginning to relax a little more now. Everyone was smoking cigarettes and feeling a little closer to everyone else. Maybe, I thought, the men would stop talking about me behind my back now. Maybe with all that blown-away flesh the killing of the corporal from Georgia wouldn't mean that much anymore.

He was just another body, he thought, just like the rest of them, the ones who had all been blown to pieces. For some crazy reason he began feeling a lot better about everything. The more the better, he thought, the more that looked like the corporal the better. Maybe, he thought, they would get confused and forget in all the madness that he had murdered the kid from Georgia. . . .

[Kovic's unit fought a North Vietnamese/Viet Cong unit in a village.]

I had started walking toward the village when the first bullet hit me. There was a sound like firecrackers going off all around my feet. Then a real loud crack and my leg went numb below the knee. I looked down at my foot and there was blood at the back of it. The bullet had come through the front and blew out nearly the whole of my heel.

I had been shot. The war had finally caught up with my body. I felt good inside. Finally the war was with me and I had been shot by the enemy. I was getting out of the war and I was going to be a hero. I kept firing my rifle into the tree line and boldly, with my new wound, moved closer to the village, daring them to hit me again. For a moment I felt like running back to the rear with my new million-dollar wound but I decided to keep fighting out in the open. A great surge of strength went through me as I yelled for the other men to come out from the trees and join me. I was limping now and the foot was beginning to hurt so much, I finally lay down in almost a kneeling position, still firing into the village, still unable to see anyone. I seemed to be the only one left firing a rifle. Someone came up from behind me, took off my boot and began to bandage my foot. The whole thing was incredibly stupid, we were sitting ducks, but he bandaged my foot and then he took off back into the tree line.

For a few seconds it was silent. I lay down prone and waited for the next bullet to hit me. It was only a matter of time, I thought. I wasn't retreating, I wasn't going back, I was lying right there and blasting everything I had into the pagoda. The rifle was full of sand and it was jamming. I had to pull the bolt back now each time trying to get a round into the chamber. It was impossible and I started to get up and a loud crack went off next to my right ear as a thirty-caliber slug tore through my right shoulder, blasted through my lung, and smashed my spinal cord to pieces.

I felt that everything from my chest down was completely gone. I waited to die. I threw my hand back and felt my legs still there. I couldn't feel them but they were still there. I was still alive. And for some reason I started believing, I started believing I might not die, I might make it out of there and live and feel and go back home again. I could hardly breathe and was taking short little sucks with the one lung I had left. The blood was rolling off my flak jacket from the hole in my shoulder and I couldn't feel the pain in my foot anymore, I couldn't even feel my body. I was frightened to death. I didn't think about praying, all I could feel was cheated.

All I could feel was the worthlessness of dying right here in this place at this moment for nothing.

The back yard, that was the place to be, it was where all the plans for the future, the trips to Africa, the romances with young high-school girls, it was where all those wonderful things took place. Remember the hula hoop, everyone including my mother doing it and my sister, yes my sister, teaching me the twist in the basement. Then out on the basketball court with all the young fine-looking girls watching. Then back on the fence for a walk around the whole back yard. Up there! Can you see me balancing like Houdini? Can you see me hiding in a box, in a submarine, on a jet? Can you see me flying a kite, making a model, breeching a stream?

It was all sort of easy, it had all come and gone, the snowstorms, the street lamps telling us there was no school at midnight, the couch, the heater with all of us rolled up beside it in the thick blankets, the dogs, it was lovely. Getting nailed at home plate, studying the cub scout handbook, tying knots, playing Ping-Pong, reading National Geographic. *Mickey Mantle was my hero and Joan Marfe was the girl I liked best. It all ended with a bang and it was lovely.*

There was a song called "Runaway" by a guy named Dell Shannon playing one Saturday at the baseball field. I remember it was a beautiful spring day and we were young back then and really alive and the air smelled fresh. This song was playing and I really got into it and was hitting baseballs and feeling like I could live forever.

It was all sort of easy.
It had all come and gone.

RON KOVIC
Photo taken February 1990 at the Good Stuff Cafe,
Hermosa Beach, California.

SELECTED BIBLIOGRAPHY

Adams, Timony Dow. *Telling Lies in Modern American Autobiography.* Chapel Hill: University of North Carolina Press, 1990.

Addis, Patricia K. *Her Story: An Annotated Bibliography of Autobiographical Writings by American Women.* Metuchen, N.J.: Scarecrow Press, 1983.

Andrews, William L. *Sisters of the Spirit: Three Black Women's Autobiographies of the Nineteenth Century.* Bloomington: Indiana University Press, 1980.

———. *To Tell A Free Story: The First Century of Afro-American Autobiography, 1760–1865.* Urbana: University of Illinois Press, 1986.

Atkinson, Linda. *Mother Jones, The Most Dangerous Woman in America.* New York: Crown Publishers, 1978.

Berry, J. Bill, ed. *Home Ground: Southern Autobiography.* Columbia: University of Missouri Press, 1991.

Borg, Mary. *Writing Your Own Life: An Easy-To-Follow Guide to Writing an Autobiography.* Fort Collins, CO: Cottonwood Press, 1992.

Braxton, Joanne M. *Black Women Writing Autobiography: A Tradition Within a Tradition.* Philadelphia: Temple University Press, 1989.

Brignano, Russell C. *Black Americans in Autobiography: An Annotated Bibliography of Autobiographies and Autobiographical Books Written Since the Civil War.* Durham: Duke University Press, 1974.

Briscoe, Mary L. *et al. American Autobiography 1945–1980: A Bibliography.* Madison: University of Wisconsin Press, 1982.

Brumble, H. David. *American Indian Autobiography.* Los Angeles: University of California Press, 1988.

Bruss, Elizabeth W. *Autobiographical Acts: The Changing Situation of a Literary Genre.* Baltimore: Johns Hopkins University, 1976.

Butterfield, Stephen. *Black Autobiography.* Amherst: University of Massachusetts Press, 1974.

Coe, Richard N. *When the Grass Was Taller: Autobiography and the Experience of Childhood.* New Haven: Yale University Press, 1984.

Cooley, Thomas. *Educated Lives: The Rise of Modern Autobiography in America.* Columbus: Ohio State University Press, 1976.

Couser, G. Thomas. *Altered Egos: Authority in American Autobiography.* New York: Oxford University Press, 1989.

———. *American Autobiography: The Prophetic Mode.* Amherst: University of Massachusetts Press, 1979.

Cox, James M. *Recovering Literature's Lost Ground: Essays in American Autobiography.* Baton Rouge: Louisiana State Press, 1989.

Culley, Margo, ed. *American Women's Autobiography: Fea(s)ts of Memory.* Madison: University of Wisconsin Press, 1992.

Duncan, Russell. *Freedom's Shore: Tunis Campbell and the Georgia Freedmen.* Athens: University of Georgia Press, 1986.

Egan, Susanna. *Patterns of Experience in Autobiography.* Chapel Hill: University of North Carolina Press, 1984.

Eakin, John Paul. *Fictions in Autobiography: Studies in the Art of Self Invention.* Princeton: Princeton University Press, 1985.

Featherling, Dale. *Mother Jones, The Miners' Angel: A Portrait.* Carbondale: Southern Illinois University Press, 1979.

Hacker, Louis Morton. *The World of Andrew Carnegie: 1865–1901.* Philadelphia: Lippincott, 1968.

Harlan, Louis R. *Booker T. Washington: The Making of a Leader, 1856–1901.* New York: Oxford University Press, 1975.

————. *Booker T. Washington: The Wizard of Tuskegee, 1901–1915.* New York: Oxford University Press, 1983.

Holte, James Craig. *The Ethnic I: A Sourcebook for Ethnic-American Autobiography.* Westport: Greenwood Press, 1988.

Jelinek, Estelle C. *Women's Autobiography.* Bloomington: Indiana University Press, 1980.

Kaplan, Louis. *A Bibliography of American Autobiographies.* Madison: University of Wisconsin Press, 1962.

Klein, Joe. *Woody Guthrie: A Life.* New York: A.A. Knopf, 1980.

Lee, Robert A. *First Person Singular: Studies in American Autobiography.* Totowa, N.J.: Barnes and Noble Books, 1987.

Leibowitz, Herbert A. *Fabricating Lives: Explorations in American Autobiography.* New York: Knopf, 1989.

Livesay, Harold C. *Andrew Carnegie and the Rise of Big Business.* Boston: Little, Brown, 1975.

Olney, James, ed. *Autobiography: Essays Theoretical and Critical.* Princeton: Princeton University Press, 1980.

————. *Metaphors of Self: The Meaning of Autobiography.* Princeton: Princeton University Press, 1972.

Pascal, Roy. *Design and Truth in Autobiography.* Cambridge: Harvard University Press, 1960.

Payne, James Robert. *Multicultural Autobiography: American Lives.* Knoxville: University of Tennessee Press, 1992.

Pellauer, Mary D. *Toward a Tradition of Feminist Theology: The Religious Social Thought of Elizabeth Cady Stanton, Susan B. Anthony, and Anna Howard Shaw.* Brooklyn: Carlson, 1991.

Rice, Julian. *Black Elk's Story: Distinguishing Its Lakota Purpose.* Albuquerque: University of New Mexico Press, 1991.

Sayre, Robert F. *The Examined Self: Benjamin Franklin, Henry Adams, Henry James.* Princeton: Princeton University Press, 1964.

Smith, Sidonie. *Where I'm Bound: Patterns of Slavery and Freedom in Black American Autobiography.* Westport: Greenwood Press, 1974.

Spengemann, William C. *The Forms of Autobiography: Episodes in the History of a Literary Genre.* New Haven: Yale University Press, 1980.

Steltenkamp, Michael F. *Black Elk: Holy Man of the Oglala.* Norman: University of Oklahoma Press, 1993.

Stepto, Robert B. *From Behind the Veil: A Study of Afro-American Narrative.* Urbana: University of Illinois Press, 1979.

Stone, Albert E., ed. *The American Autobiography.* Englewood Cliffs, N.J.: Prentice-Hall, 1981.

Taylor, Gordon O. *Chapters of Experience: Studies in Twentieth-Century American Autobiography.* New York: St. Martin's Press, 1983.

Yurchenco, Henrietta. *A Mighty Hard Road: The Woody Guthrie Story.* New York: McGraw-Hill, 1970.